EDIBLE WEEDS HANDBOOK

A field guide to the introduced edible wild plants of New Zealand

ANDREW CROWE

PENGUIN BOOKS

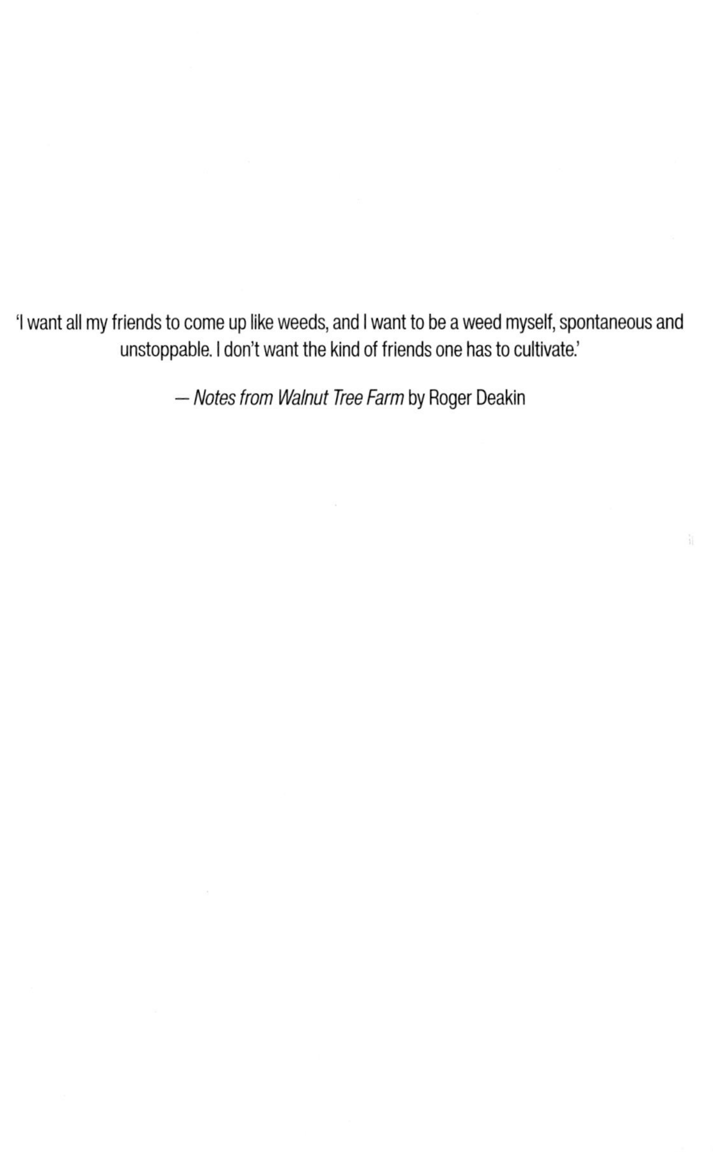

‘I want all my friends to come up like weeds, and I want to be a weed myself, spontaneous and unstoppable. I don’t want the kind of friends one has to cultivate.’

— *Notes from Walnut Tree Farm* by Roger Deakin

CONTENTS

INTRODUCTION

Why the book?

On a global level, the number of plants that have been used at some time as human food is impressive: over 7000 species are known.[1] And yet 80% of our global dietary energy requirement is provided now by just 12 plants – eight grasses (barley, maize, millet, rice, rye, sorghum, sugarcane and wheat) and just four tubers (cassava, potato, sweet potato and yam) – and over 50% of humanity's protein and energy requirements are now reliant on just three of these: wheat, maize and rice.[2]

This unprecedented contraction in food sources has brought with it a reduction in our intake of micronutrients, for the vitamin and dietary mineral content of wild edible plants is understood to be generally superior to that of cultivated vegetables.[3] In other words, humans are becoming increasingly reliant on very few plants, overlooking the significant potential of wild plants to help address deficiencies in the 40 or so vitamins and minerals that are considered essential for physical and mental development, the immune system and metabolic processes. This handbook is intended as a kind of antidote – a guide to health, history, food security and self-sufficiency.

It is founded on knowledge that has been practised and passed down for centuries, but which now risks being lost. It is this predicament that has prompted a global effort to collect and record existing traditional culinary use of wild plants, particularly among people living in isolated rural communities. Some of this practical knowledge can be traced back through classical literature for more than 2000 years and, with the aid of archaeology, further still, to wild plants that comprised much of our human diet over 12,000 years ago – or over 50,000 years ago in the case of Australia.

The primary aim of this book, then, is to distil from this global exercise any findings that are locally relevant to Aotearoa New Zealand and present them in a practical forager's field guide. Based on over 750 ethnobotanical studies from around the world, more than 1000 plants have been identified that currently grow wild in New Zealand and have a traditional history of being used as food. For simplicity, plants that are fairly rare or are less practicable sources of food have been either left out or relegated to an appendix, leaving the remainder to be arranged under 160 or so main entries.

As a seasoned forager, it came as a revelation to me how this methodical approach could turn up so many surprises; for example **madeira vine**, **coastal wattle**, or the ornamental **Ethiopian banana**, all of which are now actively spreading into the wild here. Unbeknown to most of us, all three provide important sources of food for

---

1 Royal Botanic Gardens, Kew (2020) identifies over 7000 species. Others – depending on a range of criteria – list considerably more. Kunkel (1984) lists 12,650 species as suitable, or potentially suitable, for human consumption; the Food Plants International website (https://foodplantsinternational.com/plants) lists over 35,000; while FAO (1995) claims that 'the world has over 50,000 edible plants'.

2 Agea et al. 2011.

3 Flyman & Afolayan 2006, Jones & Hughes 1983, Ranfa et al. 2014, Renna 2017, Vardavas et al. 2006.

residents based in or near the native habitat of these plants.

My own interest in edible wild plants was triggered shortly after reaching Aotearoa from England in the early 1970s, when I got lost in the bush – initially by accident and then several times deliberately to test my survival skills. This led to my first field guide (*A Field Guide to the Native Edible Plants of New Zealand*, 1981), a book that focused on plants indigenous to the country. Its aim was twofold: one, to provide a portable guide to emergency survival along the coast, in native forest and above the treeline; and two, to celebrate the considerable survival skills and ingenuity of pre-European Māori.

I was equally interested at that time in the country's introduced edible wild plants, but quickly realised that a field guide that did justice to both topics would become too unwieldy – for both the writer and the reader. I had no idea that this larger project would keep on growing to the point that my original database of local edible wild plants would run to over 1000 species.

The ingenuity of Māori following their discovery of Aotearoa is one thing, but with the arrival of Europeans there came a whole new suite of wild plants – some welcome, some not. With the loss of much native forest, a more practical source of everyday foraging would soon be provided by the country's *introduced* wild plants. These are the kind of edible plant that might come in handy nowadays when making a meal at home, for example, or when travelling – plants that are good to use in salads, as cooked greens, for making flour, fruit salads or garnishing. Knowledge of this kind might be particularly relevant in times of economic hardship or disrupted supply of more familiar, or more conventional, foods. To take a recent example: during the Bosnian War (1992–95), the unfortunate inhabitants of the capital of Sarajevo remained under siege for almost four years, yet were fortunate enough to have retained their ancestral knowledge of wild cuisine. Or looking into the future, in the uncertain times of climate change, knowledge of edible wild plants may well become more relevant, as wild plants often prove to be more resilient.

However, this field guide is not just about hard times; it concerns a sense of fulfilment that can come from taking the trouble to engage more fully with the natural world. This is nothing new. Around the globe, there are many places where edible wild plants such as those catalogued in this book continue to be gathered on a daily basis, not just through necessity but to be taken and offered for sale in local markets. Many have the potential to offer new tastes, new crops and new products.

The aim of this field guide, then, is to help readers (and the writer) to safely harvest from the wild; to provide an accessible resource for those who prefer to live a life of voluntary simplicity – one step removed from the world of packaging and the temples of trade. Or for those who simply need to find some fresh food while they get their home vege patch established.

What is a weed?

A weed can be defined as any plant growing where it is not wanted, but for the purposes of this book it refers to any introduced plant that can thrive in the wild in Aotearoa, including a few crops that are not generally thought of as weeds. Many of the plants in this book are indeed so benign that they may be encouraged in the home garden for groundcover and/or culinary use. Examples include **bitter cress**, **Cape gooseberry**, **choko**, **corn salad**, **fennel**, **Jerusalem artichoke**, **nasturtium**, **nettle**, **red amaranth**, **rocket** and **tree spinach**, all of which we have deliberately introduced to our own garden to contribute to a healthy fresh diet with minimal labour. For the same reason we leave many conventional garden vegetables to self-seed, e.g. **borage**, **cherry tomato**, **lemon balm**, **marigold**, **mustard lettuce**, **parsley** and **silverbeet**, along with several nutritious weeds such as **chickweed**, **dandelion** and **pūhā** (**sow thistle**).

In fact, there is a whole spectrum of weediness, according to how easily a plant is able to spread. And it is important to appreciate this. Several can be a real nuisance, especially the so-called 'environmental weeds' that have a tendency to invade native plant habitat, threatening native plants by out-competing them. Do take special care to not spread the seeds or tubers of these plants. This includes the seeds of **banana passionfruit** and the tubers of **Madeira vine**, both of which are now banned from sale, propagation and distribution anywhere in New Zealand due to their potential to cause serious environmental damage. For further details, see The National Pest Plant Accord (search on 'NPPA') at https://www.mpi.govt.nz.

Basics: how to know a plant is edible

What exactly does it mean to say that a plant is edible? Is it enough to google it, try the plant and feel no ill-effects the next day?

Powerful though the internet certainly is for tracking down information, it is equally efficient at disseminating errors. Many statements regarding edibility found there – and in some printed books, too – have simply been repeated from elsewhere with little or no investigation into the basis of the information or any evidence that offers a potential challenge to the claim. As in the game 'Chinese whispers', the statement 'this is thought to be edible' can quickly become 'this is edible and nutritious'.

Here I have opted for a more rigorous approach, turning, wherever possible, to those communities with the largest body of direct first-hand experience of eating the plant concerned – i.e. inhabitants of those continents where the plants originate (Europe, Asia, Africa, the Americas or Australia) – to learn about the history of traditional use there. This approach to establishing the true value of a plant for human nutrition hinges on valuing ancestral knowledge rather than reinventing it, turning to records painstakingly collected by field workers interviewing hundreds of individuals in rural areas and remote villages all over the world. The observant reader may note an apparent focus on reports collected from Italy, Turkey and East European countries and wonder why. The reason for this is that many of our introduced wild plants originate in this region – a region where foraging for wild food remains a relatively widespread tradition. Many of these countries also stand out for their food culture, where meals are traditionally shared social events that frequently last for hours. Despite the inevitable toll of the globalisation of culture, much first-hand knowledge of edible wild plants remains in Italy, for example. At least, this is my own impression.

Wherever possible, I have gone on to cross-check the findings of these researchers against independent reports from other regions, and against what has been established locally and globally about any plants that are potentially toxic or require special preparation. This is then followed up with an investigation into the nutritional qualities of the plant (which have in most cases already been quantified), and any anti-nutritional aspects, too.

'A little knowledge is a dangerous thing', they say, so the aim of this book is to provide sufficient background for the reader to explore the topic carefully and make informed decisions – including details of plants that can be deleterious to one's health under certain conditions, and those that might conceivably be confused with edible ones.

Edible, poisonous or both?

Occasionally you will come across a plant that is clearly identified in one place as being poisonous and in another as edible. This can, naturally, be quite disconcerting, for it may come as a surprise to learn that both may be correct. In reality, many plants can be classified as both edible and poisonous depending on the part under discussion and how it is prepared. Common everyday examples include apple, plum, cherry, peach and apricot – the fruit of all these may be enjoyed freely, either raw or cooked, without us ever knowing that the seeds of all are potentially toxic in large quantities. Another example is potato tubers, which are nowadays accepted across much of the world as a staple food despite the fact that any potato tuber that has turned green on exposure to light is poisonous. Similarly tomato, whose leaves, stems and green fruit are mildly toxic. The list of everyday examples also includes asparagus, whose small red berries are mildly poisonous; cashew, whose shell is sufficiently toxic to burn the skin on contact; improperly cooked kidney beans; raw cassava roots; raw taro; and the leaves of rhubarb.

Nutritional values

As you will see, chemical analyses have already been carried out on almost all the plants in this book, analyses that in most cases include assessments to quantify the plant's nutritional content. Rather than quote the original figures for each plant, they have been rated against the Recommended Daily Allowances (RDAs) for each of the nutrients concerned. For readers keen to follow up on the original measurements, sources of the original data are given in brackets.

Medicinal plants

Many wild plants – including those featured in this book – have a venerable history not just as a source of food but also as medicine, and yet the reader will find scant reference here to the therapeutic properties of the plants. Why? This is largely because it is impracticable to do justice to the topic of herbal medicine without producing a much larger book.

Health and safety

I hate to be a killjoy, but such a weighty topic as edible wild plants – a topic so 'close to the bone', so to speak – obviously requires a few safety briefings!

▶ Care with identification

'When in doubt, don't eat it!' Although this warning applies particularly to fungi, it is certainly wise to familiarise yourself first with the most toxic wild plants. If you take the trouble to learn to recognise just two, make them **hemlock** and **tutu**. Why? Because, in practice, both have been confused with edible wild plants and both are sufficiently toxic to have killed circus elephants right here in New Zealand. For this reason, both plants get special treatment in this book (pages 44 & 23).

Of the enquiries received by the New Zealand National Poisons Centre, around 5% relate to plants and fungi, with misidentification being one of the main issues. The fact that some 62% of these calls relate to children serves as a reminder of the need to educate them early about the risks. Young children are often quick to imitate and are naturally curious, yet are often unaware of the danger of tasting unknown plants. Given the risk, you will find most of the plants in this book illustrated with close-up photos of their leaves and flowers or fruit. Accurate identification does require patience, though, especially for beginners as they become familiar enough with a plant to harvest it – for the tastiest wild greens are generally harvested in spring, before the plant is in flower.

▶ Moderation

Moderation is equally important. Just because a plant is known to have health benefits does not necessarily mean that when consumed in larger quantities it is more beneficial. This caution applies particularly to a recent trend to use wild plants to make smoothies. The risk of over-consumption is, of course, not confined to wild plants. In one unfortunate incident from the 1940s, an adult chewed and swallowed a cup of apple seeds, a singular repast that led him to die of cyanide poisoning. Then there is the sad fate of Christopher McCandless, an American hiker, whose story is told in *Into the Wild* (1997) and the documentary film *The Call of the Wild* (2007). His death is generally attributed to a diet overly reliant on the seeds of **alpine sweetvetch** (**wild potato**, *Hedysarum alpinum*), which when consumed to excess can interfere with the normal functioning of proteins, due to the concentration of L-canavanine it contains.

▶ Allergies

Even important food plants – including **celery**, **strawberry**, **tomato**, **basil**, **kiwifruit**, **avocado**, **potato**, **peach**, **wheat**, **soy** and various **nuts** – have been known to trigger allergies in an unfortunate few. Such individuals should take special care.

▶ Photodermatitis

An unpleasant skin reaction (rashes or blisters) can also result from simple contact with certain plants that contain furanocoumarins, especially if contact is followed by exposure of the skin to sunlight. These plants include **fig**, **lime**, **celery**, **parsnip**, **angelica**, **parsley** and several of their wild relatives, such as **giant hogweed** (*Heracleum mantegazzianum*) whose hollow stalks are unfortunately sometimes used by children as telescopes or peashooters, and the rarer **cow parsnip** (*H. sphondylium*). An allergic skin reaction is also possible from relatively innocuous plants such as **parsnip palm** (*Daucus decipiens*, sometimes grown for fodder).[4]

▶ Waterborne parasites

In farming areas, liver fluke (*Fasciola hepatica*) cysts may attach themselves to aquatic plants such as **watercress**, so these plants should ideally be cooked to avoid contracting any disease from them.

▶ Pollution from herbicides

Given New Zealand's 'clean green' image, its use of herbicides such as Roundup is surprisingly widespread, so do take care to avoid harvesting near unnatural-looking patches of dead vegetation, especially along the edges of paths and roadways. And avoid harvesting from areas that appear to have been sprayed with blue or red herbicide dyes.

▶ Heavy metals and hyperaccumulators

Mine sites or areas where old mines have previously operated are also a concern as the mining process involves crushing rocks into fine powder, which frequently releases 'heavy metals' into the soil and water. It is therefore unwise to forage (or grow your vegetables) nearby. Of particular concern are arsenic, cadmium, mercury and lead, all of which are highly poisonous. A similar caution applies to landfill sites and to land adjacent to old timber houses, where lead paint may have been used or where treated timber may have been burnt. These risks are particularly high with some of our leafy vegetables, including **lettuce** and **brassicas**, but can be of concern also with wild plants harvested from these same areas, including several that grow in water, like **watercress**, **water plantain** and **alligator weed**. For this reason it is important to avoid areas that may be polluted by wastewater

---

4 The occasional skin reaction from **parsnip palm** (also known as *Melanoselinum decipiens*) is due to the presence of monoterpenes, such as limonene and β-pinene (Grayson 2000, Mendes et al. 2009). Most phototoxic species belong to the carrot, citrus and fig families (Bonamonte et al. 2021).

effluent, waters fed from mine sites, and waters from geothermal sites, where hot-spring systems can become a significant source of heavy metal pollution downstream.[5]

▶ Nitrates

Another potential issue is New Zealand's high use of synthetic nitrogen fertiliser and high dairy-cow stocking rates. Both of these can lead to nitrate accumulation in plants, which can be of concern with respect to farm animals, particularly cattle. A clear risk has also been identified for residents of some rural areas who take their drinking water from bore-wells.[6] However, there is currently no evidence of a risk to humans from nitrate in plants – with the possible exception of infants under the age of 3–6 months.[7] For this reason, researchers advise that home-prepared infant food containing vegetables – and this includes wild plants, of course – should be avoided until the infant is three months or older.[8]

▶ Oxalates, also known as oxalic acid

Oxalic acid is an organic compound found in many plants that, when consumed, can hinder the absorption of minerals, particularly calcium. In practice this becomes an issue only when the plant's oxalate to calcium ratio is greater than two. Plants in this group include **spinach**, **rhubarb**, **beet** and **sorrel**, and also wild members of the same plant families,[9] with oxalates potentially becoming more of an issue where these plants are growing in particularly dry conditions. Soaking and cooking both reduce the oxalate content, with boiling and discarding the cooking water being the most effective method.[10] It is no accident that plants in this group are often traditionally eaten with calcium-rich products, including milk and cheese, which naturally helps to offset any loss of calcium. For sensitive individuals, a high intake of oxalic acid may also lead to the formation of kidney stones. This is why the presence of oxalates is specifically mentioned in the text, even though oxalates may not be an issue for most people – especially those fortunate enough to have a resident population of beneficial gut bacteria such as *Oxalobacter formigenes*. With high-oxalate plants, moderation makes sense. For obvious reasons it is inadvisable to feature them too strongly in soups, juices, smoothies, etc.

---

5 Hot-spring systems can be a source of high concentrations of arsenic, mercury, cadmium, zinc and lead, all of which are readily picked up and concentrated in aquatic plants. Hyperaccumulator species such as these, and several others highlighted in the text, can tolerate and sequester metals such as cadmium, nickel, lead and zinc, often to levels 100 times greater than typical plants (Zhakypbek et al. 2024).

6 Ward et al. 2018.

7 Nitrates are generally reduced by cooking. The different response to nitrates in young infants is due to a much lower level of stomach acid, in which nitrates may convert into nitrites. When breastfed, the infant is not at risk, though, even when the mother consumes nitrate either in plants or in high-nitrate well water (Greer 2005, Hall 2018).

8 Chan 2011. Areas of high nitrate include Waikato, Bay of Plenty, Taranaki and Canterbury (Dymond et al. 2013).

9 Namely, Amaranthaceae and Polygonaceae. Other high-oxalate families featured in this book include Aizoaceae, Oxalidaceae and Portulacaceae.

10 Chai & Liebman 2005.

▶ Sodium and hypertension

Sodium is important to human health; however, too much in the diet may lead to high blood pressure (hypertension) and related health problems. So plants that tend to be particularly high in sodium are identified in the text. A few stand out: **pellitory-of-the-wall**, **sea rocket**, **orache**, **ice plant** and **silverbeet**, particularly specimens growing wild in salty places near the sea. Anyone who has been advised to reduce sodium in their diet should avoid these plants, or at least boil them with plenty of water so that the dissolved sodium can be thrown away with the cooking water.

▶ Coumarin and vitamin K

People taking anticoagulant drugs should note that coumarin may interfere with the efficacy of the drug, so should avoid consuming plants or herbal teas that contain it, namely **melilot** (*Melilotus officinalis* and *M. albus*) and **lady's bedstraw** (*Galium verum*). For the same reason, they may also be required to regulate their intake of vitamin K, which is found in green leafy vegetables generally and in many of the edible wild plants in this book. For the rest of us it should be noted, though, that this vitamin plays a useful role in blood clotting and the building of bones.

Arrangement

You will find the plants in this book arranged by botanical families, a grouping that is particularly helpful when it comes to understanding the chemistry of the plants – those plants that are most likely to be safe to eat, which ones are not and what kind of risks to look out for. In an effort to create a book that is comprehensive, and also accessible to the beginner, the most important plants are featured with a photo, description and distribution map, with any closely related edible plants growing wild in Aotearoa New Zealand listed under a subheading '**Local relatives**', where 'here' refers specifically to this country.

KEY TO SYMBOLS

 NOT TO BE CONFUSED WITH

 COOKING ADVISABLE or REQUIRED

 CAUTION ADVISABLE or REQUIRED

 POISONOUS

 SERIOUS WEED banned from sale, propagation and distribution

A selection of all-time favourites

Salad greens
bitter cress (page 32), chickweed (page 43), miner's lettuce (page 95), nasturtium (page 104), sorrel (page 85), three-cornered garlic (page 109), wall rocket (page 36), winter cress (page 32)

Flowers and flower petals
borage (page 30), brassicas (pages 32–37), chicory (page 59), marigold (page 52), nasturtium (page 104), pineapple sage (page 100), rose (page 133), violet (page 145)

Vegetable greens
choko shoots (page 73), fat-hen (page 18), nettle (page 106), pūhā (page 55), watercress (page 33), wild silverbeet (page 16)

Flavourings
fennel (page 47), lemon balm (page 97), spearmint (page 98)

Fruits — fresh, stewed or as jam
banana passionfruit (page 115), blackberry (page 134), Cape gooseberry (page 128), crab apple (page 138), elaeagnus (page 64), loquat (page 137), prickly pear (page 38), purple guava (page 102), woodland strawberry (page 136)

Fruit as vegetables
choko (page 73)

Root/tuber vegetables
Jerusalem artichoke (page 53), taro (page 21)

Seeds — nuts & flours
acorns (page 27), chestnuts (page 26), hazelnuts (page 28), macadamia (page 131), walnuts (page 146)

A simple key to identification
(major families of wild edibles are keyed by colour)

4-petalled flowers
cabbage family (pages 32–37)
speedwell (page 124)
cleavers (page 48)

5-petalled flowers
rose family (pages 133–141)
potato family (pages 126–130)
borage (page 30)
carnation family (pages 41–43)
mallow family (pages 92–93)
miner's lettuce (page 95)
purslane (page 132)
violet (page 145)

Many-petalled flowers
daisies and dandelions (pages 50–59)
ice plants (page 80)

Umbrella-like flowers
carrot family (pages 44–47)

Pea-like flowers or pods
pea family (pages 116–121)

Square stem
mint family (pages 96–101)
cleavers (page 48)
verbena family (page 144)

Thorns, spines and prickles
rose family (pages 133–141)
barberry (page 25)
cactus (page 38)
chestnut (page 26)
elaeagnus (page 64)
false acacia (page 119)
gorse (page 119)
thistles (pages 60–61)

A simple key by season

Many other wild edibles are available throughout the year.

Spring

(September, October, November)

apple flowers, Asiatic knotweed shoots, asparagus, avocado, bamboo shoots, banana passionfruit, barberry fruit, birch catkins, buds and sap, borage flowers, canna rhizomes, cherry flowers, clover flowers, false acacia flowers, gorse flowers, hawthorn flowers, hazelnut catkins and buds, horsetail shoots, ice plant fruit, Japanese honeysuckle flowers, loquat, monkey apple, mulberry, nasturtium flowers, phoenix palm sap, pine pollen cones, plum flowers, quince flowers, rowan flowers, spurrey seeds, strawberries, strawberry-raspberry fruit, sycamore sap, violet flowers, wisteria flowers.

Summer

(December, January, February)

avocado, barberry fruit, blackberry, blackcurrant, borage flowers, canna rhizomes, Cape gooseberry, Cape pondweed flowers, cherries, clover flowers, day lily flowers, elder flowers and fruit, false acacia flowers, fennel seeds, fig, fruit salad plant fruit, gooseberry, Japanese honeysuckle flowers, Japanese wineberry, loquat, nasturtium flowers, passionfruit, peach, pepino, plum, prickly pear fruit, pumpkin flowers, purslane seeds, raspberry, rowan, spurrey seeds, strawberries, strawberry-raspberry fruit, sunflower petals, tomato, wisteria flowers.

Winter

(June, July, August)

apple, brush cherry, canna rhizomes, choko, elaeagnus fruit, gorse flowers, Indian strawberry, kiwifruit, miner's lettuce, olives, passionfruit, plum flowers, rowan fruit, salsify root, tamarillo, violet flowers, winter cress.

Autumn

(March, April, May)

acorns, amaranth seed, apple, avocado, barberry fruit, blackberry, borage flowers, brush cherry, buckwheat and cornbind seeds, canna rhizomes, Cape gooseberry, chestnut, choko, feijoa, fennel seeds, fig, fruit salad plant fruit, grape, guava, hawthorn fruit, hazelnuts, Japanese honeysuckle flowers, Japanese wineberry, Jerusalem artichoke petals, kiwifruit, macadamia, nasturtium flowers, olives, passionfruit, pear, pepino, pine seeds, prickly pear, pumpkin, purslane seeds, quince, rowan fruit, salsify root, spurrey seeds, strawberries, strawberry dogwood fruit, strawberry tree fruit, sumac fruit drink, sunflower seeds, tamarillo, tomato, walnut.

Amaranth Family

[Amaranthaceae]

Also known as the **goosefoot** family, from a resemblance of the leaves of some members to the feet of geese. The stems, roots, leaves or flowers of many species are reddish due to characteristic betalain pigments. Includes **spinach**, **silverbeet**, **beetroot**, **quinoa**, **amaranth**, the introduced wild **saltwort** (*Salsola kali*, page 157) and **ureure** (the native **glasswort**, *Salicornia quinqueflora*). Many have a tendency to accumulate oxalates, so are best cooked, and many are unsuitable for young infants due to a tendency to accumulate nitrates – see page 10.

Common Amaranth

Amaranthus species

Description: Ranging from large, mat-like plants to about waist-high.

Where: Common in weedy places generally.

Part eaten: The tiny seeds (autumn), young leaves and shoots – preferably cooked – see below.

Nutritional value: Leaves rich in vitamins K, C, A and B9, calcium, potassium, iron and protein (USDA). Seeds rich in protein, manganese, phosphorus, magnesium and iron (USDA). Cooking reduces anti-nutrient content: tannins, oxalates and phytates in the seeds; oxalate and saponins in the leaves (Njoki, Chib).

Use: Amaranths occur worldwide, but their seeds were evidently first used as a high-yielding crop by the Mayans, followed by the Aztecs of Mexico and the Incas of Peru. In modern times, several species are still raised as 'grain' in the Americas and in Asia. These seeds are generally cooked to make porridge or ground into a flour for use in baked goods, typically mixed with grain flours at around 20% of the total flour volume. These nutty-tasting seeds can also be popped like popcorn. A single plant may produce over 100,000 seeds. In many parts of Central and South America, but also in Africa and Asia, amaranth leaves also provide an important cooked vegetable. In New Zealand, the most common species are the mat-like **prostrate amaranth** (*A. deflexus*) whose young leaves and shoots are cooked and eaten across much of South Africa and parts of Europe; **redroot** (*A. powellii*, top), whose leaves are cooked and eaten, and the tiny seeds boiled, dried and ground for use as flour by the indigenous Hopi and Zuni of North America; and **purple amaranth** (*A. blitum* subsp. *oleraceus*, below), whose young leaves and tops are among the most widely eaten vegetables in the humid tropics of Africa and Asia, also in Turkey and throughout China.

Red Amaranth

Amaranthus cruentus

Description: Also known as **Mexican grain amaranth**. A tall annual herb up to about 2 m, with dark-green to reddish leaves and vivid red or purple flowers.

Where: Cultivated, now wild among crops and gardens in settled areas.

Part eaten: Young leaves and seeds – preferably cooked.

Nutritional value: Seeds and flour ground from red amaranth are rich in protein (12.6–14.6%), calcium, phosphorus, magnesium, potassium and unsaturated fatty acids (Yánez), and the leaves rich in phosphorus, potassium, calcium, sodium, copper and zinc (Makobo). Cooking reduces the anti-nutrient content of both seeds and leaves (Ogundare, Osei-Owusu).

Use: A native of Nicaragua to Central Mexico, where a Mesoamerican archaeological site at Coxcatlan Cave in the Tehuacán Valley reveals that this amaranth was cultivated as a grain crop from as early as 2500BC – possibly even 4000BC. Nowadays these seeds are generally ground into flour, popped like popcorn, cooked as porridge, or – with the addition of honey or sugar – made into a kind of candy called alegría (see photo, above). Its leaves have gone on to become one of the main green vegetables of tropical Africa, India, Bangladesh, Sri Lanka and the Caribbean. In South Africa the plant is grown commercially for canning and sold in supermarkets. The young leaves and tender stems are cut and cooked or fried in oil, often mixed together with other ingredients.

Wild Silverbeet

Beta vulgaris

Description: Leaves of wild silverbeet are generally smaller than those of cultivated plants.

Where: Common behind beaches and near gardens.

Part eaten: Leaves in spring, preferably cooked to reduce the oxalic acid content. (Leaves harvested later tend to be bitter.) For people with high blood pressure, it is worth bearing in mind that plants growing near the sea tend to be high in sodium (Rana 2017). And take care to avoid harvesting from polluted sites as the plant also has a tendency to accumulate toxic heavy metals, especially lead (Sharma 2008).

Nutritional value: Leaves of wild plants rich in vitamins A and C, iron and manganese (Sánchez-Mata, Rana 2017). Although high in oxalates, this is typically offset by a high calcium content (Noonan).

Use: Native to a region extending from the UK and the Mediterranean through to India. The plant's use as a vegetable can be traced back more than 2000 years, when its leaves were enjoyed by the poet Diphilus – 'better than cabbage', he declared. To this day, its tender leaves continue to be harvested from the wild in the Mediterranean region to provide a traditional food in Spain, Italy, Cyprus, Croatia, Bosnia-Herzegovina and Turkey. In NW Tuscany, for example, they are used as a minor ingredient of minestrella soup. Elsewhere in Italy they are boiled and served on pasta, or seasoned with olive oil and lemon, or boiled and then mixed with cheese as stuffing for calzone. The plant is also cultivated in many countries, including New Zealand, as a common garden vegetable.

Orache

Atriplex prostrata (= *A. triangularis*)

Description: Leaves have a white, mealy surface.

Where: Particularly common in salty areas near the sea.

Part eaten: Young leaves, preferably cooked, as plants can accumulate oxalate and sodium (Freitas).

Nutritional value: Leaves rich in vitamin C, a fair source of vitamin A, but high in sodium (Islam).

Use: Native to the Northern Hemisphere, where charred plant remains uncovered on the shore of the Sea of Galilee allow the use of orache seeds as food to be traced back some 19,000 years. These days it is the leaves that are most often used. In Spain and Bulgaria, they are stewed or used as a pie ingredient. In response to recent famines in Africa, their value was assessed as a green leafy vegetable for cultivation on lands not currently suited for conventional agriculture. This involved a panel of judges who rated their serving – cooked for about 15 minutes with no salt added – very similar in flavour, texture and colour to spinach.

Local relatives: Young leaves and shoots of the less common *A. patula* (below) have been similarly used in Europe, while **garden orache** (*A. hortensis*) – sometimes cultivated as a spinach here, in Europe and Asia – rarely spreads into the wild.

Atriplex prostrata

Atriplex patula, various leaf forms – left and below

Fat-hen / Huainanga

Chenopodium album

Description: A whitish powder coats the underside of the leaves.

Where: Common garden weed.

Part eaten: Young leaves and tender tips in spring. High in oxalic acid (Guil), so best to boil and discard the water. Seeds also edible.

Nutritional value: Raw leaves high in vitamins A, C, B2 and B6, manganese, potassium, magnesium, and iron (USDA). Leaves also fairly high in protein (Wehmeyer). Seeds a good source of energy, protein, fat and carbohydrate (Choudhary).

Use: A native of North Africa and Eurasia, where this plant has been providing humans with food for thousands of years. Nowadays its young leaves and tips continue to be cooked and eaten as a spinach throughout much of the world, mixed with butter or cream, or used in omelettes, risotto or fried in olive oil. In the 1860s the plant reached Aotearoa New Zealand, where it was quickly adopted by Māori as a new source of greens. In Morocco the plant can be found for sale by street vendors, and in parts of North India it is deliberately cultivated, not just for the leaves and young shoots for use in soups, curries and paratha-stuffed bread but also for its seeds, which are cooked with rice or roasted and ground to make porridge – much as **quinoa** (*C. quinoa*) seeds supply a gluten-free grain here today. Indeed, in Denmark, the culinary use of fat-hen seeds can be dated from the remains of a prehistoric granary to the first century AD.

Nettle-leaved Fat-hen

Chenopodiastrum murale (= *Chenopodium*)

Description: Rather like a nettle, but lacks the stinging hairs.

Where: Widespread.

Part eaten: Young leaves. High in oxalic acid (Sánchez-Mata), so best to boil and discard the water.

Nutritional value: Fresh leaves rich in vitamins A and C, magnesium, copper and manganese (Sánchez-Mata, Guil) and fairly high in protein (Wehmeyer).

Use: Native to North Africa and Europe through to India. In Spain the leaves are traditionally collected as a pot-herb in spring and summer. In West Africa the young leaves are sometimes used in sauces. In India the leaves and tender stems are both used as a vegetable, while in Pakistan the whole plant, including the seeds, is eaten.

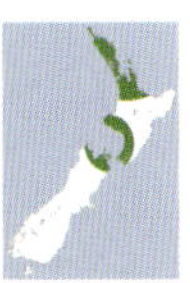

Tree Spinach

Chenopodium giganteum

Description: To 1 m or more; young leaves and shoots covered with purplish dust.

Where: Cultivated as a vegetable, occasionally wild.

Part eaten: Tender shoots and young leaves, preferably cooked – to reduce oxalic acid (Khatun).

Nutritional value: Plant rich in vitamins A, C and K, calcium, iron, phosphorus and potassium (Khatun).

Use: Native to the Himalayas through to Korea, including India, where the young shoots are a traditional wild green, in curries or fried. As the name suggests, the young leaves are widely used as a spinach.

Alligator Weed

Alternanthera philoxeroides

Description: Sprawling plant with hollow, reddish, fleshy stems, opposite leaves, papery white flowers.

Where: In warm wet places, including stream banks and ditches, where it can form floating mats in deep water to become a serious nuisance, especially in waterways (despite concerted efforts to control its spread).

Part eaten: Tender shoots, preferably cooked to reduce oxalate content. It is important to AVOID collecting from potentially polluted sites, as the plant has a known tendency to accumulate heavy metals, including lead and cadmium (Khandker).

Nutritional value: Leaves rich in vitamin C and minerals, especially iron (Mahbub).

Use: A native of South America, now common elsewhere. Although problematic for cattle (Collett), the plant is safe for people (Khandker). In Indonesia the young tops are eaten either steamed as a cooked vegetable or as a traditional salad. In North India and Bangladesh the shoots are likewise traditionally cooked as a vegetable and are even available in Dhaka from the local market.

Arum Family [Araceae]

Also known as **aroids**. Includes **kape (giant taro)**, **giant swamp taro**, **arrowleaf elephant ear**, **konjac** and **elephant foot yam**, all of which produce edible starchy underground parts containing needle-shaped crystals of calcium oxalate (raphides), and are hence eaten only after cooking. Otherwise, they cause stinging and burning of the mouth and throat. Interestingly, these same 'catch in the throat' crystals also occur in **kiwifruit** and **pineapple**, but in much smaller quantities.

Fruit Salad Plant

Monstera deliciosa

Description: Also known as **Swiss cheese plant**. Evergreen vine with large holey leaves, bearing a large cream-white hooded flower.

Where: An ornamental plant that has now been spread over much of the North Island, largely through the dumping of garden waste.

Part eaten: The cream-coloured pulp of the RIPE fruit, but only after the greenish hexagonal scales have started to fall off. Unripe fruit is strongly irritating to the throat due to needles of calcium oxalate. As the fruit ripens, the water-soluble oxalic acid content decreases to a safe level (Peters). But do be patient: the fruit can take 10 months to ripen!

Nutritional value: One fruit provides 25% of the recommended daily intake of vitamin C and is a fair source of calcium and potassium (Barros 2018).

Use: A native of Central America, where the Mayans used the roots as strong cordage for baskets and fish traps; they evidently had little or no appreciation of the fruit, though – possibly due to the fact that there it is often borne up to 20 m above the forest floor. Following the plant's introduction to England as a decorative house plant in 1752, harvesting became much more practicable. Nowadays the fruit is offered for sale in the markets of Portugal, Florida, Hawai`i and Algeria. If the fruit is picked a little early, it may be left with the base of it in water in a dark place, or placed in a paper bag to ripen. If the scales don't come off easily, the fruit (or that part of it) is still not ripe. When ripe, scrape away any small black fibres between the edible segments within the fruit. Applying a little citrus juice can help loosen these. When fully ripe, the fruit of this monstrous vine tastes like a combination of banana and pineapple. Indeed, 'delicious monster' is a literal translation of the plant's botanical name.

ripe fruit

taro corms

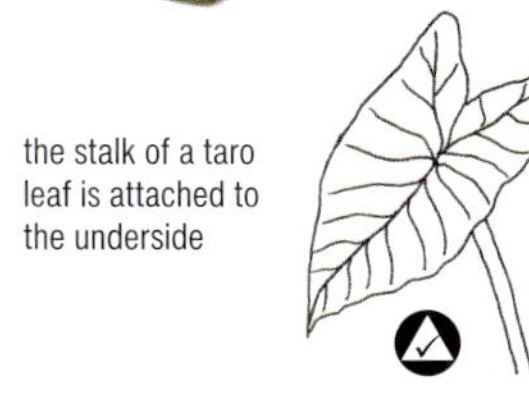

the stalk of a taro leaf is attached to the underside

Taro

Colocasia esculenta

Description: Leaves droop at an angle to the stalk, which is attached to the underside of the leaf (as shown).

Where: Introduced to New Zealand by Māori for food, but now commonly found in the wild in damp places, mostly north of the Bay of Plenty.

Part eaten: Underground part (corms), leaves, flowers and leaf stalks, all of which must be COOKED for 15–20 minutes, or until soft, to destroy the irritating calcium oxalate crystals they contain. TIP: Test corms for softness with a skewer.

Nutritional value: Cooked corms are a good source of vitamins B6 and E, manganese, phosphorus and potassium. Cooked leaves are rich in vitamins K, C, A, B1, B2, B9, manganese and potassium (USDA).

Use: A native of Asia, this is one of the most ancient cultivated crops, with evidence in New Guinea of plantations dating back 7000–10,000 years. From this region, taro went on to provide a lifeline for the settlement of the Pacific, with Polynesians and their ancestors carrying shoots of it aboard their sailing canoes, island by island, to all three corners of the Polynesian Triangle, including Aotearoa New Zealand. Indeed, the indigenous Pacific name, in its various forms – taro, talo, dalo, kalo – is shared across this entire region. Throughout Oceania, but also in Asia and tropical Africa, the corms are roasted, baked or boiled as a staple food. Throughout this wider region the cooked leaves and stalks are also eaten as a leafy vegetable or in sauces, stews, purées or soups. In the Pacific region, at least, cooked corms are pounded into a paste and left to ferment, while in the Solomon Islands, Papua New Guinea and Vanuatu the cooked flowers are also popular.

Local relatives: Although none of the following can be eaten raw, the cooked stems and leaves of **arum lily** (or **calla lily**, *Zantedeschia aethiopica*) are eaten in South Africa; in times of famine the dried 'root' of **Italian arum** (*Arum italicum*) has been boiled as food in several Mediterranean countries; the 'root' of the **cunjevoi lily** (**elephant ear**, *Alocasia brisbanensis*) is traditionally soaked, pounded and roasted as food by indigenous Australians; and the much rarer **kape** (**giant taro**, *Alocasia macrorrhizos*) is an emergency food crop of Pacific islanders. It must, however, be stressed that all four plants are toxic if eaten raw.

Asparagus Family

[Asparagaceae]

This family includes members as diverse as the **Pacific Island cabbage tree** (*Cordyline fruticosa*), whose sweet underground part is cooked and eaten in the Pacific; **Spanish dagger** (*Yucca gloriosa*), whose flowers are eaten in the Caribbean region; **century plant** (*Agave americana*), whose flower stem is cooked and eaten, and sweet sap drunk, in Mexico; and **butcher's broom** (*Ruscus aculeatus*), whose young shoots are eaten as asparagus in Europe. Note, however, that the asparagus family also features a few poisonous members, including **lily of the valley** (*Convallaria majalis* – page 164) and **bluebell** (*Hyacinthoides* species).

Wild Asparagus

Asparagus officinalis

Description: The shoots that appear in spring should not be confused with those of the highly poisonous tutu (opposite). ▶

Where: Throughout, in abandoned gardens and along some roadsides; often coastal.

Part eaten: Fleshy young shoots or 'spears' that emerge from the soil in spring – usually cooked. NOT the small berries, which are mildly poisonous.

Nutritional value: Raw shoots rich in vitamin K, iron, vitamins B9, B1 and B2 (USDA).

Use: A native of Europe and western Asia. Its young shoots are cultivated as a vegetable in cooler countries around the world, where they are generally eaten boiled, stir-fried or in soups. There is a much longer tradition, though, in Mediterranean countries – including Spain, Italy, Croatia, Bosnia and Herzegovina – of harvesting these shoots from the wild. In Spain they are eaten in omelettes or with scrambled eggs. In Sicily they are traditionally boiled and seasoned with oil and lemon, or pan-fried with bay leaves, pepper and cloves. The plant has since spread into the wild in many other countries, including the USA, where foraging for its shoots also became popular, inspiring the title there of a classic wild food book, *Stalking the Wild Asparagus* by Euell Gibbons.

Local relatives: A far more common asparagus, an invasive feathery-leaved forest weed known as the **climbing asparagus** (*A. scandens*), has no known food use; however, the young shoots of its sprawling cousin, the so-called **asparagus fern** (*A. setaceus*) are reputedly eaten by the Sotho people in its native region of South Africa.

berries

Dangerous asparagus lookalike

Tutu shoots

Coriaria species

Description: Shrubs or small trees with leaves in opposite pairs. In spring, the plant sends up succulent asparagus-like shoots, which look deceptively inviting.

Where: Common along forest edges throughout New Zealand.

POISON: Tutu has killed several circus elephants here in New Zealand. In 1868, the first of these found a very fine crop of succulent young plants, fed for four hours, took a long drink, then fell to the ground and died. Tutu has also poisoned many cattle, sheep, dogs and a few people. As recently as 2014, one man cooked and ate a tutu shoot; he later woke up in hospital with severe pain, seizures, a dislocated shoulder and loss of memory, but was fortunate enough to live to face the embarrassment. 'It looked like big asparagus,' he said. As every person who eats wild plants needs to know, all parts of this plant are very poisonous (except for the juice of the swollen flower petals – and then only after straining out the tiny, black, highly toxic seeds).

Banana Family

[Musaceae]

Members are non-woody, tree-like plants native to the tropics of Africa and Asia, and include **bananas** and **plantains** (*Musa* species), both of which are widely cultivated for their edible fruit. In many countries their flowers and the inner core of the banana 'trunks' are also commonly eaten finely chopped and cooked as a vegetable. TIP: When cutting, take care with the sap as this often leaves a black stain on clothes.

edible enset corm · inedible fruit · flower

Ethiopian Banana

Ensete ventricosum

Description: Also known as **Abyssinian banana**, **ornamental banana** or **enset**. A large, banana-like plant that grows for 5–6 years before producing a mass of short, stubby, inedible banana-like fruit, each packed with chunky, black seeds.

Where: Planted in the North Island as an ornamental, but self-seeds readily. Wild plants spreading noticeably since 1996.

Part eaten: Pulp of the 'trunk' (pseudostem), young shoots and bulb-like base of the trunk (corm).

Nutritional value: Raw pseudostem and corm rich in soluble carbohydrates and starch, but low in protein. Most parts rich in phosphorus, potassium, calcium, magnesium, iron and manganese (Yemata).

Use: A native of the Ethiopian highlands that was first domesticated there some 10,000 years ago, and which now serves as a staple/co-staple food for almost 10 million people. Its main sustenance derives from a starchy pith in the lower section of the large trunk; however, the plant also produces a giant underground corm that is packed with edible starch. To prepare the trunk part, it must first be scraped to separate the starchy pulp from the fibre. This pulp is often subjected to fermentation, too, before being dried to make a kind of flour that forms a basic ingredient of local bread or porridge. In parts of Ethiopia the pulp of the trunk, together with the young shoots, are simply boiled and eaten as a vegetable that tastes somewhat like potato.

Local relatives: Among the true **bananas** (*Musa*) grown here, few grow wild. One exception is the **Darjeeling banana** (*M. sikkimensis*), which likewise bears short plump fruit each packed with hard black seeds; although this fruit is seldom used in its native Sikkim, the flower buds are harvested there as a vegetable.

Barberry Family

[Berberidaceae]

Includes over 600 species of **barberry** shrubs from around the world, many cultivated specifically for their edible fruit. Best known among them is the so-called **European barberry**, which has proved particularly popular in Iran, where some 20,000 tonnes of barberry fruit is harvested annually, about half of this destined to be consumed in dried form.

Himalayan Barberry

Berberis glaucocarpa

Description: Spiny shrub, evergreen or semi-deciduous, with yellow flowers (Oct–Nov). Berry reddish black, with an obvious white bloom.

Where: Very common as a hedge and along roadsides.

Part eaten: RIPE fruit (Nov–Jun). Unripe fruit mildly toxic. Mind the thorns.

Use: Native to Nepal and the Western Himalayas. In North India the ripe fruit is traditionally collected near the northern border. They are generally quite tart, but are great mashed up as an ingredient of salad dressing.

Darwin's Barberry

Berberis darwinii

Description: Spiny evergreen shrub with yellow or orange flowers (Jul–Feb). Stiff, dark, shiny, holly-like leaves with spines beneath. Berries dark purple to black with a waxy bloom.

Where: Very common along roadsides.

Part eaten: RIPE fruit (Oct–Apr). Unripe fruit mildly toxic. Mind the thorns.

Nutritional value: Fruit rich in potassium and zinc (Damascos).

Use: A native of Argentina and in Chile, where the ripe fruit is collected in the plant's native Andean region for making jams, tea, liquors and ice creams.

Local relatives: European barberry (*B. vulgaris*) was originally planted here for its tart fruit for jams/jellies and juices and can now be found growing wild around some old South Island homesteads. Similarly, **Oregon grape** (*B. aquifolium*) of western North America, whose ripe fruit is a traditional food of several of the indigenous tribes, has spread into the wild around old gardens, churchyards and along roadsides.

Darwin's barberry

Beech, Oak and Chestnut Family

[Fagaceae]

A family of trees named after the **common beech** (*Fagus sylvatica*), whose seeds are not recommended as food due to their potential to cause mild gastrointestinal upset. New Zealand's native beech trees, which belong to a different family [Nothofagaceae], likewise provide no human food. The most important food plants in this family are the various kinds of **chestnut** trees, which are widely grown in cool climates for their edible nuts. Previously, acorns from oak trees were also an important source of food.

coarse ground chestnut flour

Sweet Chestnut

Castanea sativa

Description: Large deciduous tree with simple leaves, unlike **horse chestnut** (*Aesculus hippocastanum*, below), which has hand-shaped leaves and nuts that are mildly poisonous.

Where: Commonly planted along roadsides and in public parks, found in and around abandoned homesteads and occasionally wild.

Part eaten: Dehusked nuts collected from the ground in autumn (Mar–May). TIP: Slit the skins before roasting; otherwise, they are apt to explode.

Nutritional value: Raw unpeeled nuts are an excellent source of vitamin C, manganese, vitamins B6, B1, B9 and B2, phosphorus and potassium (USDA), with around 30% starch (Vaughan).

Use: A native of the eastern Mediterranean region, long cultivated in Europe for its nuts, which are commonly offered for sale, particularly in England, Germany, France, Spain, Italy, Bosnia, Hungary, Bulgaria and Turkey. Although the nuts can be peeled and eaten raw, they are best roasted, fried, boiled or steamed. Under normal conditions raw nuts don't keep well, but do if peeled and dried. They can then be milled into flour for making bread, cakes, pastries, porridge, puddings and desserts, or used as a thickener in soups. If you are serious about any of this, get a chestnut peeler machine; once peeled, they also freeze well and can be enjoyed right through the winter.

Local relatives: Japanese chestnut (*C. crenata*), **Chinese chestnut** (*C. mollissima*) and **American chestnut** (*C. dentata*) also produce edible nuts. Although these species are occasionally planted here, none are known to grow wild.

horse chestnut

instant acorn coffee

acorn flour

acorn cookies

English Oak

Quercus robur

Description: Large deciduous tree, easily recognised from the acorns in autumn.

Where: Widely planted throughout, but also wild in and around parks and plantations.

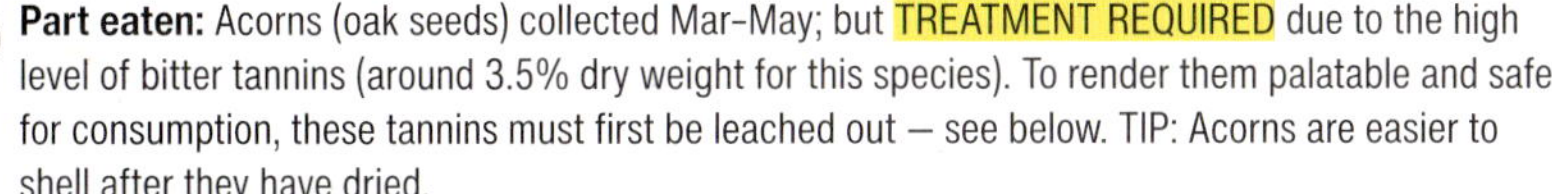

Part eaten: Acorns (oak seeds) collected Mar–May; but TREATMENT REQUIRED due to the high level of bitter tannins (around 3.5% dry weight for this species). To render them palatable and safe for consumption, these tannins must first be leached out – see below. TIP: Acorns are easier to shell after they have dried.

Nutritional value: Fresh acorns from this species typically contain 35% starch, 8% sugar, 2–4% proteins, up to 4% fat, 2% resin, 6–9% tannin (Grlić) and 6.19 % dry weight protein (Özcan).

Use: Despite the name, English oak is native to all of Europe and Iran, where acorns remained an important food until the Second World War when their use became more strongly associated with extreme poverty and famine, or with pigs. However, their use as a staple food by humans can be traced back much further – more than 10,000 years, in fact – to archaeological sites in Spain and NW Africa. Nowadays, Polish firm Dary Natury is enjoying considerable success in selling acorn coffee and acorn flour from this species of oak. Its acorns have long been traditionally eaten also in Spain, the Czech Republic, Hungary, Estonia, Romania, Bulgaria, Bosnia, Turkey and Iraq. The key lies in reducing their tannin content. One way to do this is to chop the acorns, then soak them in several changes of cold water until the water no longer turns brown. (Don't boil them, as this tends to bind the tannin into the starch, resulting in acorns that taste far too bitter.) The chopped acorns can then be dried, ground and mixed into flour to make bread, porridge or biscuits. For example, to make 12 tasty acorn biscuits (pictured), take the flour from 15 leached acorns, add an equal quantity of white flour, 1 dessertspoon each of golden syrup, margarine and water; 1 teaspoon of ground ginger and a sprinkle of sugar. Mix and bake for 15 minutes at 180°C.

Local relatives: Other oaks in New Zealand whose processed acorns are traditionally eaten elsewhere include **Turkey oak** (*Q. cerris*), whose acorns are collected for this purpose in Eurasia; **holm oak** (*Q. ilex*) from the Mediterranean region; **pin oak** (*Q. palustris*) and **red oak** (*Q. rubra*), both from North America.

Birch and Hazelnut Family

[Betulaceae]

Deciduous trees and shrubs, including several that produce commercially available foods: nutritious nuts from the **common hazel** or **cobnut** (below), **Asian hazel** (*Corylus heterophylla*) and **filbert** (*C. maxima*), and syrup and beer from the sap of various species of **birch** (*Betula pendula*, *B. pubescens*, *B. papyrifera*).

Hazelnut

Corylus avellana

Description: Large deciduous shrub. Leaves covered with soft hairs on both surfaces.
Where: Planted in cooler areas for the nuts, and occasionally found wild.
Part eaten: Nuts (autumn); catkins and buds (spring).
Nutritional value: Nuts rich in protein, energy, vitamins E, B1, B6, B9 and K, manganese, phosphorus, iron, zinc, potassium and calcium (USDA). Leaves very rich in vitamin C (Jones).
Use: A native of Europe and western Asia, where the wild nuts are traditionally collected as food, particularly in France, Belgium, Spain, Italy, Austria, Germany, Estonia, Slovakia, Czech Republic, Romania, Bulgaria and Turkey. Although sometimes eaten raw, hazelnuts are more often roasted – a practice that evidently dates back thousands of years: in 1994, a 7500-year-old pit was identified on an island off Scotland that contained the charred remains of some 30,000–40,000 nuts. In modern times, the culinary use of hazelnuts extends to their use in cakes and chocolates, breads, biscuits, muesli, ice cream, yoghurt, nut butter and chocolate spreads such as Nutella. A homemade version of this (illustrated above) can be made (with considerably less sugar) from roasted, ground nuts and a few squares of dark chocolate. Hazelnuts are also an ingredient in some vodka-based liqueurs, and a flavouring in coffee, and can also be pressed to make a strongly flavoured oil for cooking and skincare. The dried catkins (long, droopy male flowers) can even be ground into flour as a bread ingredient – a traditional use recorded from Eastern Europe – in Estonia, Slovakia and Bulgaria, at least.

Birch

Betula pendula

Description: Also known as **silver birch**. A large deciduous tree with papery white bark peeling off in flakes.

Where: Planted in cold areas, but also common wild, particularly in inland and eastern parts of the South Island.

Part eaten: Catkins (Sep–Nov), emerging leaves (when still about the size of your little fingernail), and the rising sap (all in spring).

Nutritional value: New leaves rich in vitamins A and C (Redžić 2006, Grlić). Sap of this species is rich in glucose, fructose, sucrose and calcium, while the concentration of minerals reflects the chemical composition of the soil where trees grow (Kūka).

Use: Native to much of the Northern Hemisphere, where the sweet rising sap is traditionally tapped in spring, after snowmelt, while the ground is still frozen, a practice recorded from Norway, Sweden, Finland, Lithuania, Russia, Ukraine, Latvia, Poland, Czech Republic, Slovakia, Hungary, Romania and Scotland. Initially a small twig is broken off to check that the breakage readily becomes wet. A hole is then drilled into the trunk about 50 cm above ground level and about 5 cm deep, and a small gutter or tube inserted to channel the sap into a bucket. Sap is drunk fresh, or fermented to make a beer or wine for use in summer. In one recipe the sap is flavoured with cloves and lemon peel. The tiny new leaves and buds are also eaten – in Norway and the Czech Republic, at least – and, during the Bosnian War, the catkins were used to make porridge and bread. In times of famine, the inner bark was even ground into flour in the Czech Republic.

Borage Family

[Boraginaceae]

Bristly herbs with round stems. Many members contain pyrrolizidine alkaloids, some of which have proven quite toxic when eaten in large quantities, leading to caution regarding long-term or excessive use. The best-known example is **comfrey** (*Symphytum officinale* – page 150), whose leaves were formerly promoted as a vegetable.

Borage

Borago officinalis

Description: Roughly hairy plant with sap smelling of cucumber. Blue flowers.

Where: Commonly grown in home gardens, but also wild.

Part eaten: Flowers (Sep–May) as a garnish. Excessive or prolonged use of the leaves as a vegetable is NOT recommended due to the presence of small amounts of toxic pyrrolizidine alkaloids (De Smet, Burrows).

Nutritional value: Flowers are rich in protein, polyunsaturated fatty acids and total carotenoid content (Fernandes).

Use: A native of the Mediterranean region. The delicate blue flowers taste of cucumber and may be used sparingly to garnish salads, fruit salads, soups, desserts and cakes, or frozen in ice cubes (pictured) as a decorative addition to cold drinks or iced tea. Although the leaves are widely used as a vegetable in the plant's native region – including Portugal, Spain, Italy, Czech Republic, Slovenia, Croatia, Bosnia-Herzegovina, Greece, Cyprus, Turkey, Lebanon, Tunisia and Morocco – this is not recommended, due to small amounts of a toxin whose effects on the liver are potentially cumulative.

Local relatives: In New Zealand, the name 'borage' is also loosely applied to two related plants, **Paterson's curse** (*Echium plantagineum*) and **viper's bugloss** (*E. vulgare*). Although nectar from the flowers of both is traditionally sucked from the flowers – at least in Spain – using these plants as a vegetable is inadvisable, again due to the presence of pyrrolizidine alkaloids.

Buttercup Family

[Ranunculaceae]

Many members of this family – including **monkshood** (*Aconitum napellus*), **larkspur** (*Delphinium* species) and **Lenten rose** (*Helleborus orientalis*) – contain toxins. These substances range from being sufficiently toxic to serve as arrow poisons to those (below) that are rendered perfectly harmless by the simple act of cooking or drying.

Old Man's Beard

Clematis vitalba

Description: Deciduous woody vine. Unlike native **clematis** vines, which flower Aug–Nov, this introduced clematis flowers Dec–May.

Where: A troublesome weed in native forest, often climbing high and smothering the trees.

Part eaten: Young shoots in spring – COOKED, as the whole plant contains an acrid-tasting, toxic, irritant protoanemonin that is destroyed by heat (Paura 2021).

Nutritional value: Rich in vitamin C (Jones).

Use: A native of Europe, where the young shoots are traditionally harvested in spring and stewed as a vegetable. Although cooking methods vary by region, these shoots are never eaten raw – always cooked. In rural Tuscany they are stewed or used in frittata. In Bologna the shoots are cooked and served in salads, or pan-fried in omelettes, or in mixed vegetables. In Sicily they are served as a boiled vegetable with a little olive oil, salt and vinegar, or used in omelettes, pie fillings or as a cooked ingredient in salads. In neighbouring Sardinia the preference is for eating them in omelettes, soups or fried.

Local relatives: None of New Zealand's native clematis has a known food use.

Lesser Celandine

Ficaria verna (= *Ranunculus ficaria*)

Description: Fleshy leaves. Flowers Jul–Oct.

Where: Damp places, often in semi-shade.

Part eaten: Shoots and leaves, gathered before flowering. These are eaten COOKED as raw stems, and flowers in particular contain protoanemonin (Bonora), an acrid-tasting toxin that is destroyed by heat.

Nutritional value: Leaves rich in antioxidants (Karpiuk), including vitamin C and carotenoids; also soluble sugars (Luta).

Use: A native of the Mediterranean region and Europe. As the plant matures it becomes poisonous, unless cooked. The leaves are traditionally collected in spring and eaten in Italy, Turkey, Estonia, Slovakia, Hungary and Romania. In the northern and central regions of Italy, they are added to a blend of pot-herbs, boiled or used in soups, in pies, omelettes and vegetable raviolis or as a side dish. In Hungary the leaves can even be found for sale in local markets.

Local relatives: Although buttercups should NOT be eaten raw, especially when flowering, in NE Italy the spring leaves of **creeping buttercup** (*R. repens*) are collected and boiled along with a mixture of wild herbs to be sautéed with butter or lard and garlic to make a special dish known as pistic.

Cabbage, Cress and Mustards

[Brassicaceae]

Also known as **brassicas**. Members have four-petalled flowers and a distinctively pungent flavour – due to the glucosinolates they contain. Includes **broccoli**, **Brussels sprouts**, **cauliflower**, **Chinese cabbage**, **kale**, **kohlrabi**, **mizuna**, **radish**, **rocket**, **swede**, **turnip** and various kinds of **mustard** and **cress**. Many members are prone to accumulate toxic heavy metals, so do take special care not to harvest these plants from polluted sites: near mine and landfill sites or busy roads, for example.

Winter Cress / Toi

Barbarea intermedia

Description: Shiny leaves with a cress-like taste. Yellow flowers Oct–Feb(–May).

Where: Common throughout.

Part eaten: Leaves, buds and flowers.

Nutritional value: Leaves of *B. verna* rich in calcium, iron and vitamins A, B, C, E and K (Rana 2017).

Use: A land cress of Europe, North Africa and Asia. In northern India, for example, the tender leaves are used in vegetable curries. Around 1852 this cress reached New Zealand, where it was promptly taken up by Māori as a new form of greens called **toi**, with leaves and tops being cooked in much the same way as those of pūhā. The sharp flavour of the leaves is great in salads, sandwiches and in any recipe that calls for watercress. We have taken the trouble to transplant some from the wild into our own garden.

Local relatives: Similar, less-common species of **winter cress** (e.g. *B. verna* and *B. vulgaris*) found here have been used elsewhere in much the same way.

Bitter Cress

Cardamine hirsuta

Description: Leaves often very small, but can reach 15 cm. Cress-like taste. Tiny white flowers (Aug–Dec). Seedpods flick out seeds when touched.

Where: Common throughout.

Part eaten: Leaves and flowers.

Nutritional value: Very rich in minerals, especially iron, calcium, magnesium, manganese, zinc and copper (Konsam).

Use: A native of Europe, parts of Africa and much of Asia, whose leaves and flowers have a pungent, peppery flavour similar to watercress. In Italy the young leaves are traditionally consumed raw in salad, or as an ingredient in vegetable soups, or boiled and sautéed with other spring herbs. In Bulgaria the leaves are also used in salads and in pies, while in Turkey the leaves are generally boiled first and added to salads, or cooked with onion. In Cameroon the leaves are boiled in soup, and in northern India the shoots can sometimes be found for sale in local markets. The region of its culinary use extends still further to the northern slope of the Qinling mountains in Central China.

Local relatives: Other wild cresses here include **wavy bittercress** (*C. flexuosa*), which is eaten in Italy; **panapana** (the native **New Zealand bittercress**, *C. debilis* = *C. dolichostyla*), used as an edible cress by European settlers here as early as 1848; and – less common still – the pink-flowered **cuckoo cress** (*C. pratensis*) of Europe.

Watercress / Kōwhitiwhiti

Nasturtium officinale

Description: Aquatic plant with hollow stems and white flowers Nov–Feb. Crushed leaves smell of cress.

Where: Common in sunlit streams.

Part eaten: Tender young leaves. Avoid thermal areas and old mine sites as the plant has a tendency to pick up heavy metals, including cadmium (Prasad), and slow-flowing streams in or near farms where liver fluke cysts may attach themselves to the plants. The cysts are killed by cooking for several minutes at 60°C (Dreyfuss); the use of potassium permanganate alone is not effective (Ashrafi).

Nutritional value: Leaves are low in sodium, and rich in vitamins A, C and K, potassium and calcium. High oxalic acid is largely offset by high calcium content (Sánchez-Mata, USDA).

Use: A native of North Africa, Europe and Central Asia. The culinary use of watercress can be dated back more than 2000 years to the time of Xenophon of Athens (over 350 BC). English herbalist John Gerarde (1597) went on to recommend: 'Water-Cresse being boiled in wine or milke, and drunke for certain daies together, is very good against the Scurvy.' The practice of gathering its young tender leaves remains throughout the Mediterranean region, with records from Portugal, Spain and Italy, to Slovenia, Bosnia-Herzegovina, Turkey, Cyprus, Lebanon, Jordan, Egypt, Tunisia, Algeria and Morocco. Although generally eaten raw, in Algeria and Morocco the leaves are more often cooked. The plant reached New Zealand around 1852.

Local relatives: Less-common wild edibles include **one-rowed watercress** (*N. microphyllum*); **creeping yellowcress** (*Rorippa sylvestris*) and **poniu** (the native **marsh cress**, *R. palustris*).

Twin Cress

Lepidium didymum (= *Coronopus didymus*)

Description: Leaves soft, with pungent cress smell when crushed. Inconspicuous flowers. Seeds in pairs.

Where: Common throughout.

Part eaten: Young leaves, sparingly due to strong taste.

Nutritional value: Rich in glucose, unsaturated fatty acids, proteins, vitamins A, B2, B9, B6, C and K, potassium, iron, magnesium, phosphorus, copper and zinc (Kinupp 2008, Singh 2019).

Use: A native of South America whose leaves are now enjoyed as food by rural communities across at least four continents. In Africa the peppery leaves are eaten by the Transkei and KwaZulu people (raw or cooked), and in rural subtropical areas of South America by Polish migrants. In India the young shoots are sometimes used in salad, though more commonly cooked to remove the bitter content, and eaten as spinach or as an ingredient in chapati dough. In the Czech Republic and Pakistan the leaves are generally eaten raw.

Local relatives: Less common wild edibles include **Argentine cress** (*L. bonariense*), **garden cress** (*L. sativum*), and the native **nau** (**Cook's scurvy grass**, *L. oleraceum*).

Wild Turnip / Pōwhata

Brassica rapa

Description: Yellow flowers Sep–Feb.

Where: Common throughout.

Part eaten: Young leaves, flowers, flower buds. Avoid polluted sites as this plant is a known accumulator of toxic heavy metals (Ahmad 2018).

Nutritional value: Leaves are rich in vitamins A, C, B6, B9, E and K, calcium, copper and manganese (USDA).

Use: Turnip is native to a region that extends from the Mediterranean to Iran; by 1699 it had evidently reached England, where diarist John Evelyn advises his readers: 'Take their Stalks (when they begin to run up to Seed) as far as they will easily break downwards: Peel and tie them in Bundles. Then boiling them as they do Sparagus, are to be eaten with melted Butter.' The plant's popularity remained, as botanist Pierpoint Johnson (1862) reports: 'The tops or green leaves . . . form a very wholesome vegetable, great quantities are now sold in London for such use.' Around this time (1860s) the plant reached New Zealand, where it was quickly adopted by Māori as a new form of wild greens under a wide range of names, including **pōhata**, **horuhoru**, **keha**, **kōrau**, **kotami**, **nanī**, **paea**, **pora**, **rearea**, **ruruhau**, **tairua** and **taumairangi**.

Local relatives: Wild cabbage (*B. oleracea*) began supplying greens here around the same time, under the names **paea**, **hāria**, **nanī**, **nīko**, **puka** or **rearea**. See also **rape** (*B. napus*, page 157) and **Indian mustard** (*B. juncea*, page 155).

Wild Radish

Raphanus raphanistrum

Description: Flowers white, pink or pale yellow with purple streaks on each petal (Oct–Apr). Leaves and stem rough and bristly.

Where: Very common throughout.

Part eaten: Flowers, shoots and leaves.

Nutritional value: Leaves rich in iron, calcium, magnesium, potassium, vitamin C and carotene (Wehmeyer).

Use: A native of the Mediterranean, Europe and Central Asia. The leaves are traditionally collected as a vegetable in Spain right through to Turkey and north to Belarus. Due to their rough texture, they are generally eaten cooked. When boiled, they serve as an ingredient of Italian vegetable pies or stuffing for fried ravioli, or as greens served on pasta or as a side dish. In Sardinia the boiled leaves are a traditional ingredient of local soups and salads, or are sautéed with olive oil, lard or bacon. The flowers are no less edible and are enjoyed raw in Spain, and in Sicily where they are eaten either raw or boiled and dressed with olive oil and lemon juice, or stir-fried with garlic and chilli, or in the preparation of a pasta sauce. In my own kitchen the flower buds serve as an effective substitute for broccoli. Traditional Turkish recipes often combine the boiled shoots and leaves with yoghurt, crushed garlic or lemon juice.

Local relatives: The **garden radish** (*R. sativus*) and its bulkier, milder-tasting cousin, the **daikon**, which are both grown here, are only rarely found in the wild.

Hedge Mustard

Sisymbrium officinale

Description: Small yellow flowers (Oct–Jan).
Where: Common throughout.
Part eaten: Flowers, shoots and young leaves.
Nutritional value: Rich in vitamin C, potassium, calcium (Shad) and carotene (Cerne).
Use: A native of North Africa, Europe and Kazakhstan. From the writing of botanist Pierpoint Johnson (1862) we know that it was formerly cultivated in Great Britain as a pot-herb. The young leaves and flowers can be eaten either raw or lightly cooked and have a pungent, mustard-like taste. In southern Italy and Sardinia the whole plant continues to be foraged from the wild. In Sicily the flowering shoots are generally boiled and dressed with olive oil and lemon juice, or used in soups, or battered, or fried with oil and garlic. The young shoots and leaves are also appreciated in Croatia, Bosnia-Herzegovina, Turkey and Morocco. In Ethiopia, prior to the advent of relief aid and a loss of much of the local knowledge, the plant provided an important local source of food.
Local relatives: A less-common relative here is **tumbling mustard** (*S. altissimum*), whose leaves are collected for food in western and central Turkey.

Cabbage Family

Hoary Mustard

Hirschfeldia incana

Description: To 1 m, flowering Dec–Jun.
Where: Neglected land, especially near ports.
Part eaten: Young leaves and flowering shoots.
⚠ Avoid harvesting from soils contaminated with old house paint as the plant is a known accumulator of lead (Auguy).
Nutritional value: The plant is rich in vitamins A and C (Salvatore).
Use: A native of the Mediterranean region, where the young leaves and flowering shoots supply a traditional form of greens. In Spain the tender stems are collected in winter and spring and stewed. In SE Italy the leaves and shoots are commonly boiled and served on pasta or in *pancotto* (where old bread is boiled with various wild greens, and then dressed with olive oil). In Sicily the flowering shoots are a traditional ingredient in omelettes or scrambled eggs. In Dalmatia (southern Croatia) the plant even features in wild vegetable mixes sold in most of the local markets.

Sea Rocket

Cakile edentula & *C. maritima*

Description: Fleshy leaves. Flowers lilac or white Oct–Feb.

Where: Common along the beach near high tide.

Part eaten: Leaves, flowers, immature seedpods – sparingly raw due to strong, spicy taste, or cooked.

Nutritional value: *C. maritima* is high in vitamin C and iron (Sánchez-Mata), magnesium, manganese and sodium (Guil-Guerrero 1999).

Use: Two almost identical kinds are found in New Zealand. **European sea rocket** (*C. maritima*) is a native of Western Europe and the Mediterranean, where its spicy leaves are eaten in salad or pickled, while **American sea rocket** (*C. edentula*) is from the east coast of North America, where the Iroquois of the St Lawrence River used the powdered roots with other flour to make bread in times of famine. The flowers, raw leaves and buds have a very hot mustard-like flavour, but have been used sparingly in the USA for salads. I have done the same, treating them more as a spice; however, fishermen along the coast of southern Labrador would gather and cook great quantities of the young plants.

fleshy leaves

Wall Rocket

Diplotaxis muralis

Description: Also known simply as **wild rocket**. Yellow flowers Oct–May.

Where: Throughout.

Part eaten: Flowers and leaves.

Nutritional value: Young leaves rich in potassium, calcium and magnesium (Santos).

Use: Native to Europe and North Africa. In Europe, greens gathered from wild plants appear in restaurants and cafés, where they are used in salads and other dishes as a mild substitute for commercial rocket. The practice probably spread from Italy, where the spicy, cress-like leaves and flowers are still traditionally collected from the wild and eaten in salad. In the Liguria region its leaves feature in a traditional blend of pot-herbs used in soups, filling for pies, omelettes and vegetable raviolis or simply as a boiled side dish.

Local relatives: Sand rocket (*D. tenuifolia*), which is grown commercially as a 'baby leaf rocket' salad green, is much less common in the wild here, as is **arugula rocket** (*Eruca vesicaria* subsp. *sativa*).

Shepherd's Purse

Capsella bursa-pastoris

heart-shaped seedpods

Description: Small white flowers Sep–Jan, followed by heart-shaped (purse-like) seedpods.
Where: Common throughout.
Part eaten: Tender rosettes of young leaves in spring; also flowers and seedpods.
Nutritional value: Plant high in protein compared with other wild herbs. Fresh tender leaves rich in vitamins A and C, potassium, calcium, iron and manganese, often also magnesium, and yet low in sodium, with a desirably low oxalic acid/calcium ratio (Sánchez-Mata, Zennie). Potentially unsuitable for very young infants, due to a tendency to accumulate nitrates (Bianco 1996) – see page 10.

Use: A native of North Africa and Eurasia that reached the Americas with the Spanish colonists, which led to it being cultivated there as a vegetable. As botanist Pierpoint Johnson (1862) explains: 'when cultivated in a rich soil, [it] attains a size much greater than that it usually grows to as a weed in our fields and gardens, and, so improved, is much used in America as a green vegetable, being largely raised about Philadelphia for sale in the markets'. In the Mediterranean region, including Spain, Italy, Slovenia, Croatia, Bosnia-Herzegovina, Cyprus, Turkey, Palestine and Morocco, the leaves are more commonly collected from the wild – eaten raw in salads or with bread, or boiled in soups, or with pasta or rice. The flowers and seedpods are also eaten. Eaten raw, all parts have a peppery cress-like taste, which becomes more cabbage-like after cooking. The plant is a popular vegetable across much of Asia too. In Pakistan, the Indian Himalayas, Korea and China it is considered a delicacy. Indeed, in Shanghai it is even cultivated.

Honesty

Lunaria annua

Description: Flowers Oct–Nov, followed by coin-like seedpods.
Where: Common near gardens.
Part eaten: Young leaves and shoots.
Nutritional value: Rich in vitamin C, with significant anti-inflammatory potential (Katanić Stanković).
Use: A native of southern Europe, including Italy, where the leaves are traditionally boiled along with other vegetables or used fresh in salads, at least in the central regions of Marche and Tuscany. In Bosnia and Herzegovina, too, the young shoots are traditionally used as a cooked vegetable.

Cactus Family

[Cactaceae]

Plants with succulent swollen stems, usually bearing spines or sharp prickles. Almost all are native to the Americas, where they are adapted to thriving in very dry conditions. Food plants include the Central American **dragon fruit** (*Selenicereus undatus*) and **prickly pear** (below), both of which provide edible fruit.

Prickly Pear

Opuntia ficus-indica & *O. monacantha*

Description: Also known as **Indian fig**. Bears fleshy pads covered with spines.

Where: Along cliffs and sandy beaches.

Part eaten: Pulp of ripe fruit (Jan–Apr) – in moderation, as undigested fibre from the seeds can obstruct the bowel. Young green pads also eaten. CAUTION: The fruit is covered in tiny, barbed spines, so gardening gloves are useful. Once picked, the fruit can then be rubbed in sand or with a rough cloth to remove these.

tiny barbed spines

Nutritional value: Fruit rich in calcium, magnesium, zinc, iron and vitamin C (Mutwa).

Use: Native to Central and South America, from where it was introduced to the Mediterranean region, Africa, Asia and Australia. In their native region and in Malta, Spain, southern Italy, Greece, Turkey, Israel, Saudi Arabia, Yemen and much of North Africa they are cultivated for their juicy fruit, which is eaten raw or cooked. The pulp of the fruit may also be dried, stewed, or made into jellies, jams, candy, preserves, juice, wine, vinegar or liqueur. In Mexico the immature, soft pads are harvested, too, as a vegetable – before the spines have hardened – and sliced into strips (skinned or unskinned) and fried with eggs and jalapeño chillies. In addition, the flowers can be cooked as a vegetable or used to make wine.

Canna Lilies

[Cannaceae]

These plants have large, tropical blooms which may bring to mind images of exotic lilies, but in the botanical sense these are not true lilies. This family belongs to the Zingiberales order so are really more akin to **ginger** (*Zingiber officinale*), **banana** (*Musa*) and **arrowroot** (*Maranta arundinacea*).

Canna Lily

Canna indica (= *C. edulis*)

Description: Showy red flowers (Nov–Apr), followed by large, round black seeds that look like shotgun pellets, which is why the plant is also known as **Indian shot**.

Where: Common garden escape on roadside and railway embankments.

Part eaten: Underground part (all year), usually cooked, though can also be eaten raw.

Nutritional value: Fresh rhizomes rich in starch, sugar (mostly glucose and sucrose), protein and potassium (Ruskin 1989).

Use: A native of tropical and subtropical America, including Peru, where remains of cooked rhizomes have been found in dry coastal tombs dating back to 2500 BC. These underground parts of the plant can be huge – sometimes as long as a person's forearm – and are cooked and eaten as a vegetable, or peeled, dried and milled for use in noodles, cakes and candies. In Vietnam, for example, the flour is used to prepare a pasta-like food. In Indonesia one can frequently find cooked young rhizomes for sale by street hawkers. Bakery products prepared from canna starch differ from those from wheat, being generally much lighter, spongier and crispier.

canna starch noodles

Cape Pondweeds

[Aponogetonaceae]

Members of this family are all aquatic plants with a milky sap, and include several with edible tubers, notably **Madagascar laceleaf** (*Aponogeton madagascariensis*), a native of Madagascar, and the **floating lace plant** (*A. natans*) of Asia, whose tubers, seeds, young shoots and flowering spikes are used in that region as food.

canned waterblommetji

Cape Pondweed

Aponogeton distachyos

Description: Leaves float on the water surface, while the small, sweetly scented white flowers are borne on stalks standing erect, clear of the water.

Where: In still and slow-flowing waters. CAUTION: As with all aquatic plants, it is important to avoid harvesting from polluted water.

Part eaten: Primarily the flowering spikes (Dec); the roasted roots can also be eaten.

Nutritional value: Flowers rich in protein, dietary fibre, iron, vitamin C and folic acid (Pieterse).

Use: A native of South Africa, where the flower spikes are a traditional source of food of Khoisan hunter-gatherers – a food later adopted in the 1700s by the Dutch settlers, among whom these edible flower spikes evolved into a kind of cultural symbol for the Afrikaners under the name waterblommetjie. These spikes feature in current tourist literature there as a popular ingredient in a local lamb or mutton stew known as waterblommetjie bredie, which can be found on the menus of many local upmarket restaurants. A decline in wild populations from herbicide runoff and urban expansion led to the plant being cultivated there in lakes and behind artificial dams, where the flower spikes are harvested and distributed as a canned product or frozen, or sometimes eaten pickled or as a spinach or asparagus substitute, in salads, soufflés, casseroles, fritters, sweet cakes and on toast. Less commonly, the corms or 'roots' (1.5–6 cm long) are also collected, then peeled and boiled or roasted, although the tough skin with its dense covering of black hair can be difficult to remove – even after boiling. The creamy-white inner part is starchy and tastes nutty and slightly sweet.

Carnation Family

[Caryophyllaceae]

A family best-known for its ornamental flowers like **sweet William** (*Dianthus barbatus*) and **carnation** (*D. caryophyllus*), whose flowers are also sometimes eaten. The roots of others, such as **soapwort** (*Saponaria officinalis*), contain sufficient saponins to serve as a substitute for soap, while the quantity of saponins in others, such as **chickweed** (page 43), is considerably less – at levels deemed therapeutic in the diet (Oladeji).

Bladder Campion

'bladder' at base of flower

Silene vulgaris

Description: Velvety grey leaves. Flowers (Nov–Jan) with an inflated base or 'bladder' and five white petals, each with a slit in the end.

Where: Farmland, gardens and roadsides. More common in the South Island.

Part eaten: Young leaves and stems, usually cooked. Not recommended for those with a tendency to kidney stones, due to high oxalate content (Sánchez-Mata). CAUTION: Avoid harvesting from mine sites or areas where treated timber has been burnt, as the leaves have a strong tendency to accumulate arsenic (Baroni).

Nutritional value: Young leaves and stems a good source of dietary fibre. Low in sodium, and rich in potassium, manganese and vitamins K and B9; sometimes also calcium, vitamins C and E (Sánchez-Mata). Antioxidant properties greater than those of blueberries (Vanzani). Remarkably rich in essential fatty linolenic and linoleic acids (Alarcón).

Use: A native of Eurasia. Around the Mediterranean particularly, the tender leaves and stems are traditionally a popular food. Their use in the UK can be dated back at least to 1862, when botanist Pierpoint Johnson noted that 'the young shoots resemble green peas in taste, and make a very good vegetable for the table when boiled'. Independent records of its use as wild greens have also been collected from Morocco, Spain, France, Italy, Germany, Austria, Slovenia, Belarus, Croatia, Bosnia and Herzegovina, Greece, Cyprus, Turkey, Lebanon, Egypt and North India. In Spain and Italy, at least, it is deliberately cultivated in home gardens as a vegetable and occasionally offered for sale there. Although the tender leaves are sometimes eaten raw in salads, they are more often cooked in omelettes or scrambled eggs, or used as a filling for pies and pasta.

Local relatives: Of the other common campions here, **white campion** (*S. latifolia*) enjoys a similar use in Spain, Croatia and Herzegovina, and **red campion** (*S. dioica*) is appreciated as a vegetable in England, Italy and Syria.

Spurrey

Spergula arvensis

Description: Fine-stemmed, with small, five-petalled white flowers (Sep–May).

Where: Common in gardens and farmland, sand dunes, roadsides and riverbanks.

Part eaten: Tender young plant, and tiny seeds (Sep–Jun).

Nutritional value: Plant low in fat and sugar, but high in potassium, calcium, sodium and essential amino acids, including leucine, isoleucine and histidine (Sundarapandian).

Use: Native to a region stretching from Morocco north into Siberia and Scandinavia, where Carl Linnaeus observed during an expedition to Lapland in 1732: 'In times of great scarcity, when nothing better is to be had than seeds of Spurrey (*Spergula arvensis*) from the fields, these seeds, after being dried, are ground and baked, along with a small proportion of corn. The bread thus made proves blackish, but not bad.' Stomach contents of bodies recovered from bogs in Germany and Denmark reveal that the oil-rich seeds were consumed as food in this region in prehistoric times, too, from at least as early as the 3rd century BC. Tiny though the seeds are, one plant can produce an enormous quantity of them: 1000–10,000. In India the young plant is more often used as a vegetable – a use recorded from many regions of the subcontinent, including Tamil Nadu, where farm labourers harvest it from the potato and carrot fields.

tiny black seeds (2x magnified)

tiny white flowers (3x magnified)

flowers with five notched petals (2x magnified)

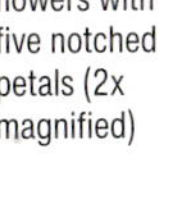

Chickweed / Kohukohu

Stellaria media

Description: Leaves opposite. Stems weak with an elastic filament within and a single line of hairs running up one side. White flowers with five notched petals (Sep–Feb). Unlike **scarlet pimpernel** (page 157), which has a square stem and red flowers. ▶

Where: Very common throughout.

Part eaten: Leaves and young stems. Moderation recommended for those deficient in calcium or with a tendency to kidney stones, as the plant is relatively high in oxalic acid with a high oxalate/calcium ratio (Guil-Guerrero 1996).

Nutritional value: Rich in vitamins C (Zennie) and K (Jansson), carotenoids (Guil), potassium, phosphorus, magnesium, calcium, iron, manganese and zinc (Civelek), containing all the essential amino acids (Shan).

Use: Native to a region extending from Morocco, India and China north to Iceland and Siberia. British botanist Pierpoint Johnson (1862) informs that 'it has been much applied in England as food for caged-birds and poultry; but in some parts of the country it is occasionally put in broths and stews,' to which herbalist Maud Grieve (1931) adds 'the young leaves when boiled can hardly be distinguished from spring spinach, and are equally wholesome [and] may also be used uncooked with young Dandelion leaves to form a salad'. Similar uses have been recorded from Iceland throughout most of Europe, Turkey, Lebanon, North India, Korea and China. In Japan, it is available in local supermarkets during the celebration of the ancient New Year festival of Nanakusa-no-sekku as one of the seven herbs customarily eaten at that time. By 1832, chickweed had reached New Zealand, where it soon became a new source of greens for Māori. It reached North America, too, where the dried leaves are nowadays packaged as a herbal tea.

Thyme-leaved Sandwort

Arenaria serpyllifolia (= *Stellaria*)

Description: Five-petalled white flowers (Nov–Feb).

Where: Tussock land, riverbeds, roadsides, sandy coastal sites.

Part eaten: Leaves, stems and flowers.

Use: This native of temperate Eurasia and North Africa is a traditional ingredient in soup for the inhabitants of the North Jeolla Province of South Korea, and is collected from the wild and eaten as a pot-herb in the Qinling Mountains district of northern China.

Carrot Family

[Apiaceae, also known as Umbelliferae]

Members have umbrella-like flowers, a hollow stem, a taproot and typically have a strong smell when crushed. Included are several important herbs, spices and vegetables – **ajwain**, **angelica**, **anise**, **asafoetida**, **caraway**, **carrot**, **celery**, **chervil**, **coriander**, **cumin**, **dill**, **fennel**, **lovage**, **parsley** and **parsnip**. Native members include **taramea** (**speargrass**, *Aciphylla* species), whose roots were traditionally eaten by Māori. However, the family also contains two of the world's most poisonous plants: **hemlock** (*Conium maculatum*, below), which is quite common in New Zealand; and **hemlock water-dropwort** (*Oenanthe crocata*), which is thankfully unknown here. Several contain furocoumarins, which can cause photodermatitis on contact, especially during the warmer months, when the sunlight and photoactive compounds are both stronger.

Dangerous carrot lookalike

Hemlock

Conium maculatum

Description: Up to 2 or 3 m tall. Crushed leaves have an unpleasant smell (*unlike* **parsley** and **wild carrot**). Stem smooth, light green with purple spots or blotches. Flowers Sep–Jan, after which the plant dies.

Where: Roadsides, riverbeds, marshy land, forest margins.

POISON: In 399 BC, when Greek philosopher Socrates was charged with 'impiety and the corruption of the young', he was condemned to death and given a cup of poison hemlock to drink. Indeed, all parts of this plant are poisonous, particularly the root and seeds. Despite the plant's unpleasant taste, children may mistake the leaves for parsley, chew the seeds, or make peashooters or whistles from the stems. So far, no one in New Zealand is known to have been killed by the plant, although one young boy in Ashburton did have a near-miss some years ago, when he ate hemlock leaves as a make-believe vegetable. Less fortunate have been several cows, sheep and one circus elephant, all of which have died here in New Zealand.

Wild Carrot

Daucus carota

Description: Also known as **Queen Anne's lace**. Stem hairy, with white flowers in a flat cluster, often with a single red-purple one in the centre (Aug–May). Crushed leaves and root smell of carrot – unlike the poisonous **hemlock** (opposite).

hairy stem

Where: Particularly common in dry places.

Part eaten: Young leaves, seeds as seasoning, and young roots where these have thickened up sufficiently in a rich soil.

Nutritional value: Leaves of wild plants very rich in vitamin K, calcium, iron (Sánchez-Mata), and antioxidants, including β-carotene and vitamin C (Vardavas, Alpinar). Roots of wild carrot have proven richer than cultivated ones in terms of protein, lipids, carbohydrates, vitamin C and calories (Redžić 2010).

Use: This is the humble ancestor of the cultivated carrot. Despite its whitish roots being usually thin and wiry, these are still traditionally used in soups in parts of Europe. The seeds are also used as flavouring in stews, soups, fish and sauces, and tender young leaves are served as wild greens. This spring growth provides a fresh wild vegetable, or salad ingredient in Sardinia, for example, where it is dressed with olive oil and salt. In NW Tuscany, Italy, wild carrot greens serve as an ingredient of minestrella soup (a traditional dish consisting of many greens). Similar uses are recorded from Bosnia and Herzegovina, Hungary, Greece, Turkey, Spain, Czech Republic, northern China, Korea and Indonesia.

Water Celery

Helosciadium nodiflorum (= *Apium*)

Description: Also known as **fool's watercress**. The long, hollow stems lie flat, often on water. Flowers (Nov–Feb) very small and white. Unlike watercress, crushed leaves smell of carrot.

Where: Usually in water. CAUTION: Avoid collecting from polluted water, e.g. from stormwater ponds.

Part eaten: Leaves and stems. Due to high oxalate content, boiling is recommended. For this reason, best avoided by those with kidney problems.

Nutritional value: Young leaves and stems rich in vitamins E, B9 and antioxidants (Sánchez-Mata).

Use: Over most of this plant's native range – from Portugal, Spain, Sardinia, Italy, Cyprus and Turkey to Lebanon, Jordan, Tunisia and Morocco – the tender leaves and stems are traditionally collected in winter and spring to be eaten either raw in salads or cooked. Popular recipes involve their use in omelettes, as a turnover filling, as a dough stuffing or to flavour soups and stews.

Local relatives: The so-called garden **celery** (*Apium graveolens*) is also sometimes found growing wild in wet areas, and **tūtae kōau** (the native **New Zealand celery**, *A. prostratum*) is common along the coast and equally edible.

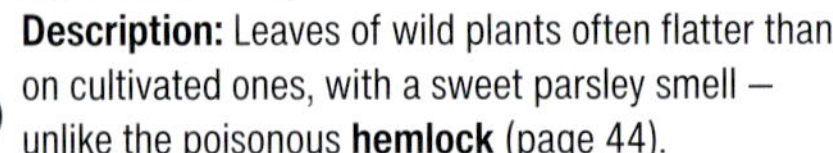

Wild Parsley

Petroselinum crispum

Description: Leaves of wild plants often flatter than on cultivated ones, with a sweet parsley smell – unlike the poisonous **hemlock** (page 44).

Where: Occasionally common in wild places and gardens.

Part eaten: Leaves (in moderation if pregnant). CAUTION: In some sensitive individuals, contact with the plant can trigger photodermatitis.

Nutritional value: Fresh leaves exceptionally rich in vitamins and minerals, especially vitamins A, B9, C and K, iron, magnesium, calcium and potassium (USDA).

Use: This is the origin of the cultivated parsley and a native of the Mediterranean region. In Crete, Southern Italy and Sicily, at least, its leaves are still traditionally collected from the wild. In New Zealand the parsley is best known as a decorative garnishing, but Mediterranean cooks are typically more adventurous. In Sicily, Tunisia and Turkey the leaves of both wild and cultivated plants are widely used as seasoning, often in soups and fish dishes. In Sardinia the leaves appear as an ingredient in cake and bread. Parsley leaves also taste surprisingly good fried for half a minute in oil or butter.

Local relatives: Hedgehog parsley (*Torilis nodosa*), whose boiled leaves are consumed as a wild vegetable in Croatia, is far less common here in New Zealand.

Parsley Dropwort

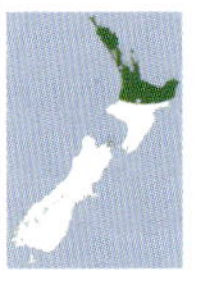

Oenanthe pimpinelloides

Description: Hairless plant. White flowers Oct–Apr.

Where: An aggressive and persistent weed of open land.

Part eaten: Leaves, which are generally eaten cooked.

Nutritional value: Rich in minerals, including phosphorus, potassium, magnesium, calcium, iron, manganese and zinc (Civelek).

Use: A native of the Mediterranean region. In Italy (Tuscany, Sicily and Sardinia, at least) and throughout much of Turkey the leaves are traditionally gathered as greens. They have a strong parsley-like taste, so are generally boiled first until tender. They are often eaten with eggs and leave a pleasantly fresh aftertaste.

Local relatives: Java water-dropwort (*O. javanica*), which is far less common here in New Zealand, has been cultivated for thousands of years in Asia as a vegetable.

Florence fennel (a popular cultivar of fennel)

Fennel

Foeniculum vulgare

Description: Tall herb up to around 2 m, with feathery leaves, and large flat bunches of small yellow flowers (Nov–May). All parts have a distinctive anise smell when crushed.

Where: Very common along roadsides, riverbeds, coastal cliffs, overgrown gardens and tracksides.

Part eaten: Tender leaves, particularly in spring, and seeds (summer and autumn).

Nutritional value: Leaves relatively high in available carbohydrate and generally a good source of dietary fibre, calcium, manganese, and vitamins A, C and B9; sometimes also potassium, magnesium and vitamin K (Sánchez-Mata).

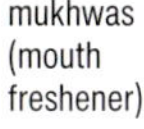

mukhwas (mouth freshener)

Use: The native region of fennel extends from the Mediterranean to Nepal. Although widely dismissed in New Zealand as a useless weed, it has been used as a medicinal plant at least since Roman times, and is still highly regarded not only as a garnish or spice but also as a vegetable. In his classic book *Acetaria, a Discourse of Sallets* (1699), John Evelyn promoted it to his English audience: 'The Stalks are to be peel'd when young, and then dress'd like Sellery. The tender Tufts and Leaves emerging, being minc'd, are eaten alone with Vinegar, or Oyl, and Pepper.' Similar uses remain current throughout the Mediterranean region today, with independent records from Portugal, Spain, France, Italy, Greece, Croatia, Bosnia-Herzegovina, Cyprus, Turkey, Lebanon, Palestine, Jordan, Egypt, Tunisia and Morocco, where the leaves continue to be collected from the wild for use as a vegetable or as seasoning – especially to garnish fish – or as a herbal tea. The tender leaves and stems are chopped finely and added raw to salads or cooked in olive or pumpkin pies, or spanakopites (spinach pies). Along the Adriatic coast of Croatia, adjacent SW Herzegovina and Turkey, wild fennel greens are so popular that they are commonly offered for sale in the local markets. The small, anise-like seeds are used for seasoning bread, pastries, soups, stews, meat, olives, boiled chestnuts and figs, or used in digestive liqueurs, and as a common spice in Malaysian cuisine, too, and in many traditional dishes of North India. They also feature in mukhwas (shown above), a colourful Indian mix of seeds used as a mouth freshener or digestive aid to finish a meal. The yellow flowers – with their mild, sweet anise flavour – are used in fruit pies, desserts and cold soups, or simply as a garnish.

Local relatives: Florence fennel or finocchio is a cultivar of the same plant, whose swollen, bulb-like stem base (pictured above left) is nowadays a popular vegetable.

Coffee Family

[Rubiaceae]

This family includes two commercially important species of **coffee** (*Coffea arabica* and *C. canephora*); New Zealand's native **taupata** (*Coprosma repens*) – whose seeds have likewise been roasted as a coffee substitute; the **noni** fruit tree (*Morinda citrifolia*); and **cinchona**, whose bark provided the original anti-malarial drug, quinine.

Cleavers

Galium aparine

Description: Climbing herb with weak, square-angled stems. The whole plant including the small round 'fruit' is densely covered with hooked hairs. No special smell. Tiny white flowers Jul–Mar.

Where: Very common among shrubs and along hedgerows. Dies off in summer.

Part eaten: Young leaves in spring – cooked (to dissolve the rough hairs of silicon). Seeds roasted as a coffee substitute.

Nutritional value: Leaves low in energy value but high in dietary fibre. Comparatively low in potassium (Abbasi 2015), but rich in vitamin C (Jones).

Use: The common name 'cleavers' – also **stickyweed** and **Velcro weed** – describe how the plant clings to the passer-by, especially to their clothing. These clingy hooks are quickly melted by boiling water – a few seconds is enough to render the plant edible. The plant is native to North Africa and Eurasia, including the UK, where diarist John Evelyn was recommending it as far back as 1699: 'Clavers, Goose-grass, *Aparine*, or *Philanthropos Dioscor*. &c. the tender Winders, with young Nettle-tops, are us'd in Lenten Pottages.' Indeed, the tradition of using its boiled young leaves as a vegetable is recorded across much of Europe, to Pakistan, Jammu and Kashmir and on to the Qinling Mountains in northern China. The ripe fruit, too, has long provided a substitute for coffee; in Croatia, for example, it is first dried, then roasted on a low fire, before being beaten or ground to a brown powder whose constituent alkaloids do actually include caffeine (Butnariu). This makeshift coffee was particularly appreciated in the early 1990s, during the siege of Sarajevo, when it would be covered with boiling water and left to steep, then served warm with the addition of powdered milk. Other traditional uses of the plant derive from the barbed stems themselves, a tangle of which formerly served as a rough sieve for straining milk, and – as with the related **bedstraws** – were sometimes dried for use as a stuffing for mattresses. An alternative name, **goosegrass**, refers to another food use – a fondness for the plant among chickens and geese.

Currants and Gooseberries

[Grossulariaceae]

This family includes around 200 kinds of currants and gooseberries, including several deciduous shrubs that are grown commercially for their edible fruit, e.g. **blackcurrant**, **red currant**, **white currant** and **gooseberry**.

Blackcurrant

Ribes nigrum

Description: Thornless deciduous shrub, strongly aromatic when bruised. Fruits dark purple to black.

Where: Cultivated in colder areas, and now found growing wild in the South Island on scrub-covered hillsides and roadsides.

Part eaten: Ripe fruit (Dec–Feb). Leaves brewed as tea.

Nutritional value: Fruit very rich in vitamin C, manganese and iron (USDA).

Use: Native to the cooler regions of Europe and Asia, where the small black fruits are traditionally gathered in the wild and eaten fresh, a practice recorded from England, Sweden, Finland, Estonia, Belarus, Slovakia, Hungary and Bulgaria right through to the Indian Himalayas. The fruit is often juiced or made into jam, or used in puddings, tarts, fruit salad and sauces. In Russia and Ireland they may be soaked in spirits. Nowadays the dried leaves are also a popular ingredient of herbal teas or tea blends.

Local relatives: Equally common in the South Island is the **red currant** (*R. rubrum*), whose fruits are collected for food in Western Europe; while the **flowering currant** (*R. sanguineum*) – whose fruit was used by the indigenous Nlaka'pamux of British Columbia and by many tribes in Washington state – is very common.

Gooseberry

Ribes uva-crispa

Description: Spiny deciduous shrub with translucent green fruit (sometimes yellow or dark red).

Where: Cultivated in colder areas, now common in the wild along South Island roadsides, etc.

Part eaten: Ripe fruit (Nov–Feb) and young leaves. TIP: To avoid the spines, use gardening gloves.

Nutritional value: Fruit rich in vitamin C (USDA).

Use: Native to Central Europe and NW Africa, from where the plant has spread with the help of cultivation as far north as the Arctic Circle. In much of Europe the ripe fruit continues to be collected from the wild and is eaten fresh or cooked in tarts and pies, or made into jellies, sauces, chutneys and jams. Young, tender leaves are also eaten in salads.

Daisy Family: Daisies

[Asteraceae: Asteroideae]

These plants have daisy-like flowers with a central disc. The group includes several important food crops – **sunflower**, **Jerusalem artichoke**, **yacón** and **stevia**, and some less well-known edibles like **dahlia** (page 151). Others, such as **ragwort** (*Jacobaea vulgaris*) and **coltsfoot** (*Tussilago farfara*), are unsuitable as food due to the poisonous pyrrolizidine alkaloids they contain. Pollen from the flowers of many can trigger allergies in those who suffer from asthma or hayfever.

Daisy

Bellis perennis

Description: Low-growing with small daisy flowers (Sep–Mar).
Where: Very common in lawns and farmland.
Part eaten: Young leaves in spring.
Nutritional value: Rich in iron, calcium, potassium, magnesium and vitamins A, E (Ranfa) and C (Redžic 2010).
Use: This is the humble lawn daisy and is a native of Europe and West Asia. Its use as an edible spring green can be traced at least as far back as the 18th century. It seems to be most popular in Italy, with independent records from Umbria, western Friuli, Liguria, NW Tuscany – and Sicily, where it serves as an ingredient of various traditional vegetable soups. In Germany, Czech Republic, Bosnia-Herzegovina, Bulgaria and Turkey the spring leaves are also eaten raw in salads and, in Turkey, can even be found for sale in local markets. The plant continues to enjoy popularity in Italy, with top chefs using its flower buds and petals raw in salads, in soups or as garnish or in tea. I personally find them too acrid.

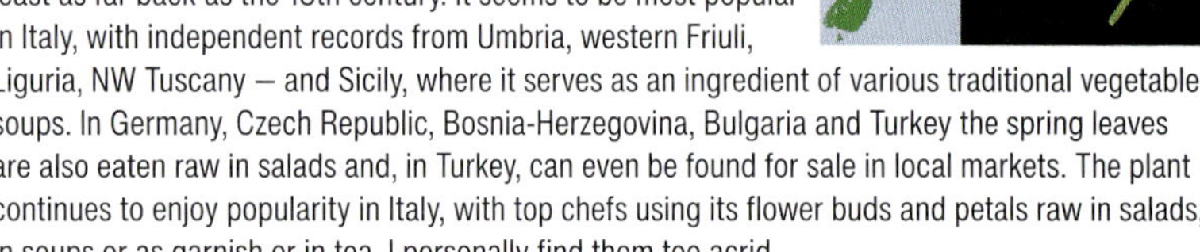

Ox-eye Daisy

Leucanthemum vulgare

Description: Waist-high plant with large daisy flowers Aug–May.
Where: Very common throughout.
Part eaten: Young leaves before flowering; also the flowers themselves.
Nutritional value: Leaves especially rich in vitamins A and C (Zennie).
Use: Although native to northern Eurasia this tall daisy has spread into Africa, where the young leaves nowadays make an important contribution to food baskets and livelihoods in the smallholder and subsistence farming communities of Cameroon, eaten raw or cooked, finely chopped and added to salads. In 1862, Pierpoint Johnson recommended using the leaves in salad, a use that remains current in Europe, including the eastern Riviera (NW Italy) and Bosnia. Similarly, in NE Italy young leaves are traditionally gathered in spring and boiled, then sautéed in a regional dish known as pistic. The flowers too are eaten in Italy and are currently popular with top chefs in the country.

Cobblers' Pegs

Bidens pilosa

Description: Small daisy flowers (Aug–May). Long, hooked seeds.
Where: Common north of Bay of Plenty.
Part eaten: Tender tops cooked. Boiling for five minutes significantly reduces antinutrient content, including tannin and phytic acid (Essack). Old leaves too bitter.
Nutritional value: Leaves rich in fibre, protein and minerals, especially magnesium (Odhav).
Use: A native of tropical and subtropical America, from where the plant has since spread across much of the globe. It is now enjoyed as a vegetable across much of sub-Saharan Africa, where the young shoots and leaves are cooked, or parboiled and dried in the sun to store as a powder for use in the dry season. Its value to Africans is reflected in the impressive number of countries from which independent records of its use have been collected. These include rural areas of Sierra Leone, Liberia, Ivory Coast, Benin, Nigeria, Cameroon, Ethiopia, DR Congo, Uganda, Kenya, Tanzania, Zambia, Malawi, Mozambique, Zimbabwe, Botswana and South Africa. Although the resinous flavour and aftertaste are not universally enjoyed, the tender tops are now used in Assam (India), in China, and in Java (Indonesia) – where they can be found for sale in local markets.
Local relatives: Beggar's ticks (*B. frondosa*) – whose young leaves and stems are eaten cooked in Japan – is common from around Christchurch north.

long, hooked seeds

Galinsoga

Galinsoga parviflora

Description: Small daisy flowers, each with five notched white petals (Oct–Apr).
Where: Common garden weed.
Part eaten: Young tops, best boiled for five minutes to reduce antinutrients, including phytic acid and oxalic acid.
Nutritional value: Leaves a good source of iron, calcium, magnesium, potassium and vitamin A (Wehmeyer).

Use: A native of Central and South America, from where it has now spread through much of the world, including Africa and Asia, where the leaves, stem and flowering shoots are harvested before flowering and cooked as a pot-herb, or added to soups and stews. The rural inhabitants of Uganda, Tanzania, Malawi, Zambia, Zimbabwe and South Africa often collect the plant for the kitchen when weeding their crops. In SE Asia, too, Tibetans in the Shangri-La region of what is now known as Yunnan, China, eat the young stems and leaves either boiled or stir-fried. In Indonesia the young tops are eaten steamed with rice. The plant is used as a vegetable, too, in Jammu and Kashmir in the NW Himalayas.
Local relatives: The stems, leaves and flowers of the similar – and equally common – *G. quadriradiata* are gathered in Mexico, where they are eaten fresh.

Yarrow

Achillea millefolium

Description: Pleasant-smelling herb with feathery leaves. White flowers Dec–May.
Where: A garden plant now common in the wild, particularly in drier areas of the South Island.
Part eaten: Flowers. Young leaves as garnish or chopped finely and used sparingly.
Nutritional value: Plants rich in protein and potassium (Dragomir). Young leaves rich in vitamin C (Redžić 2006). Overall vitamin content – A, E, K and D – highest in the flowers (Keser).
Use: Native to most of the Northern Hemisphere. In Russia, Romania, Estonia and Croatia the leaves and flowers are traditionally infused to brew a herbal tea, and in Sweden the leaves were previously used as a substitute for hops in the preparation of beer. The plant is currently making a comeback in northern Europe, where a foraging enterprise in southern Sweden is collecting the leaves and flowers for a leading restaurant in Copenhagen. The feathery leaves taste bitter, so are generally chopped finely and added sparingly to salads, or more popularly cooked: remove leaves from the tough stems and boil for five minutes.

Marigold

Calendula officinalis

Description: Roughly hairy leaves. Flowers orange or yellow Oct–May.
Where: Common garden plant, found wild near settlements.
Part eaten: Petals (and young leaves).
Nutritional value: Fresh flowers high in carotenoids and recommended as a healthy source of colourants for the food industry (Petrova).
Use: A native of the western Mediterranean that has since been distributed across much of Europe and beyond. The most commonly used part is the petals of the flower, which are used in broths and soups in Britain and Holland and as a substitute for saffron for colouring butter, cheese, rice, etc. An extract has sometimes been fed to hens to make their egg yolks golden. The petals are eaten raw in salads, too, or sprinkled as a garnish, a tradition recorded from the Bologna region of northern Italy and from Bulgaria. The fresh young leaves are less commonly used but are appreciated in the nearby border region of eastern Serbia.
Local relatives: The flowers of the less common **Mexican marigold** (*Tagetes erecta*) are marketed in Korea as a slightly bitter food; and are used in Thailand for salads, frying and in light curry. Its petals are likewise used as a food dye.

Jerusalem Artichoke

Helianthus tuberosus

Description: Up to 3 m tall with yellow flowers like small sunflowers.

Where: Cultivated, and now common in the wild.

Part eaten: Underground part (tubers) and flower petals (April).

Nutritional value: Raw tubers rich in inulin, iron, phosphorus, potassium and vitamin B1 (USDA). Flowers rich in antioxidants (Petrova).

Use: A native of North America, where the indigenous population traditionally collected its tubers from the wild to eat raw, boiled or fried; in the Great Lakes area, the Wyandot people even cultivated them. The plant was later taken to Europe for cultivation, where it escaped into the wild, providing tubers for the rural population, who eat it raw, cooked or pickled. Nowadays, they are still foraged in Spain, Sicily, Belarus, Hungary, Romania, Croatia, Bosnia-Herzegovina, Bulgaria and Turkey. Used in much the same way as potatoes, they make excellent soup or fried like hash browns (chopped/diced with onions). Being rich in inulin, a starch-like fibre, they provide food bulk and micronutrients without the associated calories. The petals can also be used as natural colourants.

Sunflower

Helianthus annuus

Description: Unbranched stem, often much shorter on wild plants (0.4–2 m tall).

Where: Cultivated for seeds and oil and as an ornamental, now spreading into the wild.

Part eaten: Flower petals (Jan–Mar) and seeds (Mar–Apr).

Nutritional value: Seeds rich in protein, unsaturated fats, vitamins E, B1, B2, B3, B5, B6 and B9, manganese, magnesium, phosphorus, zinc, iron and potassium (USDA).

Use: A native of the Americas, where the hulled seeds have been used as food by indigenous people for thousands of years; indeed, evidence there of cultivation can be dated back to 900 BC. Culinary use of the flowers is probably more recent and certainly less well known; in Korea nowadays they are marketed for food throughout much of the year. The petals are eaten raw or cooked, and young flower buds lightly boiled or steamed with an artichoke flavour. The tender leafstalks can also be boiled as a vegetable.

Edible garden escapes

In Europe and Turkey the tender leaves of **corn marigold** (*Glebionis segetum*) are eaten raw or cooked, while in Europe and Asia the leaves, tender shoots, stems and petals of **annual chrysanthemum** (**edible chrysanthemum** or **chop suey green**, *G. coronaria*), are eaten – although the latter rarely grows wild here in New Zealand.

Daisy Family: Dandelions

[Asteraceae: Cichorioideae]

Members of this group have dandelion-like flowers, with strap-like petals squared-off at the ends, typically overlapping all the way to the centre. The stems and leaves contain a bitter-tasting milky juice. Included are several popular food crops: **lettuce**, **endive**, **chicory**, **salsify** and **scorzonera**. It is advisable for those with asthma, allergies or hayfever to avoid the flowers.

Dandelion / Tawao

Taraxacum officinale agg.

Description: Hollow unbranched stem with a single flowerhead. Milky sap. Yellow flowers Sep–May.

Where: Very common throughout.

Part eaten: Young leaves (in spring before they become too bitter), root and flowers or flower petals. Leaves high in oxalates; eaten raw, oxalic acid/calcium ratio is high (>5), so may rob the body of calcium. Hence, boiling is recommended, and leaves are best avoided by those with a tendency to kidney stones (Sánchez-Mata).

Nutritional value: Raw leaves rich in vitamins K and A and a good source of vitamins C, B1, B2 and B6, potassium, iron and magnesium, and yet low in sodium (USDA). Roots contain inulin (Lim).

Use: Mention of the plant's culinary use in Greek mythology implies its use as a vegetable for some 2000 years. In 1699 the English diarist John Evelyn recommended the leaves 'macerated in several Waters, to extract the bitterness', reporting that it is 'sold in most *Herb-Shops* about *London* [and] justly esteem'd an excellent *Vernal Sallet*'. In France it has been deliberately cultivated for food from at least 1879. The leaves have remained a popular vegetable in Europe, boiled as a spinach or as an ingredient of vegetable pie, soups or omelettes. Used in salads or sandwiches, raw leaves should be finely chopped, young and tender, or blanched; otherwise, they tend to be too bitter. The roots are also roasted and ground to make a kind of coffee or coffee additive, and the flowers and petals make a colourful garnish or are brewed to make a dandelion wine or ale. The plant reached New Zealand around 1852, where Māori gave it the name **tawao**.

Local relatives: Young leaves and flower buds of **tohetaka** (**native dandelion**, *T. magellanicum*) were also traditionally used as food by Māori.

dandelion root coffee

Sow Thistle / Pūhā

Sonchus oleraceus

Description: Soft leaves. Yellow flowers in clusters (Nov-Jan).

Where: Very common throughout.

Part eaten: Leaves, best in spring, before the flowers appear. The leaves are high in oxalates, so boiling is recommended, and they are best avoided by those with a tendency to kidney stones.

Nutritional value: Tender leaves rich in potassium, manganese and vitamin B9; sometimes also calcium, iron and vitamin C (Sánchez-Mata); and rich in antioxidants generally – more so than blueberries (Vanzani, Alpinar, Jimoh 2011).

Use: This – the commonest pūhā or pūwhā in New Zealand nowadays – is a native of Europe, North Africa, and North and West Asia. It became established here in New Zealand along with the first European settlers around 1830, effectively replacing the indigenous pūhā (*S. kirkii*) as the preferred spinach of Māori. Māori typically harvest the plant all year, often washing out much of the bitter-tasting milky sap by rubbing the stems and leaves together in running water before boiling them for 20–30 minutes. The plant's use as a vegetable can be traced back much further, though, to some 2000 years ago when it was used by the Greek physician Galen. It remains a popular wild green today throughout much of the Mediterranean region, including Portugal, Spain, Sardinia, Italy, Slovenia, Croatia, Bosnia-Herzegovina, Greece, Cyprus, Turkey, Jordan, Egypt, Tunisia and Morocco. In southern Italy the demand for its leaves in salads, or for boiling or frying, is such that they are offered for sale in the local open-air markets. The plant is used similarly throughout Africa, much of the Himalayan region of Pakistan and India, and in China and South Korea, where it is most commonly used as a cooked leafy vegetable.

Local relatives: Two other European species of pūhā – **prickly sow thistle** (right, *S. asper*) and **perennial sow thistle** (*S. arvensis*) – can be used in the same way. The original **pūhā** (**New Zealand sow thistle**, *S. kirkii*), a native shore species, is now rare.

prickly sow thistle

Hawkbit

Leontodon saxatilis (= *L. taraxacoides*)
Description: Unbranched stem. Flowers Nov–Apr.
Where: Common throughout.
Part eaten: Young leaves.
Use: A native of Europe and Morocco. In Spain its basal leaves are traditionally collected in winter and spring and eaten either raw in salads or stewed.
Local relatives: Autumn hawkbit (*L. autumnalis*), whose young leaves and root are eaten either cooked or raw in salad in Bosnia, is much less common here.

Hawksbeard

Crepis capillaris
Description: Flowers in loose clusters atop a leafy, branching stem (Sep–Mar).
Where: Abundant throughout.
Part eaten: Young leaves.
Nutritional value: Leaves of the related *C. vesicaria* are rich in vitamins C, K (Vardavas), B1, carotenoids and fibre (Panfili).
Use: A native of Europe. In Italy the leaves are among those traditionally gathered in spring, boiled and stewed, or used in vegetable soups, or boiled and sautéed. Culinary use of the young leaves is recorded also from Bosnia and Herzegovina, where they are traditionally included in salads, or added to pasta and rice or cooked vegetables. As such, they were particularly appreciated during the 1992 siege of Sarajevo – the longest siege of a capital city in modern times (1425 days) – when the fried root also served as a surrogate for coffee.
Local relatives: Similar uses are recorded for the less common **beaked hawksbeard** (*C. vesicaria*).

Catsear

Hypochaeris radicata

Description: Leaves roughly hairy. Sparingly branched leafless stems. Flowers Nov–Mar.

Where: Very common throughout.

Part eaten: Leaves of young plants.

Nutritional value: Leaves rich in vitamin C (Jones) and minerals, especially iron and calcium (Zeghichi).

Use: A native of Europe and North Africa, whose virtue as a pot-herb was noted over 2000 years ago by Theophrastus. As British botanist Pierpoint Johnson (1862) explains, it 'may be boiled as a pot-herb, and has been cultivated in gardens, but has fallen into disuse'. On the European mainland, though, its leaves have continued to be widely used in much the same way as dandelion – in salads, fried or boiled, or used in vegetable pies, omelettes and soups. Records of such uses have been collected from many regions of Italy, and from Spain, Croatia and Crete. In Sicily the flowers are also sometimes included.

Local relatives: Smooth catsear (*H. glabra*), whose young leaves are traditionally eaten in Italy and Spain, is far less common here.

Oxtongue

Helminthotheca echioides (= *Picris*)

Description: Rough, prickly leaves. Flowers Jan–Mar.

Where: Very common roadside plant.

Part eaten: Leaves of young plants – cooked.

Nutritional value: Leaves rich in iron, potassium, calcium, magnesium and manganese (Guil-Guerrero 1999).

Use: A native of the Mediterranean region, where the leaves are appreciated as a spring vegetable. In southern Italy and Croatia they are offered for sale in some local open-air markets. From Spain across to Italy, including Sardinia and Sicily, and right through to Greece the leaves are boiled, used in soups and omelettes, or as an ingredient of vegetable pie. Due to their rough texture the leaves are not eaten raw; however, a few minutes in boiling water melts their prickliness.

Nipplewort

Lapsana communis

Description: Branching stem, small flowers Dec–Mar.

Where: Common throughout.

Part eaten: Leaves of young plants.

Nutritional value: Fresh leaves rich in vitamin C and carotene (Jones, Grlić, Bussmann 2020).

Use: A native of western Eurasia and North Africa. 'The young leaves,' notes John Lightfoot (1777), 'are eaten by the inhabitants of *Constantinople* raw as a sallad. In some parts of *England* the common people boil them as greens, but they have a bitter and not agreeable taste.' Lightfoot may have been trying older leaves for, in mainland Europe – Italy, Bosnia-Herzegovina and Bulgaria, at least – rural residents are still eagerly collecting the young foliage for use in soups and/or salads.

Prickly Lettuce

Lactuca serriola

Description: Upper leaves twist on their sides to align north–south, and midribs not red – *unlike* those of the less-common **acrid lettuce**. Flowers Jan–Mar.

Where: Scattered throughout.

Part eaten: Tender young shoots and leaves in spring (otherwise, too bitter).

Nutritional value: Spring leaves very rich in vitamins A and C (Zennie). Indeed, generally contain more vitamin A than do cultivated lettuces (Mou).

Use: A native of Eurasia and North Africa, whose tender young shoots are collected in spring over much of this region. They taste similar to dandelion leaves so are often eaten along with other, blander-tasting greens. They are generally cooked, especially in North India, but in several Mediterranean countries (including Spain, Italy, Croatia, Herzegovina and Turkey) they are also enjoyed raw in salads. Its native range extends as far east as China, where wild plants are collected for the same purpose.

Local relatives: The related **garden lettuce** (*L. sativa*) is rarely found in the wild. Leaves of the less common **acrid lettuce** (*L. virosa*) are not recommended – see appendix.

Wall Lettuce

Mycelis muralis (= *Lactuca*)

Description: Thin stems much-branched towards the top. Flowers Dec–Mar.

Where: Very common in shade from Coromandel southwards, often on walls.

Part eaten: Young leaves (before flowering). Later, the leaves become too bitter.

Nutritional value: Leaves rich in calcium and potassium (Clabby).

Use: A native of NW Africa and Europe. In Umbria, Central Italy, the young leaves are used in the same way as dandelion, eaten in vegetable soups or raw in salads.

Chicory

Cichorium intybus

Description: Finely ribbed stems. Flowers blue or pinkish (Dec–Mar).

Where: Planted as a forage crop, now common along roadsides and in farmland.

Part eaten: Tender leaves (prior to flowering, when they become too bitter). Roasted roots as a coffee substitute. ⚠ Flowers as a garnish. Avoid harvesting from polluted sites as the shoots have a tendency to accumulate toxic heavy metals, including cadmium (Abe 2008).

Nutritional value: Tender leaves a good source of dietary fibre and vitamin K, and often of potassium and calcium, vitamins C, B9 and A; low in oxalates (Sánchez-Mata, USDA). The root contains up to 17% inulin, a 'sugar' that can be useful in the management of diabetes (Couri).

Use: A native of the Mediterranean region to the Lesser Himalayas and northern Europe. Theophrastus, writing more than 2000 years ago, noted its use as a pot-herb, as did diarist John Evelyn (1706), who describes it as: 'being very bitter, a little *edulcorated* [made more palatable] with *Sugar* and *Vinegar*, [it] is, by some, eaten in the Summer, but more grateful to the Stomach than the Palate'. In Europe the young leaves are still collected from the wild, not in summer but in spring – for use in salads, pies, ravioli or stews or sautéed. The leaves may be boiled several times to reduce the bitterness. It is the root that is harvested in summer – for roasting as a coffee substitute. The flowers are nowadays added to salads, or frozen into ice cubes to add to drinks. In southern Italy and Dalmatia, wild chicory is offered for sale in the open-air markets. In the Lesser Himalayas young leaves are cooked in diluted milk.

Salsify

Tragopogon porrifolius

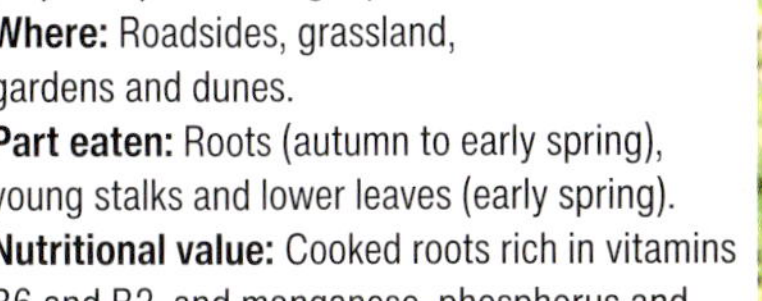

Description: Leek-like leaves, milky sap, purplish flowers (Sep–Mar) and strong taproot.

Where: Roadsides, grassland, gardens and dunes.

Part eaten: Roots (autumn to early spring), young stalks and lower leaves (early spring).

Nutritional value: Cooked roots rich in vitamins B6 and B2, and manganese, phosphorus and potassium (USDA).

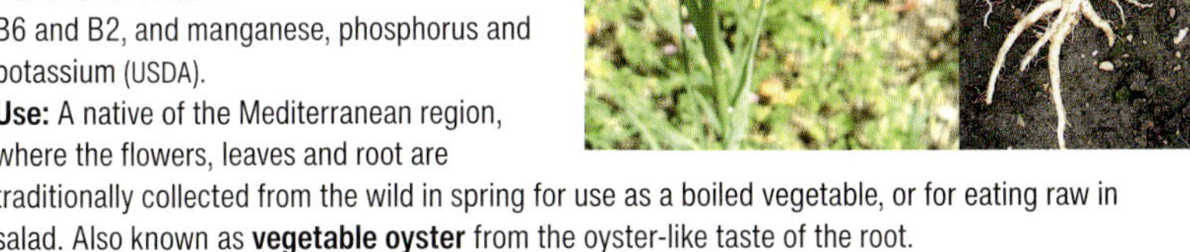

Use: A native of the Mediterranean region, where the flowers, leaves and root are traditionally collected from the wild in spring for use as a boiled vegetable, or for eating raw in salad. Also known as **vegetable oyster** from the oyster-like taste of the root.

Daisy Family: Thistles

[Asteraceae: Carduoideae]

Thistles are a subfamily of the daisy family and comprise plants that are generally spiny or bristly, with flowerheads wrapped in layers of overlapping bracts with bristly points. Many have a bitter taste. Examples include **globe artichoke**, **cardoon**, **safflower** and the less well-known **cabbage thistle** (*Cirsium oleraceum*), whose young stems and leaves are grown as food in Japan and India.

Burdock

Arctium minus

Description: Floppy leaves with hollow stalks. Reddish-purple thistle-like flowers Jan–Apr, with bur-like hooks that cling to clothing.
Where: Common south of Tauranga.
Part eaten: Leaves, roots, and young stems (in spring).
Nutritional value: Spring greens rich in vitamin C (Burrell). Roots rich in carbohydrate in the form of inulin – up to 27% (De Smet).
Use: The plant's native region extends from Morocco to Siberia, where the stems are harvested for food in spring – before becoming stringy. In Spain, SW Italy and eastern Turkey they are peeled like thin cardoon stems and enjoyed fresh in salads, or cooked like asparagus. In Spain the tender leaves are also eaten; and in Italy the roots, too.
Local relatives: In Egypt, Iraq and Japan, roots of the **greater burdock** (*A. lappa*) are even cultivated as a vegetable, and in Britain they are still a popular ingredient of various brands of dandelion & burdock cordial, beer and gin; however, this plant is much less common in New Zealand.

Scotch Thistle / Pūngitangita

Cirsium vulgare

Description: Prickly leaves and reddish-purple thistle flowers Nov–Mar.
Where: Abundant throughout.
Part eaten: Young stems and spring leaves. The white nutty base of the inside of the flower.
Nutritional value: Whole plant rich in potassium (Dragomir).
Use: Native to a region that extends from Algeria to Siberia. In Turkey the young stems are a traditional food, and in Italy the young leaves (trimmed of prickles) are traditionally collected in spring for use in soups, filling for pies, omelettes and vegetable ravioli or simply as a side dish.
Local relatives: The **cotton thistle** (*Onopordum acanthium*, also sometimes known in Europe as **Scotch thistle**) is used in the same way, but is less common in New Zealand.

Californian Thistle

Cirsium arvense

Description: Also known as **creeping thistle**. Bears clustered, pale purple flowerheads (Dec–Feb).
Where: Very common throughout.
Part eaten: Young shoots, leaves and peeled stems.
Nutritional value: Leaves rich in vitamins C (Jones) and K (Jansson).
Use: Although common in California nowadays, this thistle is actually a native of Eurasia, where the young shoots and leaves are still traditionally collected in spring – a use recorded from Estonia, Belarus, Hungary, Spain, parts of Italy, Croatia and Turkey, where they are trimmed of prickles and stewed in vegetable soups or served as a boiled vegetable. In Hungary and NW Pakistan harvesting may also include the peeled semi-mature stems.
Local relatives: Less common in New Zealand are **marsh thistle** (*C. palustre*), whose leaves and peeled stems are also eaten in Europe; **winged thistle** (*Carduus tenuiflorus*), whose basal leaves and tender stems are peeled and eaten either raw or stewed in Spain and Morocco; **slender winged thistle** (*C. pycnocephalus*) whose peeled stems are eaten raw or cooked in Sardinia; and **nodding thistle** (*C. nutans*), whose peeled stems are eaten in Turkey.

Variegated Thistle

milk-like markings on leaves

Silybum marianum

Description: Also known as **milk thistle**, as the very large leaves appear marbled with white, milk-like markings. Red-purple flowers Nov–Jan.
Where: Common throughout.
Part eaten: Trimmed leaves and peeled midribs (in spring), preferably boiled, due to relatively high oxalate content. Potentially unsuitable for very young infants, due to a tendency to accumulate nitrates (Burrows) – see page 10.
Nutritional value: Leaves rich in potassium, antioxidants and vitamin B9 (Sánchez-Mata).
Use: Native to Central Asia through to Ethiopia. In the Mediterranean countries of Spain, Italy, Greece, Cyprus, Turkey, Jordan, Palestine, Tunisia and Morocco this thistle is traditionally eaten as a vegetable. As diarist John Evelyn says of its use in Britain in 1699: 'Disarm'd of its Prickles, and boil'd [it] is worth Esteem: The young Stalk . . . (sold in our Herb-Markets) being peel'd and soak'd in Water, to extract the bitterness, boil'd or raw, is a very wholsome *Sallet*, eaten with *Oyl*, *Salt*, and *Pepper*: some eat them sodden in proper Broath, or bak'd in Pies, like the *Artichoak*; but the tender Stalk boil'd or fry'd, some prefer; both nourishing and restorative'. The leaves are no less popular collected before the flowering shoot begins to grow (trimmed of the prickles), as are the peeled midribs of the lower leaves. Gardening gloves can be handy!

Day Lily Family [Asphodelaceae]

A family that includes day lilies, whose flowers are a popular food in China, **asphodels** and **aloe** – a gel from which is nowadays being used commercially as an edible coating to maintain freshness of cut food products. Another important member is the native **harakeke** (**New Zealand flax**, *Phormium tenax*), whose nectar was traditionally collected as food by Māori.

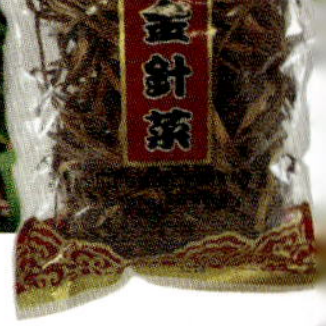

dried day lily flowers

Orange Day Lily

Hemerocallis fulva

Description: Flowers Dec–Jan, each flower typically lasting just one day.

Where: Widely grown as an ornamental plant, but also wild in scattered sites across the North Island, and around Nelson, Greymouth and Hokitika.

Part eaten: The flowers, flower buds, young leaves, young shoots and young tuberous roots. Although completely harmless as a food for people, the plant can cause acute renal failure in cats.

Nutritional value: Raw flower buds rich in potassium, magnesium, vitamins A and C. Tender leaves rich in vitamins A and C (Ershow).

Use: Although culinary use of this flower is almost unknown here or in Europe, it is a well-known food plant in its native region of Japan, Korea and China, where the flowers are collected from the wild and eaten raw, cooked as green beans, or dried in the sun for thickening soups. The young white tubers are also eaten – either raw in salads or cooked – and the young spring shoots are added to salads, or steamed as asparagus. In Korea, these shoots are commonly offered for sale for this purpose – a use that has recently spread to California and Florida, where the plant is now cultivated specifically for this purpose.

tuber-l root

Local relatives: Less common in the wild here is the **onion-leafed asphodel** (*Asphodelus fistulosus*), whose leaves, stems and bulbs have been cooked and eaten in North Africa and France.

Dogwood Family

[Cornaceae]

A family noted for its ornamental flowering trees. Important food plants include the so-called **Cornelian cherry** (*Cornus mas*), which is cultivated in southern Europe for its fruits, used in tarts, jam or sauce, or eaten dried.

Strawberry Dogwood

Cornus capitata (= *Dendrobenthamia capitata*)

Description: Small evergreen tree to about 6 m, with strawberry-like fruits.

Where: Grown as an ornamental tree in gardens and street sides, but has spread into the wild from birds eating the fruits. More common from Nelson north.

Part eaten: Ripe fruit (Mar–Apr).

Nutritional value: Fruit rich in crude fibre, carbohydrate, calcium, magnesium, sodium, iron (Mishra) and phosphorus (Saha).

Use: Also known as **Himalayan dogwood**, as this tree is a native of the Himalayan region. The fruit is sweetish, often with a slight bitterness. In remote regions of NE India it constitutes an important part of the food supply, where it is enjoyed raw or used for making preserves and fermented drinks. Further north, in what is now known as China, Tibetans of the Shangri-La region also frequently collect the wild fruit to eat fresh, or to make into jam or a sweet liqueur.

Elaeagnus Family

[Elaeagnaceae]

Also known as the **Oleaster** family. The leaves and shoots of most members are covered with tiny, silvery or brownish scales. The family includes **buffalo berries** (*Shepherdia* species) of North America, whose fruit was traditionally gathered as food by the first Americans, eaten either fresh or dried for winter; **sea buckthorn** (*Hippophae rhamnoides*), cultivated for its edible fruit in China; and the so-called **Russian olive** (*Elaeagnus angustifolia*), which is cultivated for the same purpose in southern and central Europe.

Elaeagnus

Elaeagnus × reflexa (= *E. pungens* var. *reflexa*)

Description: Tangled shrub, often spiny. Leaves silvery beneath, usually dotted with brown scales.

Where: Common, spreading from neglected gardens and farms, often covering nearby trees and shrubs.

Part eaten: Ripe fruit (Jun–Aug).

Nutritional value: Fruit very rich in vitamins and minerals, especially vitamins A, C and E, and also lycopene (Mariod), which may have health benefits.

Use: A native of central and southern Japan, widely planted here in New Zealand as a hedge in the 19th and early 20th centuries. Its long, arching shoots proved hard to keep under control and birds spread the seed, leading to the plant becoming a pest in some regions. In rural China the fruit of this species is often eaten raw, especially by children when herding livestock. I have often eaten them myself here in New Zealand. Elaeagnus fruits in general are used for the production of juice, herbal tea, wine, sauce, dessert, candy, fruit leather, jam and jelly.

Elderberry Family

[Adoxaceae]

Besides the **European elder** (below), this family includes **American elder** (*Sambucus canadensis*) of eastern North America, whose flowers and ripe fruit are enjoyed as a drink, and **nannyberry** (*Viburnum lentago*), whose fruit is likewise collected and eaten in North America.

Elder

Sambucus nigra

Description: Deciduous shrub or small tree with hollow stems, soft leaves and fragrant white flowers, followed by shiny black fruits.

Where: Very common throughout.

Part eaten: Flowers (Nov–Jan), and ripe berries (Jan–Mar) when cooked, dried or fermented. Leaves and stems poisonous.

Nutritional value: Fruit rich in vitamins C and B6, iron (USDA), anthocyanins (Veberic), antioxidants generally (Jabłońska-Ryś), with up to 7.5% glucose and fructose (Knudsen).

CAUTION: berries edible only when cooked, dried or fermented

Use: This elder is native to Europe through to western Iran. Across much of this region the ripe fruit and flowers are traditionally used as food and for making various beverages, including wine. In Italy, for example, the fruit is commonly made into syrup, jam and spirits, while the flowers are used to prepare liqueurs, vinegar, syrup, or fried as an ingredient of frittata or incorporated into pancakes powdered with sugar. Similar uses are recorded from Greece, Cyprus, Tunisia, Spain, Portugal, Belarus, Russia, Czech Republic, Slovakia, Hungary, Romania, Bosnia, Bulgaria and Turkey. In 1699 John Evelyn of England recommended a 'Small Ale in which *Elder-Flowers* have been infus'd [that] is by many esteem'd so salubrious and palatable, as it is of late grown into so great Vogue, that it is to be had in many of the Publick Eating-Houses about Town'. Archaeological evidence from Dorf Ehrenstein near Ulm in Germany reveals that the fruit was being collected as food in that region more than 4000 years ago. It was presumably eaten cooked, as the raw fruit has a cloying taste.

Ferns and Fern Allies

[Polypodiopsida]

The fiddleheads and rhizomes of various species of fern are eaten in many countries, including New Zealand, where several native species were traditionally eaten by Māori.

Common Polypody

Polypodium vulgare

Description: Leaflets of the fronds are divided right down to the stalk, unlike those of the native **pāraharaha** (**hound's tongue fern**).

Where: Rock faces and road banks, where it is spreading to become a nuisance and is consequently banned from sale, propagation and distribution.

Part eaten: Underground part (rhizome).

Nutritional value: Rhizomes contain the glycoside osladin, a sweetener 500 times sweeter than sucrose (Yamada).

Use: A native of Eurasia – including Poland, Bosnia and Slovakia, where the rhizomes provided an important famine food during the 19th and early 20th centuries. Nowadays these serve more often as a children's snack food – a use recorded in recent times from Romania, Estonia, Croatia, Slovakia and the Czech Republic. In another traditional use reported from Hungary, these rhizomes were wrapped in a rag and given to babies to chew at teething, and ground roots soaked in water provided a sweet drink. Use of the rhizomes as food is also recorded from Sicily and the Friuli region of NE Italy.

Ladder Fern

Nephrolepis cordifolia

Description: Bears potato-like tubers.

Where: A garden plant that has spread into the wild in warmer areas, especially from Tauranga north. Now banned from sale, propagation and distribution.

Part eaten: Tubers (all year).

Nutritional value: Tubers rich in carbohydrate, calcium (Gauchan), and antioxidants (Hadi).

Use: A native of the tropics, including India and Nepal, where the tubers are traditionally used as food. In NE India, where foraging for wild plants remains a common practice among members of tribal communities, the boiled tubers serve as an ingredient of vegetable salad; indeed, the fern is deliberately cultivated there specifically for this purpose. Similar uses are recorded in Nepal, where the tubers are cleaned and eaten either raw or roasted. In Nigeria, too – where the plant is evidently introduced – the tubers are eaten after boiling in salted water. To my taste they rate more as a survival food, though, for they have a fibrous coating and a bitter taste. This taste and a crisp texture remain even after boiling. Also known as **tuber sword fern**.

Local relatives: The much rarer native **ladder fern** (*N. flexuosa*) bears no tubers.

horsetail tubers

Field Horsetail

Equisetum arvense

Description: Creeping rhizomes spread to form a colony, which sends up asparagus-like shoots in spring.

Where: Damp ground, including riverbanks and around lakes and ponds, where it often becomes a pest whose spread is very hard to control. Now banned from sale, propagation and distribution.

Part eaten: Tubers and spring shoots, preferably cooked due to the presence of thiaminase, a heat-sensitive enzyme that destroys vitamin B1 (Burrows).

Nutritional value: Rich in vitamins C and E, potassium, copper and zinc (Nagai).

Use: A native of the subarctic and temperate Northern Hemisphere, where the fertile shoots and tubers are (or traditionally have been) eaten over an extraordinarily large area, with independent records collected from Iceland, the Faroe Islands, Norway and Russia down through Estonia, Poland, Hungary, Slovakia, Bulgaria and Italy and right across to Japan. In North America, too, the shoots and tubers are traditionally eaten by indigenous peoples, including those based in Alaska. When it came to collecting the edible nodules or tubers, the Yup'ik of western Alaska proved particularly enterprising, often obtaining them by raiding underground caches collected by lemmings and other tundra rodents. The shoots are best collected immediately after they first emerge from the ground and while still white (as in the photo). Later, they become too stringy. The coarse brown bracts that surround each node are tough and should also be peeled off.

Local relatives: Edible wild relatives here in New Zealand include the much less common **rough horsetail** (*E. hyemale*), whose rootstocks were similarly used as a traditional food by the indigenous Hoh and Quileute of North America.

fertile shoots (spring)

Fig and Mulberry Family

[Moraceae]

Most members are trees or shrubs, all of which contain a sticky, milk-like sap or latex, which – in some species – is used as glue or for caulking boats. Included are several important fruit trees: various kinds of **fig**, **mulberry**, **jackfruit** and **breadfruit**. The fibrous inner bark of some, including breadfruit and the **paper mulberry** tree (**aute**, *Broussonetia papyrifera*), are used to make tapa cloth.

Fig

Ficus carica

Description: Deciduous tree with smooth bark and a milky sap.

Where: Planted for its edible fruit, and now found wild in warmer areas from birds and mammals scattering the tiny seeds in their droppings.

Part eaten: Ripe fruit (Jan-May) and tender young leaves. Also unripe figs when cooked. Sensitive individuals should take care with the milky white sap as contact can cause a skin reaction (photodermatitis).

Nutritional value: Fruit (fresh or dried) a good source of dietary fibre. Low in vitamins A and C, but a reasonably good source of vitamin B6 (USDA).

Use: The plant's native range extends from Greece to the Western Himalayas including Pakistan, where the young leaves are traditionally cooked in diluted milk, and unripe figs boiled in water as a vegetable. It transpires that figs are one of the oldest fruit crops in the world: archaeological evidence of carbonised sterile fruits from an early Neolithic village in the Lower Jordan Valley can be dated to 11,400 to 11,200 years ago. These days the fruit is eaten fresh or dried or used to make jam. Low-grade figs can also be converted into alcohol. Immature figs are surprisingly good stir-fried with onion, or grilled when ripe with blue cheese – a favourite in our household.

Local relatives: Following the arrival in New Zealand of the specialised pollinating wasp for the majestic Australian **Moreton Bay fig** (*F. macrophylla*) in 1993, this tree has begun to spread quite quickly. Although its fruit is small, one tree can bear a lot of fruit; when ripe, these make good jam. The corresponding pollinating wasp for the Asian **climbing fig** (**creeping fig**, *F. pumila*) has not yet reached here; consequently, its fruits typically remain dry and inedible.

Black Mulberry

Morus nigra

Description: A deciduous tree with large soft leaves, growing to 10 m, and bearing blackberry-like fruit.

Where: Planted in parks and gardens, or as a street tree, and found growing wild only occasionally.

Part eaten: Ripe fruit (late spring to early summer).

Nutritional value: Fruit especially rich in vitamin C, and a good source of iron (USDA).

Use: A native of Iran, now cultivated and wild throughout much of Europe, North Africa and Asia, where the ripe fruits are often enjoyed fresh, but also frozen, dried, stewed or used for the production of wine, syrup, sauce, jam and fruit tarts or pies.

Local relatives: The so-called **white mulberry** (*M. alba*) of China is best-known for its leaves, which are a primary food for the caterpillar of the domestic silk moth, from which raw silk is produced. Its fruit – which can be white, pink, deep purple or black – is similar and is an equally worthwhile source of food for humans.

Geranium Family

[Geraniaceae]

A family best-known for its showy garden plants. Members are typically hairy, aromatic herbs, with five-petalled flowers and long, straight, pointed, beak-like seed capsules, inspiring the names storksbill and cranesbill. Food uses include the flowers of several **pelargoniums** and **geraniums**, used decoratively and as flavouring. Native species include **matua-kūmara** (*Geranium solanderi* and *G. retrorsum*), whose swollen root was formerly eaten by Māori.

Storksbill

Erodium cicutarium

Description: Stem reddish and hairy. Pink or white flowers (Sep–May). Long seed pod, shaped like the bill of a stork.

Where: Very common throughout.

Part eaten: Young leaves in spring.

Nutritional value: Leaves rich in vitamin C (Jones), protein, magnesium, calcium, phosphorus and potassium (Howard, Bilić).

Use: This is a native of North Africa and Eurasia. Along much of the Adriatic coast young plants are traditionally harvested for food – from Herzegovina (where they are for sale in some of the wild vegetable mixes) and neighbouring Croatia, through to western Friuli (NE Italy), where they are cooked in a traditional spring mixture of wild herbs. The plant is also a popular vegetable in Turkey, where it is among the wild edible plants sold in the markets of İzmir. In this western region of Turkey the fresh aboveground part is fried, sometimes with eggs, or added as stuffing in saç böreği, a stuffed Turkish flatbread similar to the Indian spinach paratha. In the Black Sea region of Turkey the leaves are traditionally eaten raw as salad or mixed with cheese and meat and roasted. When the plant reached North America along with passing Spanish explorers in the early 1700s, it was soon adopted as a food by the indigenous population, who ate it raw or cooked. Likewise, the Mapuche community in Patagonia relishes the leaves in stews (pucheros).

Musky Storksbill

Erodium moschatum

Description: Often musk-scented, sticky to the touch. Pink or white flowers (Sep–Nov).

Where: Very common throughout.

Part eaten: Young leaves in spring.

Nutritional value: Leaves rich in vitamin A, with 2.5% protein (Cowan).

Use: A native of the Mediterranean region, where the young leaves are traditionally used as a wild vegetable, at least in Morocco, Lebanon, Sicily and Turkey.

Cut-leaved Cranesbill

Geranium dissectum

Description: Leaves deeply dissected. Pink flowers Nov–Feb. Seed capsules beak-like, like the bill of a crane.

Where: Throughout.

Part eaten: Leaves.

Nutritional value: Fresh leaves rich in vitamin C (Jones).

Use: A native of Europe and the Mediterranean, including the Aegean region of Turkey and Central Anatolia, where the leaves are traditionally roasted with yoghurt and eaten as a vegetable, or thinly sliced and wrapped in unleavened flatbread (yufka) with oil, cheese, mincemeat, potatoes, eggplant and parsley, and often cooked on a simple tin plate.

Local relatives: The native **matua-kūmara** (*G. solanderi* and *G. retrorsum*), whose swollen roots were traditionally eaten by Māori.

Dove's Foot Cranesbill / Namunamu

Geranium molle

Description: Soft, flexible leaves. Pink flowers Sep–Feb. Seed capsules beak-like, like a crane's bill.

Where: Common throughout.

Part eaten: Young leaves in spring.

Nutritional value: Fresh leaves rich in vitamin C (Jones), potassium and calcium (Civelek).

Use: A native of Europe and the Mediterranean, where the leaves are traditionally collected in spring for inclusion in the soups of NW Tuscany and Liguria (NW Italy). Similarly, in Dalmatia (southern Croatia) and SW Herzegovina its boiled leaves are eaten. In the Black Sea region of Turkey the leaves are traditionally roasted. The plant was an early arrival in New Zealand, first recorded in 1852, where it was given the Māori name **namunamu**.

Edible garden escapes

The flowers of ornamental geraniums and pelargoniums are edible. The blossoms of the common **zonal pelargonium** (*Pelargonium* × *hortorum*, right) are widely enjoyed in China and Korea, while those of pelargoniums generally are used by some of the top chefs in Italy. In addition, the leaves of the pink or lilac-flowered **lemon-scented geranium** (*P. crispum*) are used to line cake pans to give the pastry a lemony fragrance, or added to soups, fruit salads and jellies.

Gourd Family

[Cucurbitaceae]

Members of this family are tendril-bearing vines that may either trail along the ground or climb over trees. Cultivated fruits and vegetables in this group include **choko**, **watermelon**, **rock melon**, **honeydew melon**, **pie melon**, **marrow**, **zucchini**, **pumpkin**, **squash**, **cucumber**, **kiwano** (African horned cucumber), **bitter gourd** and **snake gourd**.

Pumpkin

Cucurbita maxima

Description: A sprawling vine.

Where: Widely cultivated and occasionally wild in and around settlements.

Part eaten: The pumpkin (late autumn), its hulled seeds, long tendril shoots, tender leaves, and flowers (Nov–May). TIP: When harvesting the flowers, it is a good idea to leave the female ones (with a tiny pumpkin developing at the base) and a few male flowers to pollinate them! Otherwise you will miss out on the pumpkins themselves.

Nutritional value: Fruit rich in potassium – a good thing if you suffer from high blood pressure. Seeds rich in protein. Raw flowers rich in vitamin C (USDA).

Use: A native of central and northern South America, where domestication for the edible seeds can be traced back some 10,000 years though archaeological evidence found in the caves of Guilá Naquitz in Mexico. The vine is better known nowadays, though, for its edible fruit – a popular vegetable that can be steamed, baked or used as an ingredient in pies or soups. In Zimbabwe a porridge is also made from pumpkins mixed with maize. The flesh can be dried and ground to a powder and stored to use as an ingredient in bread and cakes. The husked seeds are popular raw, roasted or as a bread ingredient. Less well known here in New Zealand is the use of its flowers, long tendril shoots and tender young leaves as a vegetable – usually cooked. Blossoms (usually male ones with stamens removed) are commonly sold for this purpose in local markets in SE Asia, where they may be dipped in batter and fried.

Local relatives: Pie melon (*C. ficifolia*), **marrow** (*C. pepo*) and **watermelon** (*Citrullus lanatus*) are equally edible but much less common in the wild.

Choko

Sechium edule (= *Sicyos edulis*)

Description: Climbing vine. Fruit solid inside (as above), unlike that of moth plant – below.
Where: Cultivated for food, but wild plants occasionally found climbing trees and hedges.
Part eaten: The choko itself and its seeds (late autumn to early winter), also young leaves, stems, tender shoots, and tuberous roots of plants when at least two years old.
Nutritional value: Fruit especially rich in vitamin B9, and a reasonably good source of vitamin C and zinc (USDA). The tuberous root may contain about 20% carbohydrate (Vaughan).
Use: This vine originates from Central America, where it was cultivated by the Aztecs for its edible fruit in pre-Columbian times under the name **chayote**. From there it has since been distributed to many countries, where the fruit is widely offered for sale as a vegetable. Older fruit often requires peeling and tastes starchy, like a potato, but the taste of young fruit is mild, more like a zucchini. Although this may be eaten raw in salads, it is more often steamed, fried (with cheese and garlic is good), or used in curries and soups or sliced and pickled in vinegar. With a little lemon, cinnamon and sugar, it also makes a good substitute for apple in fruit pies, etc. Surreptitiously serving a choko version of apple crumble to friends who profess to hate choko made for one hilarious evening here! The tender seeds are great fried or roasted; and young leaves and tendrils stir-fried and eaten as 'dragon-whiskers' – highly recommended.

Mildly toxic lookalike

Moth Plant

Araujia sericifera

This pest plant has a milky sap and bears a choko-like fruit that is filled with silky hairs (like kapok). Although the fruit itself is only mildly toxic, its leaves and stems can cause digestive and neurological problems. The milky sap is also a strong skin irritant (which incidentally responds better to rinsing off with milk than with water).

Grape Family

[Vitaceae]

This family includes some 80 kinds of fruiting **grape** (*Vitis* species), most of which are native to the temperate Northern Hemisphere.

Grape

Vitis vinifera

Description: Deciduous woody vine that climbs via tendrils to form tangled thickets on trees. Fruit on wild vines is generally small and black.

Where: Widely cultivated, and commonly wild in the North Island, scrambling through trees and bushes, particularly around old gardens and along roadsides.

Part eaten: Fruit (Mar–Apr), shoots and leaves.

Nutritional value: Fruit rich in sugar and vitamin K (USDA).

Use: A native of the Mediterranean and Middle East with an extraordinarily long culinary history, with traces of tartaric acid in Neolithic pottery vessels at Hajji Firuz Tepe in the northern Zagros mountains of Iran allowing the use of grapes to be traced back to at least 5000 BC. Although best known for the fruit – enjoyed fresh or dried, pressed for juice, fermented as wine, or made into jams and jellies – the shoots and young leaves are also widely used as a vegetable. In eastern Mediterranean countries grapevine leaves (first blanched in boiling water) are commonly stuffed with various ingredients – such as rice, pine nuts and fresh herbs – to make a range of dishes including the Greek dolmades and Turkish dolma (illustrated).

Grasses

[Family: Poaceae]

This is the world's most economically important plant family, providing **sugarcane** and **bamboo** and all our cereal crops, including **wheat**, **rice**, **oats**, **barley**, **rye**, **sorghum**, **maize** and various kinds of **millet**. Besides these, New Zealand has over 30 species of wild grass whose stems, young shoots, rhizomes or seeds have a history of being used as human food, often in times of famine. As few of these (apart from bamboo) provide practical or worthwhile everyday sources of food, further discussion of them is relegated to the appendix of this book (page 152).

Bamboo

Bambusa and allied species
[Subfamily: Bambusoideae]

Description: Tall woody grasses with a hollow, jointed stem.

Where: Widely cultivated and also common wild.

Part eaten: Young shoots up to around 15 cm high cut close to soil level (spring and early summer – later, they become too tough and bitter); these must, however, still be treated to remove the bitter-tasting and potentially toxic cyanogenic glycosides by cooking, canning, soaking, drying or fermentation (Chongtham, FSANZ, Rawat 2015) – see below.

Nutritional value: Shoots low in fat and calories yet rich in vitamin B6, B1, manganese, zinc, potassium and protein (USDA).

Use: Of the more than 1400 known species of bamboo, most are native to SE Asia, where several are grown commercially for their edible shoots. Although the shoots of a few are edible raw, most require processing to remove the bitter taste, which is generally achieved by boiling, soaking, drying or fermentation. The emerging shoots are cut when they reach about 15 cm in length; the hard, and often hairy, leaf sheaths are then removed before boiling the shoots to remove any bitterness. Depending on the species, this can involve slicing up the shoots first, adding salt to the cooking water and boiling for up to half an hour. With the bitterness gone, the shoots are like asparagus and are used in stir-fries and soups or as a pickled condiment. Worldwide, an estimated two million tonnes or more of bamboo shoots are consumed each year, mostly in China but also in India, Japan, Thailand, Malaysia, Vietnam, Indonesia, etc. Bamboo leaves are also useful: they are traditionally used in Asia as scouring material for cleaning cooking utensils.

Local relatives: Shoots of all the common bamboo species here have been used elsewhere as food, but especially the thin shoots of **walking stick bamboo** (or **fishpole bamboo**, *Phyllostachys aurea*) and **arrow bamboo** (*Pseudosasa japonica*), both of which are chopped into small pieces in Indonesia, then boiled or fried in vegetable oil along with other vegetables and meat.

Gunnera Family

[Gunneraceae]

Members of this family are typically huge herbs of damp places with very large, toothed leaves whose veins radiate out from the centre.

Chilean Rhubarb

Gunnera tinctoria

Description: Giant rhubarb-like plant. Leaf stalks up to 1 m long, studded with short conical, often reddish, prickles – unlike the similarly large-leaved **bear's breeches** (*Acanthus mollis*), which is more of a medicinal plant.

Where: Cultivated as a waterside plant, but commonly spreading into the wild nearby, especially in high rainfall areas, so now banned from sale, propagation and distribution.

Part eaten: Young leaf stalks, peeled. CAUTION: Take care not to get scratched.

Nutritional value: Leaf stalk high in protein, crude fibre and antioxidants (Zamorano), but low in vitamin C (Petzold).

Use: A native of southern South America. In Argentina the young leaf stalks are peeled and eaten either raw in salads or cooked as a traditional vegetable by the indigenous Mapuche people. In Chile these slightly acidic stalks have been used for making ice cream and salads.

Heather Family [Ericaceae]

Members of this family typically thrive on poorly drained, acid soils and include several food plants, including **blueberry**, **cranberry**, **bilberry**, **huckleberry** and the native **tāwiniwini** (**snowberry**, *Gaultheria* species), whose fruit was traditionally eaten by Māori. The family also includes a few toxic plants such as **rhododendron**, whose unpalatable leaves are *poisonous* (as is honey made from the nectar of its flowers).

Strawberry Tree

Arbutus unedo

Description: Medium-sized evergreen tree with white bell-shaped flowers (Feb–Aug) and strawberry-like fruit.
Where: Widely planted, and also commonly spread by birds.
Part eaten: Ripe fruit (Mar–May) – best when slightly overripe.
Nutritional value: Raw fruit rich in sugars, dietary fibre, α-linolenic acid (an omega-3, essential fatty acid), quinic acid, malic acid and anthocyanins, standing out among wild fruits for antioxidant potential. Rich in vitamins C and E; also magnesium, potassium, calcium, and very low in sodium (Sánchez-Mata, Lim, Alarcão-E-Silva).
Use: Native to the Mediterranean region, where the wild fruit is traditionally collected and eaten raw as a snack or as a dessert, in jellies, jam or liqueurs. Independent records of such uses have been collected from Portugal, Spain, Italy, Cyprus, Greece, Croatia, Bosnia-Herzegovina, Turkey, Tunisia, Algeria and Morocco. The fruit is mealy and sweetish, but needs to be fully ripe or slightly overripe to have much flavour.

Heather

Calluna vulgaris

Description: Low evergreen shrub with a sweet scent, especially when in flower.
Where: Common on acidic soils in open areas around Tongariro (where it has become an invasive weed), Taranaki, Te Aroha, Aoraki Mt Cook and occasionally elsewhere.
Part eaten: Dried flowering branches (Dec–Mar) used as tea or as an ingredient in beer.
Nutritional value: Fresh leaves very rich in vitamin C (Jones).
Use: Native to a region that extends from northern Morocco to Iceland and Siberia, including the Hebrides Islands off the west coast of the Scottish mainland, where a kind of beer is brewed by fermenting a mixture of two parts heather-tops and one part malt. In Estonia the flowering branches and seeds are traditionally used in herbal teas and as an ingredient of breads. In Bosnia and Herzegovina the flowers are used similarly as a spice.

Honeysuckle Family

[Caprifoliaceae]

A family named from the large quantity of nectar that can be sucked from the tubular, scented flowers of many members, such as the **English honeysuckle** (*Lonicera periclymenum*). Members typically have their leaves arranged in opposite pairs.

Japanese Honeysuckle

Lonicera japonica

Description: Sweet-scented woody vine that can smother trees.

Where: A very common nuisance weed of forest edges, though less common in southern South Island. Now banned from sale, propagation and distribution.

Part eaten: Flowers (Sep–May), but NOT the berries, which have been known to cause digestive tract disturbances in children (Burrows).

Nutritional value: Flowers very rich in antioxidants (Araújo, Cai, Li); vitamin content negligible (Ershow).

Use: A native of Japan, Korea and China, where the vine has served as an edible-medicinal herb for over 1600 years. Popular products made from it include tea, wine, candies and toothpaste. The flowers are sucked for their sweet nectar, and used as a vegetable or made into syrup and puddings, while the flower buds and leaves are made into herbal teas that are nowadays available in dried form from Chinese stores.

Local relatives: Although the fruit of **Himalayan honeysuckle** (*Leycesteria formosa*) is reportedly eaten fresh by Tibetans in the Shangri-La region of what is now known as Yunnan, China, I personally find them too bitter to recommend.

Spur Valerian

Centranthus ruber (= *Valeriana rubra*)

Description: Fragrant flowers Nov–Jun.

Where: Very common across much of the North Island, also Nelson, Canterbury, and coastal and central Otago.

Part eaten: Young leaves.

Nutritional value: Fresh leaves rich in vitamin C (Jones), with greater antioxidant properties than blueberries (Vanzani).

Use: A native of the Mediterranean region, where the bitter leaves are used as a vegetable, particularly in Italy, a use that dates at least to the mid-19th century. In Liguria (NW Italy) the boiled leaves and shoots are commonly eaten in vegetable pie, soup, stuffing of ravioli, or served as a side dish; and in Central Italy and Sicily the young leaves are traditionally eaten raw in salad, or boiled. Personally, though, I find even the young leaves too acrid for my taste.

Local relatives: Corn salad (*Valerianella carinata* and *V. locusta*) readily self-seeds in gardens; its leaves make a great addition to salads.

Hop Family

[Cannabaceae]

This family includes **hops**; **Mediterranean hackberry** (*Celtis australis*) – a deciduous tree, only occasionally found wild here in New Zealand, whose sweet fruit is eaten raw in its native Mediterranean region; and **cannabis** or **hemp**, various species and forms of which are cultivated for a range of purposes – for fibre, for edible seeds and oil, or specifically as a mood-altering or medicinal drug.

Hop

Humulus lupulus

Description: Climbing plant that resprouts each spring, producing a fragrant green flower cone (Jan–Feb).

Where: Found mostly near where the plant is or has been cultivated, e.g. around Nelson, often scrambling over scrub or trees along forest edges.

Part eaten: Young shoots (about 20 cm long) and leaf buds collected in spring and cooked as a kind of asparagus. The female flower cones are collected in summer to impart a bitter aromatic flavour to beer.

Nutritional value: Young shoots a good source of dietary fibre, with a relatively high protein content; low in sodium and oxalates and a good source of potassium, manganese, zinc and vitamins C, E and B9 (Sánchez-Mata, Cerne). Rich in antioxidants generally (Morales 2012).

Use: Native to a region extending from Morocco to Siberia, including Europe, where the use of the spring buds or first sprouts as a tasty vegetable can be traced back at least 2000 years to the time of Pliny the Elder, author of *Naturalis Historia*. Although the plant is nowadays grown primarily for its female flower cones, which are used to impart a bitter flavour to beer, in Europe and around the Mediterranean the young shoots continue to be widely enjoyed as a vegetable, particularly in spring when the hop plantations are being pruned. Independent records of this tradition have been collected from England, Belgium, Spain, Italy, Estonia, Slovenia, Hungary, Bosnia-Herzegovina, Turkey and Morocco. The young shoots are generally boiled or steamed like asparagus, often then fried with eggs. The plant is evidently making something of a comeback nowadays in the haute cuisine of northern Europe, where these shoots are collected and sold to a leading restaurant in Copenhagen by a small southern-Swedish foraging enterprise.

Ice Plants

[Aizoaceae]

This family is named after the succulent leaves of members whose surface glistens like frost or ice. Also known as the **fig-marigold** family after the fig-like fruit and marigold-like flowers of many. Edible members include the South African and Chilean **ice plants** (below), and three native species, **horokaka** (**New Zealand ice plant**) and two kinds of **kōkihi** (**New Zealand spinach**, *Tetragonia* species). Many members contain soluble oxalates, which have the potential to rob the body of calcium; particularly so when mature and dry, making them less suitable as food at this stage.

South African ice plant flower

Chilean ice plant flower

ripe fruit

succulent leaf

cut fruit

Ice Plant

Carpobrotus edulis & *C. chilensis*

Description: Mat-forming coastal plant, with succulent, sharply three-angled leaves and large, many-petalled flowers (Oct–Feb). The South African species has yellow flowers, while the Chilean one bears purple flowers.

Where: Common on cliffs and sand dunes throughout.

Part eaten: Ripe fruit (Aug–Nov) – when soft and yellow, not when over-mature and dried up.

Nutritional value: Fruit of the African species (*C. edulis*) rich in calcium, magnesium and potassium, yet also high in sodium (Wehmeyer).

Use: Also known as **sea fig**. The yellow-flowered species is a native of South Africa, where the sour-tasting ripe fruit is a traditional food of the Khoe-San people of South Africa's Cape South Coast, and available there nowadays in local fruit and vegetable markets. The ripe fruit is also used in South Africa for making jam and chutney and its leaves are sometimes pickled. The fruit and leaves of the **Chilean ice plant** (*C. chilensis*) are harvested for local consumption in South America, and in California the indigenous Luiseño and Pomo peoples eat the fruit.

Local relatives: The fruit and leaves of the smaller-leaved native **horokaka** (**New Zealand ice plant**, *Disphyma australe*) are likewise edible.

Kiwifruit Family

[Actinidiaceae]

This family includes many shrubs and woody vines that bear edible fruit, including some 55 species of **kiwifruit** (*Actinidia* species) from the Asian region – from the Himalayas across to the Russian Far East and south to Indonesia.

Wild Kiwifruit

Actinidia chinensis var. *deliciosa*

Description: Deciduous woody climber. Fruit on wild vines is generally smaller and hairier than commercially cultivated fruit.

Where: Widely grown in the North Island and northern South Island, the vine has spread to become an invasive weed in places – partly as a result of silvereyes eating and dispersing seed from neglected or discarded fruit.

Part eaten: Fruits ripen in winter (May–Jun), and sweeten naturally after the first frost. (As commercial harvesting aims for a longer shelf life, these are picked much earlier.)

Nutritional value: Fruit particularly rich in vitamins C and K, and a good source of potassium (USDA). (Potassium can help reduce high blood pressure.)

Use: A native of South China, where the fruit, known there as **mihoutao** (**monkey peach**), has long been collected from the wild, with peasants bringing baskets of them down from the hills to sell in local markets. In 1904 the vine was introduced to New Zealand, where the taste of the fruit inspired the name **Chinese gooseberry** before it was launched onto world markets in the 1960s as **kiwifruit**. Commercial cultivation did not follow in the plant's native China until around 1980. Although the crop is now grown in Italy, France, the USA, Chile, Australia and a few other countries, more kiwifruit are grown these days in China than in any other country. In New Zealand the vines began spreading into the wild in around 1982. The ripe fruit – wild or cultivated – can be eaten alone or in fruit salads or as jam, in pies, or sauce, blended to make smoothies, brewed to make a wine or dried as a snack.

Local relatives: The much smaller, hairless, green-skinned **hardy kiwi** or **kiwi berry** (*A. arguta*, right), from China, Korea, Japan and the Russian Far East, is much less common in the wild here.

kiwi berry

Knotweeds, Sorrels and Docks

[Polygonaceae]

Members of this family typically have knot-like swellings on the stems – hence the name. Food plants include **rhubarb**, **French sorrel**, **garden sorrel**, **buckwheat**, **Vietnamese coriander** and the native **pōhuehue** (*Muehlenbeckia* species) whose 'fruit' was traditionally eaten by Māori. Many members are relatively high in oxalates.

Buckwheat

unhulled buckwheat seeds (about 5 mm)

Fagopyrum esculentum

Description: Knee-high herb with hollow stems, reddish at the base.
Where: Occasionally cultivated. Self-sown plants often spring up nearby.
Part eaten: Seeds (autumn) and leaves.
Nutritional value: Seeds rich in minerals and B vitamins, especially magnesium, manganese, phosphorus, zinc, iron and potassium and vitamins B3, B2, B5 and B6 (USDA). Shoots rich in phosphorus (Jain).
Use: A native of China, where the plant has been cultivated for thousands of years. It is now a major crop worldwide, grown primarily for its edible seeds, which are consumed as porridge, noodles and pancakes, etc. In India especially, but also in Korea, the young leaves are eaten as a cooked vegetable.

Cornbind

cornbind seeds (about 3 mm)

Fallopia convolvulus (= *Polygonum*)

Description: Also known as wild buckwheat. Scrambling vine with tiny white flowers in clusters and black, triangular seeds (unlike **bindweed**).
Where: A common weed of cultivation, often climbing the stalks of corn – especially in South Canterbury, also Hawke's Bay and Wellington.
Part eaten: Young shoots, and seeds (autumn).
Nutritional value: Leaves rich in antioxidants (Heinrich). Protein content of seeds (including lysine, an essential amino acid) comparable to that of cereals, such as barley (Harrold).
Use: The native range of this vine extends from Morocco to Kamchatka. In Spain, Belarus and Bosnia, at least, the young shoots are traditionally collected in spring for use as a cooked vegetable or in soups. In times of famine the seed has also been ground into flour – at least in the Czech Republic. Archaeological remains of stomach contents of bodies recovered from bogs in northern Germany indicate that these seeds were consumed as food from at least as early as the 12th century, their nutritional value noted by botanist Pierpoint Johnson (1862). Although Johnson judged these too small to be of much value as food, a large plant can produce 11,900 seeds, which amounts to more than 80 g of protein-rich food – equivalent to a single-serve packet of puffed barley.

Willow Weed

Persicaria maculosa (= *Polygonum persicaria*)

Description: Leaves often have a dark patch in the middle. Stem reddish; hence also known as **redshank**. Flowers all year.

Where: Common throughout.

Part eaten: Young shoots, before flowering; later, they become too bitter. Usually cooked, due perhaps to its relatively high oxalic acid content (Chistyakova).

Nutritional value: Young shoots rich in vitamin C and β-carotene (Grlić).

Use: Native from Algeria to Siberia. The leaves are collected for food in spring and, in Spain, are traditionally eaten raw; however, in the western Friuli region of Italy they are generally boiled and sautéed along with a mixture of other wild greens. In the Ağrı Province of eastern Turkey the plant is brought to market for sale, where a survey rated it among the top five of 100 wild edible species; the leaves and shoots are most often eaten cooked, stirred with olive oil and fried with chilli or garlic and various spices along with other wild vegetables. Ljubiša Grlić, an influential botanical writer from Croatia, recommends the young leaves in soup, or boiled as spinach for 5–10 minutes and eaten along with other wild vegetables.

Local relatives: Water pepper (*P. hydropiper*) – found only in wet places – is grown in Japan as a vegetable, where its leaves are not generally harvested from wild plants as these tend to have a far more pungent taste (too hot for some). **Slender knotweed** (**tūtunāwai**, *P. decipiens*) is native not only to New Zealand but also to Africa, where its cooked leaves are used as a vegetable.

note the dark patch

Vietnamese Coriander

Persicaria odorata

Description: Also known as **Asian mint**. Readily distinguished from the above by the lemony fragrance of its leaves.

Where: Grown here by some as a culinary spice, and occasionally wild.

Part eaten: Tender leaves as flavouring.

Nutritional value: Leaves rich in antioxidants (Nguyen).

Use: A native of SE Asia, where the tender leaves are traditionally used in Vietnamese cuisine in salads, soups and stews. Similar uses recorded from India, Myanmar, Cambodia, Laos, Thailand, Malaysia, Singapore and Indonesia.

Asiatic Knotweed

toxic lookalike: **tutu** shoot

Reynoutria japonica (= *Fallopia* = *Polygonum cuspidatum*)

Description: Flowers white. Leaves alternating (unlike tutu). The asparagus-like shoots (spring) are not to be confused with those of the highly poisonous **tutu** (page 23). ▶

Where: Common in parts of Westland, mostly near dwellings and gardens. Strong enough to damage concrete. Now banned from sale, propagation and distribution.

Part eaten: Peeled shoots (up to 30 cm) in spring, preferably cooked and in moderation due to a high oxalic acid content – almost twice that of sorrel (Grlić, Noonan, Shitasue). Juicing not recommended.

Nutritional value: Plant rich in vitamin C and antioxidant activity generally, and in minerals, including magnesium and iron (Shitasue).

Use: A native of eastern Asia, including Japan, where we know from the *Engi Shiki* (Regulations and Laws of the Engi era), from AD 927, that the meals of the emperor at that time included the spring shoots of this plant preserved with salt. Indeed, in the Hubei Province of Central China, its tender shoots continue to be eaten as asparagus. These sour-tasting shoots, which emerge from old roots in spring, are often peeled and eaten raw by children, but are generally eaten cooked (5 minutes is enough).

Wireweed / Mākākaka

Polygonum aviculare

Description: Often forms a mat, so is also known as **prostrate knotweed**. Tiny pink flowers (Nov–Jun), green stem and NO milky sap – unlike **euphorbia** (page 162).

Where: Common throughout.

Part eaten: Tender young leaves and stems in spring, usually cooked.

Nutritional value: Spring leaves rich in vitamin C and carotene (Grlić), fibre, calcium and potassium (Abbasi 2015).

Use: A native of the Northern Hemisphere. In Russia, Belarus, Hungary, Croatia, Bosnia and Herzogovina, Turkey, North India and China the young leaves and stems traditionally serve as a vegetable. In the Iğdır Province of eastern Turkey it is eaten raw, roasted, or boiled with bulgur (parboiled cracked wheat) before adding yoghurt. Of 210 villagers surveyed there it was rated among the top seven out of 154 local edible wild plants. In mountain regions of Pakistan the young leaves are customarily cooked instead in diluted milk.

Local relatives: The young leaves of the less-common **small-leaved wireweed** (*P. arenastrum*, left) are used in Turkey in much the same way.

Sheep's Sorrel

Rumex acetosella

Description: Often grows in dense patches. Leaves sour-tasting.

Where: Abundant throughout.

Part eaten: Young leaves (best in spring and summer).

Nutritional value: Leaves rich in vitamin C, iron, copper and manganese (Kuhnlein). Oxalic acid content about one third of that in watercress (Pereira 2013).

Use: A native of Eurasia and Greenland that has now spread around the world. The leaves have a pleasantly acid taste and are traditionally harvested from the wild in Spain, Italy, Estonia, Belarus, Hungary, Romania, Bosnia-Herzegovina, Bulgaria and Turkey, where they are often eaten raw as a snack or in salads, or cooked as an ingredient in pies or soups. In Turkey they are eaten with yoghurt as salad, sold in the markets of İzmir and even cultivated there for this purpose. Sheep's sorrel leaves are also enjoyed in Greenland by the Inuit, in Manchuria, and by the indigenous peoples of the Americas, from eastern Canada right through to Patagonia.

Garden Sorrel

Rumex acetosa

Description: Flimsy, sour-tasting leaves often shaped like an arrowhead. Flowers Nov–Jan.

Where: Cultivated as a vegetable, and occasionally wild in scattered localities throughout, usually near gardens.

Part eaten: Young leaves.

Nutritional value: Leaves rich in potassium, iron and vitamins A, B1 and C (Rana 2017). The plant generally contains less oxalic acid than spinach, with a similar oxalic acid to calcium ratio (Noonan).

Use: A native of temperate Eurasia and Morocco that features as a garden vegetable in nearly all the early British herbals, with traditional consumption recorded in many Mediterranean countries too, including Portugal, Spain, Italy, Slovenia, Bosnia-Herzegovina, Albania, Palestine and Morocco. The leaves and tender stems are often eaten raw in salads, but are also cooked in soups (in moderation), or with rice or pasta, where they are relished largely for their acidic flavour. The plant was first cultivated in New Zealand in the 19th century, occurring in the wild only occasionally since 1855.

Climbing Dock

Rumex sagittatus (= *Acetosa sagittata*)

Description: A delicate climbing vine with woody kūmara-shaped tubers and sour-tasting leaves.

Where: More common in the North Island, especially near the coast.

Part eaten: Cooked leaves. A change of water during cooking is advisable to reduce the oxalic acid content.

Nutritional value: Besides substantial amounts of carbohydrates, fibre, crude protein and moisture, the leaves contain calcium, copper, iron, magnesium, manganese, nitrogen, phosphorus, potassium and zinc (Jimoh 2010, Moteetee 2019).

Use: A native of South Africa, where the leaves are collected from the wild as a traditional spinach – a use recorded among the rural Xhosa, Zulu and Basotho people. Indeed, in Swaziland some 33% of the adult population report using this plant for greens at least once a year.

Dock / Paewhenua

Rumex obtusifolius

Description: Leaves broad and sour-tasting.

Where: Abundant throughout.

Part eaten: Leaves collected in spring, best boiled for 5 minutes with a change of water, then boiled for a further 10 minutes to reduce their oxalic acid content (and bitter taste). It is inadvisable to drink the cooking water, and not recommended for soup.

Nutritional value: Leaves rich in vitamin K, a good source of vitamins A (Sánchez-Mata) and C (Vardavas) and protein (Guil-Guerrero 2003).

Use: The plant's native region extends from Algeria to Siberia. In Spain, Italy, Turkey and Morocco the young leaves are traditionally collected as spinach. British botanist Pierpoint Johnson (1862) reports that its young leaves and shoots were at that time also used in the UK as a pot-herb. The plant reached the Americas too, where the official US Army guide to edible wild plants advises that 'you can eat [the] succulent leaves [of docks] fresh or slightly cooked,' adding that 'to take away the strong taste, change the water once or twice during cooking'.

Local relatives: The leaves of **curled dock** (*R. crispus*), **fiddle dock** (*R. pulcher*), and **clustered dock** (*R. conglomeratus*) are all similarly used across much of Europe.

clustered dock
(*Rumex conglomeratus*)

curled dock
(*Rumex crispus*)

fiddle dock
(*Rumex pulcher*)

Knotweed Family

Laurel Family

[Lauraceae]

Members are typically aromatic evergreen trees or shrubs with leathery leaves. A few are mildly toxic, including **camphor**, the fumes from which are particularly harmful to budgerigars. Important food plants in this family include **avocado**, **bay**, **cinnamon** and **sassafras**. Native members locally include **tawa** and **taraire**, whose fruit was traditionally eaten by Māori.

Avocado

Persea americana

Description: Medium-sized evergreen tree.

Where: Widely planted for its fruit, but self-seeds in the wild, particularly in the North Island.

Part eaten: Creamy pulp of ripe fruit (Sep–Apr). Picked too early, they remain bitter and rubbery. Eating the bitter seeds is not recommended (Burrows, Orabueze, Siol); and the leaves are toxic to birds and many mammals.

Nutritional value: Raw fruit rich in monounsaturated fats, exceptionally rich in vitamins B5, B6, B9 and K, and a good source of vitamins E, B3 and B2 and potassium (USDA). (Potassium helps combat high blood pressure.)

Use: Native to Central Mexico through to Costa Rica, and now cultivated in nearly all subtropical/tropical regions, where the tree has also spread into the wild. The oily pulp is generally eaten raw and makes a great substitute for butter. I can recommend avocado ice cream, too, made from 3 ripe avocados, the juice of 2 limes, ½ teaspoon lime zest, 2 tablespoons sugar, a 400 ml can of coconut cream – blend the ingredients and freeze, then cover with a sprinkling of grated chocolate and dried coconut. An oil is also expressed from the flesh, but cooking the flesh tends to spoil the flavour, making it bitter due to the tannin content. The seeds are fibrous and bitter, and are toxic to mice; despite ongoing research into their culinary potential, it is yet to be confirmed whether they can be rendered safe for human consumption.

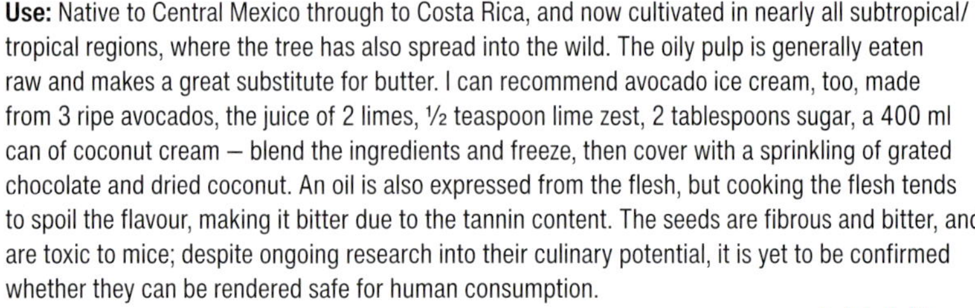

Bay

Laurus nobilis

Description: Evergreen shrub or small tree, also known as **bay laurel**. Unlike the toxic **cherry laurel** (right), the leaf tip is narrow.

Where: Widely cultivated and also common in the wild near major settlements, particularly in scrub and abandoned gardens.

Part eaten: Leaves, dried or fresh, as flavouring.

Nutritional value: Leaves rich in iron and manganese (USDA).

Use: A native of the Mediterranean region, whose sprigs were used in ancient Greece to make wreaths to signify high status (laureate). Whole leaves are traditionally used in the same region for flavouring soups, sauces and stews, meat, boiled chestnuts or olives in brine, or for making liqueur.

Lily Family

[Liliaceae]

Members of this family typically grow from bulbs, bearing strap-like leaves and large flowers whose parts are arranged in threes. The family includes **tulips** (*Tulipa* species), whose bulbs are mildly toxic; and **lilies** (*Lilium* species), many popular in Chinese and Japanese cuisine for their edible bulbs (although the stems, leaves and flowers are highly toxic to cats). (For **day lilies**, see page 62.)

Taiwan Lily

Lilium formosanum

Description: Also known as **Formosan lily**. To waist-high with nodding white flowers (Jan–Mar). Bulb breaks into segments.
Where: Spreading freely along roadsides and tracksides, particularly in the North Island. Now banned from sale, propagation and distribution.
Part eaten: Bulbs.
Nutritional value: Bulbs contain vitamin C and starch, which is readily converted to sucrose by refrigeration (Deng).
Use: This lily is a native of the island of Taiwan, where it is valued as a source of cut flowers. The bulbs are also recommended by the Taipei Botanical Garden as a nutrient-rich food. They are harvested there in the dormant period and kept in refrigerators for 50 days to sweeten them, converting the starch into sucrose; however, to my taste they are sweet enough as they are.

Tiger Lily

Lilium lancifolium

Description: To waist-high, bearing nodding orange flowers with purple-black spots (Jan–Feb). Bulb breaks into segments.
Where: Scattered throughout, mostly around settlements. (Much less common than the Taiwan lily, above.)
Part eaten: Bulbs and flowers.
Nutritional value: Raw bulbs rich in potassium and fair source of protein and phosphorus (Ershow) and carbohydrate (Sim).
Use: A native of China, Japan and Korea, where the fleshy scales of the bulb are eaten raw or cooked – a traditional favourite in Chinese cooking, particularly in summer – and a principal food in the Chinatown markets of New York. The starch-rich bulbs are generally stir-fried or deep-fried, but may also be baked, grated or ground into flour and added to sweets or soups, or pickled. In Japan the starch may be separated out by crushing the bulbs in a mortar and pestle and by repeated washing. The flowers themselves may also be used to add a delicate flavour to salads and soups.

tiger lily bulbs

Madeira Vine Family [Basellaceae]

This is a family of climbing or trailing vines. Important edible members include **ulluco** (*Ullucus tuberosus*), a native of the Andean region of South America, where it is also cultivated – primarily for its tubers. These rate second only to potato among the economically important root crops of the region and are now grown here in New Zealand on a small scale.

aerial tubers

Madeira Vine

Anredera cordifolia

Description: Also known as **mignonette vine**, **lamb's tail** or **potato vine**. An evergreen climber with delicate, fleshy, heart-shaped leaves, distinctive aerial tubers and long, tail-like bunches of fragrant white flowers (Jan–Apr).

Where: Previously cultivated in warmer areas but now banned from sale, propagation and distribution due to it spreading so freely here by pieces of rhizome and stem tubers to become a serious weed, often smothering trees, especially from Hamilton north.

Part eaten: Leaves, aerial tubers and underground rhizomes, usually cooked. TIP: The aerial tubers are easily collected from the ground as they drop off very freely, but do take care not to spread these.

Nutritional value: Leaves rich in iron, calcium, zinc, protein and vitamins A and C (Kinupp 2007, Sartori).

Use: A native of South America. In Brazil the leaves are traditionally used as spinach or dried and ground into a powder as an ingredient of bread, and the aerial tubers are cooked and eaten as a vegetable. The custom has since largely fallen into disuse, although the leaves are nowadays again being promoted there as a replacement for spinach, for example in homemade pasta, where they give the pasta a striking green hue. The leaves are tender and mild in taste. The Brazilian Ministry of Health also recommends the aerial tubers cooked or fried in a similar manner to potatoes; indeed, these do taste like a slightly glutinous version of a potato. Harvesting the underground rhizome involves a little more work, but these have a very similar texture to the aerial tubers and are used in much the same way. The World Vegetable Center recommends growing the vine as a vegetable, adding that the leaves and tender stems can be eaten raw, boiled, stir-fried with sesame oil and ginger, or in soups; while Valdirene Sartori in *Plantas Alimentícias Não Convencionais* provides recipes for vegetable pie and vegan cheese bread.

Malabar Spinach

Basella alba

Description: Also known as **vine spinach**. A fast-growing, soft-stemmed vine with thick, succulent, heart-shaped leaves.
Where: Cultivated here on a small scale, readily self-seeding in gardens as far south as Christchurch.
Part eaten: Stems and leaves, raw or cooked – all year.
Nutritional value: Raw leaves exceptionally rich in vitamin C, also vitamins A, B9, B6 and B2, manganese, magnesium, potassium, calcium and iron (USDA).
Use: A native of SE Asia – from India through to Indonesia and the Philippines – that is now cultivated as a vegetable elsewhere on a large scale, particularly in warm regions. The leaves and stems are cooked as a spinach or added to stews and soups as a thickener. As a hot-weather green it is a particularly important crop in the Philippines, Thailand, Vietnam, China, Mongolia, India, Bangladesh, Sri Lanka and many African countries, and its leaves are offered for sale in many supermarkets and farmers' markets across Asia. A red juice squeezed from the fruit can be used as ink, as a cosmetic and for colouring foods.

Mallow and Hibiscus Family

[Malvaceae]

Members of this family typically have five-petalled flowers, leaves shaped like the palm of a hand and a slimy sap. Includes several commercially important food plants – **okra (lady's fingers)**, **cocoa**, **durian**, **marshmallow** and **hibiscus** – and some important fibre plants, including **cotton** and the native **houhere (lacebark**, *Hoheria* species), the inner bark of which was traditionally used by Māori to manufacture a soft, lacy textile for making hats and headbands.

Large-flowered Mallow

Malva sylvestris

Description: Tall plant up to 1.5 m, with large purple flowers (Nov–Apr).

Where: Very common throughout most of the country, except Westland.

Part eaten: Tender leaves, flowers and immature seedpods ('cheeses').

Nutritional value: Tender leaves a good source of dietary fibre, calcium, potassium and vitamins C and E; sometimes also of magnesium, iron, copper, manganese and zinc. Desirably low oxalic acid/calcium ratio (Sánchez-Mata).

Use: A native of North Africa, Europe and SW Asia, whose use as a vegetable can be traced back at least 2000 years through the writings of Dioscorides, and Galen of Pergamon. In 1862 British botanist Pierpoint Johnson elaborated: 'The foliage when boiled forms a very wholesome vegetable; and the flat seeds, commonly called from their shape "cheeses" by country people, are likewise edible.' In Morocco, Turkey and Italy these leaves are offered for sale in some of the local markets. Some enjoy them in salads, but they are best in soups. In salad the best part is the flowers, which are added as garnish by chefs in Italy. Similar traditional food uses of the plant have been recorded from right around the Mediterranean, from Portugal across to Turkey, Lebanon, Palestine, Jordan, Egypt, Tunisia and Morocco, where the tender leaves are generally collected in spring and boiled, then seasoned with oil, or cooked in stews and soups or sautéed in olive oil. The same plant is also enjoyed as a vegetable further east in the Indian Himalayas.

Local relatives: Although the hairy leaves of the equally common **tree mallow** (*M. arborea*) are also edible, they tend to be rather dry and unappetising. The other wild mallows are less common here: **dwarf mallow** (*M. neglecta*), **French mallow** (*M. nicaeensis*) and **small-flowered mallow** (*M. parviflora*) whose young leaves, shoots and immature fruit are used as a wild leafy vegetable across much of Europe. The tender leaves and stems of **Cretan mallow** (*M. pseudolavatera* = *M. multiflora*) are likewise enjoyed as a vegetable in Morocco, Spain and Turkey.

Local garden escapes in the mallow family — edible flowers

In India the flowers of **Indian mallow** (*Abutilon indicum*, 1) are eaten; and those of the **trailing abutilon** (*A. megapotamicum*, 2) are eaten as a vegetable in their native Brazil. In Thailand **Turk's cap** (*Malvaviscus arboreus*, 3) is cultivated for its flowers, used in salads and light curry. The tender new leaves of **hollyhock** (*Alcea rosea*, 4) feature in Egyptian cookery, and in Bosnia and Herzegovina as an ingredient (along with the flowers) in pies. In Italy, Asia and many Pacific islands the flower petals of **hibiscus** (*Hibiscus rosa-sinensis*, 5) are eaten, or brewed to make a herbal tea; while in Kenya, Zimbabwe, South Africa and China the flowers, young leaves and shoots of **bladder hibiscus** (*Hibiscus trionum*, 6) are eaten raw or cooked.

Maples

[Sapindaceae]

This family is also known as the **soapberry** family as many members possess soap-like properties derived from the mildly toxic saponins they contain. Most members are trees, shrubs or woody climbers. Food trees in this family include **sugar maple** (*Acer saccharum*), **lychee**, **longan**, **rambutan**, **ackee apple** and the native **tītoki**, whose fruit was traditionally eaten by Māori.

Sycamore

Acer pseudoplatanus

Description: Large deciduous tree. Leaf stalks reddish. Winged 'helicopter' seeds.
Where: Very common, especially in eastern South Island and Stewart Island.
Part eaten: Sap in spring (flows best on warm sunny days following frosty nights).
Nutritional value: Spring sap may contain an average of 3.18% sugars, mostly sucrose (Łuczaj 2014).
Use: A native of Europe. In cooler regions of the continent the sap is tapped just as the tree is coming into leaf in spring, which involves drilling an 8–12 mm hole in the trunk about 5–6 cm deep to accommodate a short tube from which the sap can be collected in a bucket. This sap may be drunk fresh as a refreshingly sweet drink, or used to make beer or wine – traditional uses recorded from the northern European countries of Scotland, Estonia, Poland, Czech Republic, Slovakia, Hungary, Romania and Bosnia-Herzegovina. Croatian botanist Ljubiša Grlić notes that one tree can yield up to 12 litres (a bucketful) of sap per day. Boiling this liquid down will transform it into syrup, but the typical quantity yielded is meagre: around 300 ml (just over a cupful) of syrup, i.e. about 2.5% of the quantity of sap collected.
Local relatives: Likewise, the sugary sap of the less-common **box elder** (*A. negundo*) was harvested by many of the indigenous tribes of eastern Canada and southern Montana.

Miner's Lettuce Family

[Montiaceae]

Members of this family were previously included in the **purslane family** [Portulacaceae]. Like members of that family, these also typically have fleshy leaves. Edible members of the miner's lettuce family include many kinds of **spring beauty** (*Claytonia* species), whose tubers were widely eaten by the indigenous inhabitants of North America.

Miner's Lettuce

Claytonia perfoliata (= *Montia*)

Description: Low plant with pale, delicate leaves and tiny, white, five-petalled flowers (Oct–Nov).

Where: Cultivated as a salad plant and common growing wild in shady damp sites, especially in the South Island.

Part eaten: Young upper leaves and stems in spring; later, the leaves become bitter.

Nutritional value: Leaves rich in protein and vitamins A, C, B1, B2, B3 and B6, potassium, calcium, magnesium and iron (Rana 2017). Low in oxalic acid (Schelstraete).

Use: Native to a region that extends along the western side of North America from Canada to Mexico, where the plant was first used as food by the indigenous inhabitants, either as a fresh salad or cooked green. Later their custom was adopted by Europeans, especially during the 1849 California Gold Rush when miners collected the tender young leaves in late winter and spring for use in salads or cooked as a spinach, thus preventing and serving as a cure for scurvy. These days it is occasionally cultivated as greens in the USA, Cuba, Argentina, Europe and also in New Zealand. The flavour of the young tender leaves is delicate, so combines well with stronger-flavoured greens.

Local relatives: The tender young stems and leaves of the less-common **blinks** (*Montia fontana* subsp. *chondrosperma*) are collected in Europe in spring before flowering, for use in salads. The tiny black seeds of the even less common **Curnow's curse** (**redmaids**, *Calandrinia menziesii*) are a traditional food of the indigenous inhabitants of California, who roasted and ground them, then pressed them into balls as a staple food.

Mint Family [Lamiaceae]

Members of this family typically have square stems and opposite leaves; many are aromatic. Includes many culinary herbs – **basil**, **oregano**, **marjoram**, **summer savory**, **rosemary**, **sage** and **thyme** – as well as a few plants with edible tubers, such as **Chinese artichoke** and native **African potatoes**, and others that are grown commercially for their edible seeds, such as **chia** (*Salvia hispanica*).

Wild Basil

Clinopodium vulgare

Description: Softly hairy, aromatic leaves. Pinkish-purple flowers (Dec–May).

Where: Wetter areas. More common in the northern South Island.

Part eaten: Leaves and flowers.

Nutritional value: Leaves rich in vitamin C (Jones).

Use: Native to a region that extends from Morocco to Siberia. In NE Italy (western Friuli) the first flowers are collected for inclusion in a traditional spring mixture of cooked wild herbs. Similarly, in the folk traditions of Central Italy the fresh leaves are sometimes collected in winter for use as seasoning in place of the better-known culinary herb basil.

Local relatives: Although the culinary herb **basil** (*Ocimum basilicum*) is commonly cultivated here, it is rarely found growing wild.

Red Dead-nettle

Lamium purpureum

Description: Soft leaves. Reddish-purple flowers (Sep–Nov).

Where: Very common throughout.

Part eaten: Leaves and flowering tips, usually cooked. The flowers can be sucked for nectar.

Nutritional value: Leaves rich in carbohydrates, vitamin C and carotene (Redžić 2010).

Use: A native of Eurasia that can be found on the menu of the well-known restaurant Noma in Copenhagen, for which it is collected from the wild by a small southern-Swedish foraging enterprise. In fact, its use by the Swedish peasantry can be dated to at least the 1860s, when the whole plant was commonly eaten boiled as a spinach. In Italy, too, the young leaves and flowering tips are among the traditional gathered food plants of NW Tuscany and western Friuli. In nearby Bosnia and Herzegovina the young shoots are cooked as a vegetable or eaten in salad, especially during the siege of Sarajevo when they helped supplement humanitarian food aid. In Turkey, too, the herb is traditionally eaten cooked, and children like to suck a sweet nectar from the base of the flowers.

Local relatives: The leaves and flowering tips of the less-common **henbit** (*L. amplexicaule*) are cooked and eaten throughout much of Europe and Asia, but may not be good to eat raw (see page 152). The yellow-flowered **yellow archangel** (*L. galeobdolon*) is not recommended: despite occasional use of its young shoots and flowers overseas, it contains potentially toxic compounds (Egebjerg).

Horehound

Marrubium vulgare

Description: Leaves downy beneath. Small white flowers Nov–Mar.

Where: Common in drier parts of Canterbury and Otago, often in disturbed or overgrazed land.

Part eaten: Shoots and young leaves. Very bitter, so best in small quantities and cooked.

Nutritional value: Rich in antioxidant activity, calcium, magnesium and potassium (Rezgui).

Use: A native of North Africa and Eurasia, including the Mediterranean region, where the plant's reputation as a cough remedy can be traced back some 2000 years to Pliny the Elder, who advised that horehound 'dried, powdered, and taken with honey, is extremely efficacious for a dry cough'. Nowadays the name is more often associated with horehound candy drops, ale, liqueurs and tea made from the bitter leaves. In Bosnia, Sicily and other Mediterranean countries, though, the shoots and young leaves are traditionally collected in spring and summer for use in small quantities as a boiled vegetable.

Lemon Balm

Melissa officinalis

Description: Leaves lemon-scented. White flowers Dec–May.

Where: Widely planted for its scented leaves, but also common wild.

Part eaten: Flowers and leaves.

Nutritional value: Fresh leaves very rich in vitamin C, B1 (Franke), and carotene (Grlić), and natural antioxidants generally (Lin).

Use: A native of the Mediterranean region, where its fragrant leaves have been used in cooking for more than 2000 years. For most of that time it has also been cultivated, eventually reaching England where great quantities were grown around London in the mid-1700s to supply local markets. In Spain, Italy, Bosnia-Herzogovina, Croatia, Turkey and Palestine the plant continues to be collected from the wild for use either as flavouring or in salads, or to brew as a herbal tea. The plant was brought to New Zealand during the early period of European settlement, where it was first noted wild in 1904.

Spearmint

Mentha spicata

Description: Leaves with pointed tips and a distinctive spearmint smell. Pink or white flowers Jan–May.

Where: An escape from cultivation found in most settled localities.

Part eaten: Leaves and flowers as flavouring.

Nutritional value: Fresh leaves rich in vitamins A and C and in a wide range of minerals, including iron, calcium, magnesium, potassium, copper and manganese (USDA).

Use: Native to a region that extends from Europe to China, and now cultivated on a commercial scale for spearmint oil for flavouring candies, chewing gum and toothpaste. Around much of the Mediterranean the leaves and flowers are gathered to brew a herbal tea, syrup or liqueur, to flavour sauces, dressings, ice cream, salads, soups, fruit drinks and desserts, or as a garnish.

Local relatives: The slightly less-common **apple mint** (*M. suaveolens*) can be used in the same way; the leaves of **peppermint** (*M.* × *piperita*), which is not uncommon here in streams, make a popular tea. Culinary use of the very common **pennyroyal** (*M. pulegium*) requires CAUTION, for

tea made from its leaves and flowers has proven toxic to infants and small children (Bakerink), and excessive use by women attempting to induce abortion has even proven fatal (Brown).

Catnip

Nepeta cataria

Description: Also known as **catmint**. Pleasant aroma, with a peculiar attractiveness to cats. Pink or white flowers Dec–May.

Where: Widespread except in Westland and Fiordland.

Part eaten: Leaves and flowers.

Nutritional value: Herb rich in calcium, magnesium, potassium and iron (Terninko).

Use: Native to a region that extends from southern Europe to Japan. In Sicily the plant is collected from the wild in spring and winter and boiled as a vegetable. It is also traditionally used sparingly for flavouring in England (in sauces), Croatia (in tea and as a spice) and in the Spanish Pyrenees (where the plant – minus the roots – is used in the preparation of ratafia liqueurs).

Wild Marjoram

Origanum vulgare

Description: Also known as **oregano**. Woody with aromatic leaves, and pink to purplish flowers (Dec–Mar).

Where: A garden escape found in scattered locations.

Part eaten: Flowers and leaves as flavouring and to brew a tea.

Nutritional value: Fresh leaves rich in vitamin C (Jones), potassium, calcium, magnesium, iron, carbohydrates and dietary fibre (Abbasi 2015). Flowers especially rich in antioxidants (Sánchez-Mata).

Use: Throughout most of the plant's native range, from Morocco across much of Eurasia, the leaves and flowers are traditionally collected from the wild as flavouring for tea, soups and other dishes.

Local relatives: Sweet marjoram (*O. majorana*) is a slightly different plant, which is widely cultivated but not known to grow wild here. It is used in the same way.

Selfheal

Prunella vulgaris

Description: Creeping plant with mild taste and no particular smell. Violet flowers (mostly Nov–Apr).

Where: Very common throughout.

Part eaten: Young shoots, leaves and flowerheads.

Nutritional value: Fresh leaves and stem rich in protein, plant fat, carbohydrate, β-carotene, vitamins B1, B3, C and K (Rasool). Plant high in antioxidants generally and commonly used as a medicinal plant in China (Li).

Use: Native to most of the Northern Hemisphere. Nicholas Culpeper (1653) gives a pithy explanation of the common name: it is a herb 'whereby when you are hurt you may heal yourself . . . a special herb for inward and outward wounds'. Besides still being widely used for a range of ailments, it is collected for use as a cooked vegetable in Germany, Czech Republic, Bosnia-Herzogovina, South Korea and throughout much of China. The part most often used is the young shoots, but in western Friuli (Italy) the cooked flowerheads are also eaten. A tradition of brewing the plant as a herbal tea is recorded from Estonia and Bosnia, and also China, where the dried flowerheads are sold for this purpose and exported to the USA, where the Cherokee people likewise traditionally cooked the leaves as greens.

Wild Sage

Salvia verbenaca

Description: Also known as **wild clary**. Aromatic leaves; stems often purplish where exposed to sunlight. Flowers Oct–Feb.
Where: Widespread in sunny places among short vegetation, especially in parts of Canterbury and Central Otago.
Part eaten: Leaves and flowers as flavouring.
Nutritional value: Leaves and stems rich in antioxidants (Khlifi).
Use: A native of the UK and the Mediterranean region. In the NW Tuscany region of Italy the leaves are traditionally gathered for use in salads, vegetable soup and torte salate (like a quiche). The leaves are used similarly as a wild green in Dalmatia (southern Croatia) and SW Herzegovina, while in the Black Sea region of Turkey the leaves are brewed to make a refreshing tea.

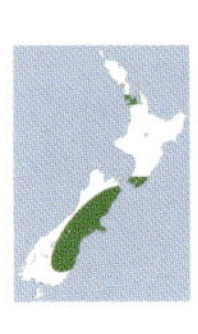

Garden Sage

Salvia officinalis

Description: Greyish leaves; distinctive sage smell when crushed.
Where: Commonly grown as a culinary herb and found wild only rarely.
Part eaten: Leaves and flowers as flavouring or as a herbal tea.
Nutritional value: Plant rich in antioxidants (Abdelkader).
Use: A native of the Mediterranean region, where the leaves have long been used to flavour meals and savoury breads, or brewed to make a herbal tea.
Local relatives: Chia (*S. hispanica*) – whose seeds are sold as a health food – is found in the wild here, but very rarely.

Pineapple Sage

Salvia elegans (= *S. rutilans*)

Description: Leaves taste and smell of pineapple. Red flowers (all year).
Where: Near gardens.
Part eaten: Leaves and flowers.
Nutritional value: Flowers, leaves and stems rich in antioxidants, including caffeic acid – more so than those of the common garden sage (Pereira 2018).
Use: A native of Mexico, where the plant is used primarily as fodder and as traditional medicine to alleviate anxiety. These days it is used to impart a pineapple-like fragrance to food, with the fresh edible flowers sprinkled in salads, drinks, cakes and desserts to add colour, or infused to make a herbal tea.

Rosemary

Salvia rosmarinus (= *Rosmarinus officinalis*)

Description: Fragrant evergreen shrub, up to shoulder-high. Leaves dark green on upper side (unlike **lavender**).

Where: A common garden herb, with wild plants becoming increasingly common in recent years.

Part eaten: Leaves for flavouring.

Nutritional value: Fresh leaves rich in calcium, iron, magnesium, potassium, and vitamins A, C, B6 and B9 (USDA).

Use: A native of the Mediterranean region, traditionally used for flavouring stews, salads, soups and casseroles. It is a favourite with roasted potatoes, kūmara, zucchini, peppers, asparagus and eggplant, for example.

Wild Thyme

Thymus vulgaris

Description: Also known as **common thyme** or **garden thyme** – the same thyme that is commonly cultivated. Semi-woody herb with small, aromatic leaves and mauve or white flowers (Sep–Dec).

Where: Dominates dry slopes in the area of Alexandra and Cromwell, with scattered patches elsewhere.

Part eaten: Flowers and leaf tips as flavouring.

Nutritional value: Fresh leaves rich in calcium, iron, magnesium, potassium, copper, manganese, and vitamins A, B2, B6 and C (USDA).

Use: In its native region of Spain and Italy the plant is traditionally collected from the wild as herbal tea, or to make a liqueur, or for seasoning olives, stews and roasted meat.

Local relatives: Creeping thyme (*T. pulegioides*) – traditionally used in the same way in the same region – is also grown here, but is far less common wild.

Edible garden escapes

The crushed leaves of **harlequin glorybower** (or **peanut butter tree**, *Clerodendrum trichotomum*) smell of peanut butter and are harvested as a wild vegetable in China and South Korea. This plant occurs wild only occasionally near old gardens in the North Island.

Myrtle Family

[Myrtaceae]

This family includes the **feijoa**, **guava** and **jabuticaba** fruit trees of South America, the **Malay apple** and several spices including **allspice**, **cloves** and the **common myrtle** (*Myrtus communis* – whose fruit and sprigs serve as flavouring). Native members include **ramarama** and **rōhutu**, which traditionally supplied Māori with a small edible fruit, and **rātā** and **pōhutukawa**, whose flowers supplied Māori with an edible nectar.

Feijoa

Feijoa sellowiana (= *Acca*)

Description: Evergreen shrub. Leaves dark and smooth on top, silvery below.

Where: Widely planted for its fruit and as a hedge, but also wild, particularly in the north.

Part eaten: Pulp of the fruit – which falls when ripe (Feb–Jun). Also the fleshy flower petals (Nov–Jan).

Nutritional value: Fruit particularly rich in vitamin C, and also in B5, B6 and B9 (USDA).

Use: A native of Argentina, Brazil and Uruguay, where its fruit is collected in the wild. By the 1920s it had reached New Zealand; however, it was not until the late 20th century that the tree reached southern Europe and the USA, from where it was distributed throughout the world as an ornamental shrub for gardens and parks. Nowadays, commercial cultivation is mainly in the USA, Australia and New Zealand, where the tree was first recorded in the wild in 2006. Although the taste of the skin itself is too strong for most, it becomes more palatable, though sour, with cooking. More commonly the ripe fruit is eaten by cutting it in half, then scooping out the pulp with a spoon, eaten directly or in fruit salads, cakes and desserts.

Purple Guava

Psidium cattleyanum

Description: Large shrub or small tree with smooth trunk. Fruit to 2 cm, dark purple, occasionally yellow.

Where: Spread by birds, pigs and possums.

Part eaten: Ripe fruit (Mar–May).

Nutritional value: Fruit rich in potassium and vitamin C (USDA), and natural antioxidants generally (Ribeiro).

Use: A native of Uruguay and eastern Brazil, and planted in many countries for its edible fruit, where it has become a serious weed, for example in the Hawaiian Islands and potentially also here. The fruit is akin to a small tropical guava, so is also sometimes known as **strawberry guava**. When fully ripe they are good to eat fresh, and – once the bone-hard seeds have been strained out – good for making jam, purée, jellies, etc.

Local relatives: The so-called **Chilean guava** (*Ugni molinae*) is cultivated here for its much smaller fruit under the name **New Zealand cranberry**, but is fairly rare in the wild. The **tropical guava** (*Psidium guajava*), which is occasionally grown in northern New Zealand for its large yellow fruit, is not known to grow wild.

Monkey Apple

Syzygium smithii (= *Acmena smithii*)

Description: Also known as **lilly pilly**. Evergreen tree with fragrant white flowers (Oct–Jan). Fruit 1–1.5 cm, white to deep purple.

Where: Commonly grown in warmer areas, but spreading into native scrub around the Bay of Islands, Auckland and Coromandel, so now banned from sale, propagation and distribution.

Part eaten: Ripe fruit (mostly Sep).

Nutritional value: Fruit contains only trace quantities of vitamins and minerals, other than copper, which helps with the uptake of iron (Lim).

Use: This tree is a native of eastern Australia, where the ripe fruit is traditionally used as a raw snack food by the indigenous people of the region, who know the tree as tdgerail (NSW) or coochin-coochin (Queensland). Despite being recommended there as a 'bush tucker' plant and for making jams, jellies, drinks, relishes, desserts, tarts, pies, cakes and even ice cream, the taste is – in my experience – too insipid.

Local relatives: Although **Malay apple** (*S. malaccense*) is strictly tropical and not found here, **rose apple** (*S. jambos*) is occasionally grown in New Zealand for its edible fruit, and can sometimes be found wild from Auckland north.

Brush Cherry

Syzygium australe (= *Eugenia myrtifolia*)

Description: Evergreen tree with white flowers (Jan–Jul), and pink-red fruit 1.5–2 cm.

Where: From Nelson north.

Part eaten: Ripe fruit (autumn and winter).

Nutritional value: Fruit rich in copper and a fair source of iron (Brand-Miller) with a similar antioxidant content to blueberries (Netzel).

Use: A native of eastern Australia, where botanist Joseph Maiden recommended the fruit in his *Useful Native Plants of Australia* (1889) as acid, making a good preserve and a red juice with similar properties to those of red grapes; 'by fermentation it yields wine possessing a bouquet', he adds. The ripe fruit can also be eaten raw or made into jams, jellies, etc.

Local relatives: The very similar **magenta cherry** (*S. paniculatum*) is equally common here; its ripe fruit likewise provided indigenous Australians with a traditional food.

Edible Eucalypts

Eucalypt trees also belong to the myrtle family. Although a few species provide food, these are not common in the wild. These include **cider gum** (*Eucalyptus gunnii*, right) whose sweetish sap was bled by Australian settlers to make a kind of cider; and **manna gum** (*E. viminalis*), from whose leaves Aboriginal Australians collected white lumps of manna (edible insect exudations) in spring and summer.

Nasturtium Family

[Tropaeolaceae]

Nasturtium means 'nose-twister'. This common name of the family derives from watercress (*Nasturtium officinale*) – a plant that actually belongs to a different family. The link lies in the fact that both are members of the same Brassicales order, many of which share pungent mustard-oil compounds (glucosinolates), giving them their characteristic mustard-like taste and smell. Cultivated food plants include **mashua** or tuberous nasturtium, whose tubers are eaten in the Peruvian Andes.

pickled seeds

nasturtium seeds

Garden Nasturtium

Tropaeolum majus

Description: Weak-stemmed scrambling plant with scarlet, orange or yellow flowers.
Where: Very common throughout, especially in moist and shady places.
Part eaten: Flowers (Oct–May), flower buds and leaves. Seeds pickled.
Nutritional value: Flowers and leaves rich in vitamin C (Cobus). Flowers – especially yellow ones – are rich in lutein, while the leaves are good sources of both lutein and β-carotene (Niizu). (Lutein is known to play a role in reducing the risk of cataract and macular degeneration.)
Use: Also known as **Indian cress**, in reference to the 'Indies', a term employed by the Spanish royal government to refer to its 'overseas possessions'. How this native of the Andes came by this name is explained by English herbalist John Gerarde (1597): 'The seeds of this rare and faire plant came first from the Indies into Spaine, and thence into France and Flanders,' adding his opinion that 'The smell and taste shew it to be a kinde of Cresses' – a link that is explained above. In Europe the plant's popularity as an ornamental continued to grow, along with its use as a 'cress' – a use that spread right around the globe. As Charles Bryant observed in 1783, 'In France [the flowers] are not only used to garnish dishes, but are mixed with Lettuce and other cold sallads, and are esteemed both pleasant and wholesome. The berries have a warm spicy flavour, and make an excellent pickle.' In fact, the pickled seeds continue to be used as a substitute for capers, and the spicy peppery flavour of the flowers, flower buds and leaves – similar to watercress – are still enjoyed in salads or sandwiches. The blossoms are rated as one of the most popular of edible flowers to this day; in Korea one can even find them for sale in the local markets.
Local relatives: Although the tubers, leaves and flowers of **ladies' legs** (*T. pentaphyllum*) are traditionally eaten in South America, this plant is much less common here.

Nettle Family

[Urticaceae]

Members of this family have inconspicuous flowers and a watery sap. Many have stinging hairs on the stems and leaves, which can cause a painful rash on contact but are rendered harmless by cooking. Several, such as the **ramie** plant of China and the **common nettle**, have tough stems that provide a useful source of fibre. Native members include the harmless **parataniwha** of streamsides and tracksides, and the potentially dangerous **ongaonga** (**tree nettle**) shrub that grows at forest edges, neither of which is known to have been used as food by Māori.

Pellitory-of-the-wall

Parietaria judaica

Description: Densely hairy with tiny pink or white flowers (Oct–Jun). Stouter and far more common than the native *P. debilis*.

Where: In cracks in city footpaths, garden walls, and on coastal cliffs.

Part eaten: Leaves and young shoots. Avoid harvesting from polluted sites, though – near busy roads or sites potentially contaminated by dust from old house paint – as the plant is a known accumulator of heavy metals, including lead and cadmium (Aksoy). Many people are also allergic to the pollen (Ciprandi).

Nutritional value: Leaves rich in minerals, especially calcium, magnesium and manganese, yet also high in sodium (Sánchez-Mata).

Use: Native to a region that extends from Morocco to Kazakhstan. In the Mediterranean region, at least, the leaves and young shoots are still used in place of commercial leafy vegetables. In the sparsely inhabited Dalmatian Hinterland region of Croatia, for example, the leaves are a traditional ingredient of mišanca, a very common local dish prepared from a mix of lightly boiled wild vegetables, often with the addition of potatoes, seasoned with salt, and olive oil or sunflower seed oil.

Local relatives: Although the longer-leaved **erect pellitory-of-the-wall** (*P. officinalis*), has a 2000-year history of being eaten as a spinach in Europe, it is much less common in the wild here in New Zealand.

nettle (*Urtica dioica*)

ongaonga (native **tree nettle**, *Urtica ferox*)

dwarf nettle (*Urtica urens*)

Nettle

Urtica dioica & *U. urens*

Description: Herb covered with stinging hairs. Inconspicuous green flowers.

Where: Very common in scattered localities throughout.

Part eaten: Growing tips and young leaves, best in spring (later, it becomes coarse and bitter). TIP: gardening gloves useful to avoid stings. The sting is completely inactivated by cooking. Not to be confused with the potentially dangerous **ongaonga** (the native **tree nettle**, *U. ferox*) of forest edges, which is much taller with long, narrow leaves (see photo).

Nutritional value: Leaves rich in calcium, manganese, phosphorus and vitamin C; sometimes also in potassium, magnesium, iron, copper and vitamins B2, B3, E and β-carotene. Relatively high in protein and very low in sodium (Sánchez-Mata).

Use: Native to North Africa and much of Eurasia, including the Mediterranean region, where the culinary use of nettles can be traced back some 2000 years to the time of Pedanius Dioscorides, Greek author of *De materia medica*, who tells us how he would boil the leaves and eat them with shellfish. Recent records of the use of the spring foliage have been collected from Portugal, Spain, Italy, Slovenia, Croatia, Bosnia-Herzegovina, Albania, Bulgaria, Turkey, Lebanon and Morocco. The plant's reputation as a wild spinach, or as a basis for nettle soups, extends north through Hungary, Romania, Slovakia and the Czech Republic to Estonia, and east through Iran to the Indian Himalayas, where harvesters sometimes use wooden forceps to avoid the stings. In Croatia and Turkey young nettle tips appear for sale in local vegetable markets, and in Spain and Denmark they appear on the menu of luxury restaurants (e.g. Hotel Exe Alfonso VIII in Plasencia, and Noma in Copenhagen). Italians have many traditional nettle recipes, employing the leaves as a filling for stuffing pasta (tortelli or ravioli) or pie (byrek), or fried with eggs (frittata). Given the rather insipid taste of nettles, their appeal lies more in helping to moderate other flavours, and in their nutritional value. In Europe young nettle leaves are also brewed to produce nettle beer, wine and herbal teas.

Olive Family

[Oleaceae]

Members of this family are typically noted for their hard wood and fragrant flowers. Most have white flowers and opposite leaves. Well-known members include **privet** (whose fruit is mildly toxic), **ash**, **lilac** and **jasmine**; the family also includes several species of native **maire** (*Nestegis*), the fruit of at least one of which traditionally provided a minor source of food for Māori.

Olive

Olea europaea

Description: Evergreen tree or shrub to 10 m tall. Fruit green, turning purple-black when ripe, containing a large, hard seed.

Where: Widely planted for the fruit, but also spread by birds and perhaps also possums.

Part eaten: CURED fruit, minus the inedible, bone-hard seed. Picked Mar–Jul. Leaves as flavouring.

Nutritional value: Fruit rich in vitamin E and monounsaturated fat (USDA).

Use: A native of Africa through to Central China, including the Mediterranean region, where olives were among the first fruit trees to be domesticated. Indeed, for some 6000 years they have remained one of the most important crops of the region. The flesh of the fruit is widely used – as a relish or in breadmaking, soups, salads, etc. and as a source of oil that is highly valued in the kitchen and as a fuel for traditional lamps. If you have ever tried eating fruit fresh off the tree, you will appreciate why it is generally cured first. This is due to a very bitter compound called oleuropein, which does reduce as the fruit ripens but must generally be removed to render the fruit edible, usually by curing the fruit in brine, dry salt, water, or lye (a mixture of wood ash and water). Many Kiwis give up at this point, yet the methods of preparation practised in homes around the Mediterranean are quite basic and surprisingly simple. Cured in brine (a concentrated salt solution), for example, olives undergo a natural fermentation that breaks down the chemical bond between oleuropein and sugars in the olive, allowing this bitter component to be leached out. The use of salt also helps reduce the chance of spoilage. For green-ripe olives the process is slightly longer than for naturally black-ripe ones, but here are the basic rules: always select fresh, hard and unbruised fruit, and use glass, stainless steel, enamelware, earthenware or plastic utensils rather than copper, brass, iron or galvanised ones. Make sure the olives are completely submerged in the brine; otherwise they will turn brown and mouldy and be unfit for eating. The basic mix for the brine is a ratio of 1 kg of olives to 1 L of water and 100 g of salt.

Local relatives: Wild olives in New Zealand fall into two groups – the **European olive** (*O. e.* subsp. *europaea*) of the Mediterranean region, and the **African olive** (*O. e.* subsp. *cuspidata*).

Onion Family

[Amaryllidaceae]

Members of this family typically grow from bulbs or underground stems, producing several strap-like or grass-like leaves. Important food plants include **garlic**, **leek**, **shallots**, **spring onions** and **chives**, all of which contain diallyl disulphides, substances that give them a distinctive, sulphurous onion or garlic smell when crushed. This feature distinguishes them from other poisonous members of the family: **daffodils**, **agapanthus**, **amaryllis** (**naked lady**) and **snowflake**.

Wild Onion

Allium vineale

Description: Also known as **wild garlic** or **crow garlic**. Up to waist-high, with long, stiff, hollow, tube-like leaves, with a groove along one side. Flowers (Oct–Nov) pinkish-green interspersed with yellowish-brown bulbils. Whole plant has a strong smell of garlic.

Where: In dry, grassy, neglected land and on roadsides, easily overlooked among grass.

Part eaten: Young leaves and bulbs. As with other kinds of onion, this plant is toxic to dogs, cats, cows, pigs and horses.

Nutritional value: Rich in phosphorus, iron, magnesium and potassium, but also high in sodium (Tegin). Leaves also rich in vitamin C (Zennie).

Use: This wild onion is native to a region that extends from Algeria to Scandinavia and Iran. Botanist C. Pierpoint Johnson records its use in 19th-century Britain in his treatise on *The Useful Plants of Great Britain* (1862): 'The leaves are used in the same manner as those of the wild garlic and are equally wholesome.' In Denmark the leaves and bulbs feature these days in the menu of at least one leading Copenhagen restaurant. They have meanwhile remained a traditional ingredient in Italian minestrella soup made in NW Tuscany, and are among the wild herb ingredients used in western Friuli, too, in a spring mixture of cooked greens, and for consumption raw in salads. In Dalmatia (southern Croatia) and in the adjacent SW Herzegovina the leaves and bulbs are likewise collected for use as a vegetable, and in Hungary too. Further east, in Turkey, the leaves are gathered for sale in the local markets for use in cheese production as an antibacterial, and also to give flavour and aroma.

Local relatives: Other wild onions traditionally harvested for food in Mediterranean countries include **wild leek** (*A. ampeloprasum*, with V-shaped leaves), **Naples garlic** (*A. neapolitanum*) and **rosy garlic** (*A. roseum*), both with grass-like leaves; however, none of these three are common here in New Zealand. Slightly more common is the **slender false garlic** (*Nothoscordum gracile*) – also with grass-like leaves – from Central and South America, whose leaves and bulbs are likewise used in that region as food. In New Zealand, one wild onion is by far the most common: **three-cornered garlic** (*A. triquetrum*), featured on the facing page. ▶

Three-cornered Garlic

Allium triquetrum

Description: Petals white with a strong green line (Oct–Nov). Leaves triangular in cross-section, with a mild smell of garlic when crushed, unlike the toxic **snowflake**. ▲

Where: Very common throughout, especially in urban areas. Spread by seed and offset bulbs carried by drains or in soil. By far the most common wild onion here.

Part eaten: Young leaves, flowers and bulbs; older leaves tend to be stringy. As with onion and garlic, etc., this plant can be toxic to dogs, cats, cows, pigs and horses.

Nutritional value: Leaves a good source of vitamin C; bulbs less so (Chapman). Leaves and bulbs rich in antioxidants generally (Menacer).

Use: A native of the western Mediterranean region, where the plant is still traditionally harvested from the wild. In Corsica and Sardinia its leaves are included in a traditional wild-herb soup recipe, and in Sardinia the minced stems are used to add flavour to salads, or sautéed in olive oil when frying eggs. The leaves and bulbs are eaten raw in salad on the Italian mainland too, or boiled or fried, or used as an ingredient in omelettes. The plant is thought to have reached New Zealand originally as a kitchen herb. By 1899 it had spread into the wild and was subsequently recommended as a healthy source of greens here during the Second World War, finely chopped and added to salads along with the bulbs, in much the same way as spring onions are used. The flowers, too, are used – as a tasty and decorative garnish on salads. The flavour of the whole plant is mild, between that of mild garlic and spring onion. In New Zealand the plant is often known as 'onion weed', despite the fact that several other wild onions are also found here – see facing page.

Oxalis Family

[Oxalidaceae]

Members of this family typically have three-part, clover-like leaflets that spread open in daylight and close at night, five-petalled flowers, and underground bulbs, tubers or carrot-like roots. Members are also sometimes known as **sourgrass** due to their sour taste from the oxalic acid they contain. Well-known edible members include **star fruit** (*Averrhoa carambola*), **bilimbi** (*A. bilimbi*), **wood sorrel** (*Oxalis acetosella*), and oca (the so-called **New Zealand yam**, *O. tuberosa*). Native species include **tūtae kāhu (white oxalis**, *O. magellanica*), whose leaves were devoured by the scurvied crew of Crozet's voyage to New Zealand in 1772.

Horned Oxalis

Oxalis corniculata

Description: Low plant, bearing small yellow flowers all year. Produces no bulbs.
Where: Common throughout.
Part eaten: Leaves, shoots, buds and flowers.
Nutritional value: Leaves and tender stalks rich in vitamin C, calcium, iron (Sengupta) and β-carotene (Begum). The plant is rich also in potassium and manganese (Abbasi 2015). Although high in oxalates, this is adequately offset by the high calcium content (Khare).
Use: Although nowadays found throughout most of the world, this plant is generally thought to be native to Central and South America, including Mexico – where it is eaten by the indigenous inhabitants. Interestingly, evidence from early herbarium specimens, literature and archaeobotany point to an origin instead in SE Asia, which coincides with where most records of its traditional uses for food are found. In Pakistan, for example, the young leaves are cooked along with other vegetables in diluted milk to add a sour tang, and in neighbouring Jammu and Kashmir the leaves are made into chutney. Further east, in the Indian state of Meghalaya, the whole plant is commonly eaten raw. Indeed, similar traditional uses have been collected throughout much of India, from Assam and Arunachal Pradesh right down to Tamil Nadu, also from Nepal, Indonesia, Korea and various parts of China, Europe (Spain, Italy, Hungary) and Africa (Ethiopia and Uganda).

Fishtail Oxalis

Oxalis latifolia

Description: Pink flowers Nov–Jun. Thick white carrot-like roots produced below small bulbils.

Where: A common garden weed.

Part eaten: Leaves and root (in moderation).

Nutritional value: Fresh leaves rich in iron (Orech) and antioxidants (Krishnan); however, *Oxalis* plants are generally high in oxalates.

Use: Native to Central and South America, including Mexico, where the plant is still traditionally eaten. The plant later spread to Africa and Eurasia, where the leaves are collected and either eaten raw as a snack or used as a wild leafy vegetable, with similar uses recorded from Spain, Kenya and Uganda. In Zimbabwe the root is also eaten – raw, mostly by children. In south India the leaves and root are more commonly cooked.

Local relatives: The **large-flowered oxalis** (*O. purpurea*), which is collected as food in its native South Africa, is also common here in New Zealand. Less common locally is **pink shamrock** (*O. debilis*), which is eaten in Argentina and North India, and **sourgrass** (*O. articulata*) whose leaves are added to salads in Turkey.

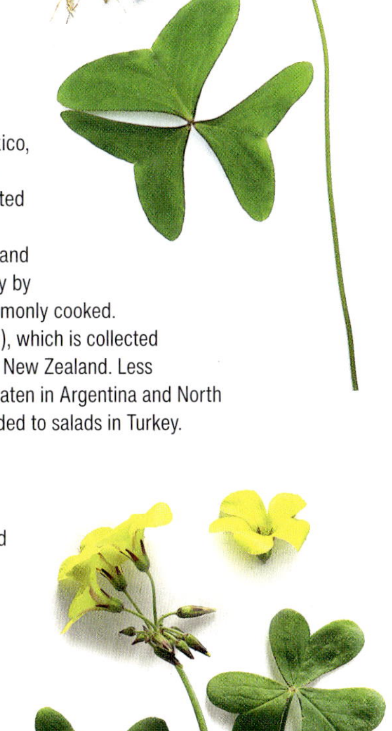

Bermuda Buttercup

Oxalis pes-caprae (= *O. cernua*)

Description: Yellow flowers all year. Produces bulbils and a white main bulb up to 3 cm long.

Where: A common garden weed.

Part eaten: Leaves, stalks, flowers and underground part, used sparingly, as ratio of oxalic acid to calcium is very high (Romojaro).

Nutritional value: Fresh leaves rich in vitamin C, magnesium, iron, copper (Wehmeyer) and potassium (Romojaro).

Use: A native of Namibia and South Africa, where the bulbs are eaten fresh or boiled and served with milk, and the leaves and flower stalks are also eaten. Similar uses are recorded from several Mediterranean countries, including Sardinia, Cyprus, Turkey and Palestine. In Spain the leaves and flower stalks are traditionally collected in spring and eaten raw as a snack. In Sicily the leaves are eaten raw in salads, and the bulbs grilled and seasoned with oil and lemon.

Local relatives: Oca, the so-called **New Zealand yam** (*O. tuberosa*), long cultivated in South America for its edible tubers, is now grown here, but seldom occurs wild.

Palms

[Arecaceae]

Palms are predominantly tropical but can also be found in subtropical and warm temperate climates and typically have a single, unbranched trunk, often tall and slender, topped by large, feathery or fan-shaped leaves. Food plants include the **date palm**, **sago**, **coconut** and several palms whose sap is bled for making syrup, sugar and wine. New Zealand is home to the world's southernmost palm, **nīkau**, whose heart was traditionally harvested as food by Māori.

Phoenix palm

Phoenix canariensis

Description: Stocky palm tree with sharp spines. Small orange-yellow fruit (Dec).

Where: Widely planted, with self-sown palms appearing in coastal areas and on islands around Auckland and Tauranga. (Seed spread by birds and water.)

Part eaten: A syrup made from the sap, which is generally collected in spring. The flesh of the fruit is also edible but is very thin.

Phoenix palm syrup

TIP: Beware the wicked spines on the fronds, which have been responsible for many injuries, often with long-lasting effects.

Nutritional value: Syrup made from the sap may contain 37.8% sucrose, 9.50% glucose, 4.80% fructose and can be a good source of potassium, with an overall vitamin content higher than that of other natural syrups (Luis).

Use: This palm is a native of the Canary Islands, off the coast of Morocco, where the sap is traditionally harvested in early spring to produce a sweet drink or palm syrup, similar to maple syrup – a practice that can be dated some 2000 years back to the time of Pliny the Elder (AD 23–79), who mentions it in his *Naturalis Historia*. Harvesting typically involves use of a ladder and a sharp knife or chisel to scoop out a bowl-shaped hollow next to the heart of the palm, where the sap can accumulate. A short pipe is then inserted into this bowl to channel the sap into a bucket overnight. In this way a single tree may provide 10 or more litres of sap, which is then boiled down into a syrup with a consistency similar to maple syrup. Nowadays, in the Canary Islands, the trunk is often banded with metal foil to keep out thirsty rats.

SAFETY TIP: falls from ladders are a leading cause of hospitalisations in New Zealand.

Local relatives: Chinese windmill palm (*Trachycarpus fortunei*) is less common in the wild, but its young flowers are eaten in China – although I personally remain unimpressed by those I have tried. Far less common in the wild is the **Australian cabbage palm** (*Livistona australis*), whose heart is traditionally eaten by Aboriginal Australians, and the **jelly palm** (*Butia* species), whose tasty fruit is enjoyed in Brazil.

Papaya Family [Caricaceae]

Members of this family belong to the same Brassicales order as the mustard family, an affinity reflected in the fact that most share similar pungent mustard-oil compounds (glucosinolates) and this accounts for the characteristic mustard-like taste and smell of their seeds. The family is named after the tropical **papaya** (or **pawpaw**, *Carica papaya*), which is grown in some frost-free areas of New Zealand, albeit rarely.

Mountain Pawpaw

Vasconcellea pubescens (= *Carica*)

Description: Evergreen tree with a single trunk. Flowers all year, some trees bearing flowers of a single sex only, others with flowers both male and female together.

Where: Commonly grown in warmer areas, now wild, especially near settlements.

Part eaten: Fruit (throughout much of the year).

Nutritional value: Fresh fruit rich in vitamins A and C, calcium and iron (Rahayu), containing a latex that is rich in papain, which is used for tenderising meat. Seeds contain sulforaphane – a compound shared with cabbage and broccoli, etc.

Use: A native of the South American Andes, from Venezuela to Bolivia, where it is commonly grown in family gardens. Indeed, a few commercial orchards in Chile produce canned fruit, juice, jam and processed sweets from it. I like to scoop out the pulp with a spoon or simply squeeze it out and eat this raw – often in fruit salad, but if you prefer to eat the fruit cooked and sweetened, the optimum boiling time to retain the high vitamin C content is 10 minutes. Although the skin is also edible, it is a bit rubbery and less tasty. According to Odilo Duarte, in *Exotic Fruits and Nuts of the New World*, the green fruit can also be boiled or baked as a vegetable, but this is hard to reconcile with their acrid taste. In my own experience they are quite inedible at this unripe stage, even when cooked.

Local relatives: Of 25 similar species from South America, **toronche** (*V. stipulata*), **papayote** (*V. goudotiana*) and **babaco** (*V.* x *pentagona*) are occasionally cultivated for their edible fruit here in New Zealand, but are not known to grow wild.

Passionfruits

[Passifloraceae]

This family takes its name from the 550 or so species of **passionfruit** (*Passiflora* species) it contains. Their common name derives from their unusual flower structure, which early Spanish missionaries in South America saw as representing the passion of Christ – the crown of thorns, the nails, wounds and the apostles. Edible members include the **giant granadilla** (*P. quadrangularis*), whose fruit can be up to 30 cm in length (the size of a gourd), right down to our native **kōhia** (**New Zealand passionfruit**, *P. tetrandra*), whose fruit is small and not very sweet – more attractive to birds than to humans.

Black Passionfruit

Passiflora edulis

Description: A vigorous evergreen vine. Flowers Jul–Mar. Fruit dark purple.
Where: Widely cultivated in warmer parts of the country, it has since spread into the wild along forest margins and shrubland in frost-free areas.
Part eaten: Pulp of the ripe fruit, including the seeds (Jan–Sep). Tender shoots (spring).
TIP: When the fruit is ripe, it has typically fallen and the hard skin is wrinkled.
Nutritional value: Raw pulp rich in vitamin C and a good source of vitamins B3 and B2, iron and phosphorus (USDA).
Use: This is the best known of all the passionfruits – a native of Brazil, Paraguay and Argentina, now cultivated in many countries, including Peru, India, Sri Lanka, South Africa, USA, Australia and New Zealand. When the fruit is fully ripe the skin becomes wrinkled and the fruit falls to the ground. Bite into this and suck out the pulp, or cut the fruit in half and scoop out the pulp to eat as is or with ice cream, yoghurt or in fruit salads, cheesecake, etc., or as juice. In the local markets of Mizoram (NE India), not only is the ripe fruit offered for sale but also the tender shoots, which are eaten boiled.
Local relatives: Two kinds of edible round **yellow passionfruit** are sometimes found here (*P. pinnatistipula*, particularly around Christchurch and Otago, and *P. edulis* f. *flavicarpa*, which is not yet found in the wild). Although the related **blue passion flower** (*P. caerulea*) is reasonably common here, its orange-coloured fruit is insipid.

Banana Passionfruit

Passiflora tripartita (= *P. mollissima*), *P. tarminiana* & *P. mixta*

Description: A vigorous evergreen vine with large pink flowers (all year). Fruit yellow.

Where: Forest margins, sometimes smothering trees to become a serious weed. Now banned from sale, propagation and distribution.

Part eaten: Pulp of ripe fruit (Sep–May).

Nutritional value: Pulp rich in antioxidants, including vitamin C (Vasco), also potassium, manganese and selenium (Leterme).

Use: A native of South America, from Panama to Peru, including Venezuela, Colombia and Ecuador, where the vine is widely cultivated for its fruit (curuba). Beneath the soft skin lies a sweet pulp that is eaten raw, or used there as an ingredient of ice cream, jams, jellies and gelatin desserts, or in refreshing drinks such as crema de curuba or sorbete de curuba. To make this popular drink, strain the pulp to remove the seeds, then blend the remaining juice with milk and sugar. In South America, this juice is also made into wine or combined with alcoholic liquors and sugar and served as a cocktail. In the Hawaiian Islands, Papua New Guinea, Australia and here in New Zealand the plant has escaped from cultivation and has spread into forests, where its vigorous vines can often smother well-established trees.

Pea and Clover Family

[Fabaceae]

One of the largest plant families, whose members typically bear seeds in a pod. Also known as legumes, many of which provide important protein-rich foods, e.g. **peas**, **chickpeas**, **beans**, **lentils**, **peanuts** and **alfalfa**. Several provide important sources of flavouring: **liquorice**, **fenugreek**, **carob** and **tamarind**. However, some (including the native **kōwhai**) are poisonous, and many others require soaking and cooking to safely remove the toxins or antinutrients they contain. For this reason, it is essential to follow all instructions given for processing, a caution that applies especially to their seeds – see note on wild **peas** (*Lathyrus*), page 156 and **vetch** (*Vicia*), page 159.

Wisteria seeds are toxic

Wisteria

Wisteria sinensis

Description: Large, strong, deciduous vine, bearing strings of violet, blue or white flowers and large pods containing large, broad-bean-like seeds that are toxic and should NOT be eaten.

Where: Widely cultivated, but spreads vigorously and is hard to eradicate, so it frequently persists in neglected gardens.

Part eaten: Flowers (Oct–Feb). NOT the seeds, which contain a poisonous proteinaceous lectin that affects the mucosal cells of the intestine (Burrows).

Nutritional value: Flowers are rich in antioxidants (Keskin).

Use: A native of China, where the flower clusters are traditionally gathered as food. In rural areas farmers are apt to eat the flowers themselves or share them with their neighbours, but many suburban gardeners sell them to earn extra cash. The washed flowers and buds may be mixed with flour, steamed and seasoned, or boiled and eaten with oil and salt. Flowers may also be folded into egg batter and made into fritters, or used for preserves or brewed into wine. Around Beijing the flowers are a common addition to cakes. Note that the bean-like seeds should NOT be eaten.

Lucerne

Medicago sativa

Description: Also known as **alfalfa**. Purple or blue flowers (Nov–May).

Where: Important fodder plant, now common in the wild.

Part eaten: Tender leaves, cooked or raw, and sprouted seeds, but NOT unsprouted raw seeds, which are mildly toxic due to the presence of canavanine.

Nutritional value: Spring leaves rich in vitamin C and carotene (Grlić). Raw sprouts rich in vitamin K (USDA).

Use: Native to Europe, North Africa through to China. Although best known as a fodder plant, the young leaves and stems are traditionally prepared as a vegetable throughout much of this region, a use recorded from Spain, Germany, the Czech Republic, northern Italy, Croatia, Moldova, Bosnia, North India and China. The seeds are generally sprouted as this significantly reduces the canavanine content – a culinary practice that originates in China and Japan.

alfalfa sprouts

Small Melilot

Melilotus indicus

Description: Long spikes of tiny yellow flowers (Sep–Jun).

Where: Very common in dry places, especially near the coast.

Part eaten: Young leaves cooked. *Melilotus* contain coumarin, so are best avoided by anyone on anticoagulant drugs. Take extra care to avoid polluted sites as the plant has a tendency to accumulate cadmium (Abbasi 2015).

Nutritional value: Fresh leaves rich in antioxidants and calcium (Abbasi 2015).

Use: Native to a region extending from the Mediterranean to China, including the Lesser Himalayas of Pakistan and neighbouring Jammu and Kashmir, where the young leaves are boiled as a vegetable.

Local relatives: The similar white-flowered **white melilot** (*M. albus*) – used in the same region in the same way – is also common in New Zealand.

Red Clover

Trifolium pratense

Description: Leaflets often with pale crescent markings. Flowers purple or dark pink.

Where: Sown as a pasture plant, but also very common wild.

Part eaten: Young leaves, flowerheads and nectar sucked from these (Oct–Mar). Unsprouted raw seeds should NOT constitute a major part of the diet, though, due to presence of canavanine (Bell).

Nutritional value: Leaves rich in fibre, vitamin C, calcium and potassium (Grlić, Lim).

Use: This plant's native region extends from Morocco to Siberia. The plant is valued primarily as a pasture plant; however, English parson-botanist John Lightfoot noted in 1777 that 'in Ireland the poor people, in a scarcity of corn, make a kind of bread of the dry'd flowers . . . reduced to powder [which they esteem] to be very wholsome and nutritive'. The young leaves – which in my opinion are not particularly tasty – have also been used in many countries as a spinach. These days the plant's main culinary use is of the young flowerheads. Typically they are eaten raw in salads and soups, but are also popular with children, who enjoy sucking out the nectar – a use recorded from Spain, Slovakia and Belarus; or simply munching on them as a snack – a use recorded from Italy, Hungary and Turkey. The flowerheads – dried or fresh – are commonly used to brew a sweet herbal tea.

White Clover

Trifolium repens

Description: Leaflets often with pale V-shaped markings. Flowers scented, white often tinged pink.

Where: Sown as a pasture plant, but also very common wild.

Part eaten: Young leaves, flowerheads (Jul–Mar) and nectar sucked from the flowers. However, unsprouted raw seeds should NOT constitute a major part of the diet, due to the presence of canavanine (Bell).

Nutritional value: Leaves rich in vitamin C (Jones), protein and minerals (Lim).

Use: Native to a region extending from Morocco to Siberia. Although valued primarily as fodder for farm animals, in 18th-century Ireland people occasionally made a kind of bread from the dried flowers. Similarly in Bosnia, especially during the siege of Sarajevo, the leaves and flowers were appreciated in fresh salads and as a vegetable, or as a herbal tea. Similarly, in North India and parts of China the plant is traditionally cooked as a vegetable. For the most part, these days, the young flowerheads are more commonly brewed as a tea, used in salads, soups or sandwiches or as an ingredient of wines and pickles. Indeed, some of the top chefs of Italy now regularly feature the flowers in their restaurant cuisine.

mildly toxic lookalike: **broom** (no prickles – see page 149)

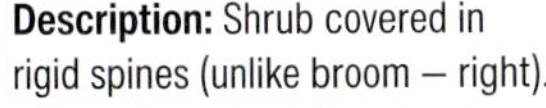

Gorse

Ulex europaeus

Description: Shrub covered in rigid spines (unlike broom – right).
Where: Abundant throughout.
Part eaten: Flowers (May–Nov) and leaf buds. TIP: Use gardening gloves!
Nutritional value: Gorse is rich in protein, carotene, calcium and sodium (Jobson).
Use: This native of Western Europe was originally introduced to New Zealand as a quick-growing hedge but is now widely derided as a useless and irksome weed. However, it enriches the soil and, as English botanist John Lightfoot observed in 1777, 'Horses, sheep, and other cattle are very fond of it, but as the spines annoy them, and prevent their feeding on it, the husbandmen in many parts of Wales bruise the tender branches, or grind them in mills for that purpose, by which means they become an excellent fodder.' Similarly, the people of Basque Country, northern Spain, traditionally chew the young shoots as food, and the flower buds are pickled elsewhere in vinegar and eaten in salads, the leaf buds brewed as tea and the flowers made into wine. The flowers serve as a trailside nibble, too, smelling curiously of coconut with a mildly bitter taste. They are also used as a dye to tint Easter eggs and fabric a beautiful bright yellow. The 17th-century herbalist Nicholas Culpeper (1653) even claims a medicinal use: 'a decoction made with the flowers thereof hath been found effectual against the jaundice, as also to provoke urine, and cleanse the kidneys from gravel or stone engendered in them'.

False Acacia

Robinia pseudoacacia

Description: Deciduous tree with spines at the base of the leaves, bearing white flowers.
Where: Widely planted as an ornamental tree and for soil conservation, but suckers freely to form small thickets in the wild.
Part eaten: Flowers only (Nov–Jan). All other parts toxic – especially bark and seeds. Indeed, children have been poisoned by sucking on fresh twigs, and by eating inner bark or seeds.
Nutritional value: Flowers a fair source of protein, and a good source of vitamin C (Redžić 2010).
Use: This tree is a native of the eastern USA, introduced to Europe as an ornamental plant in the early 17th century and later to China. Over much of its introduced range the flowers are eaten, sometimes raw, but most commonly fried in batter – a dish commonly found on Italian menus as fiori d'acacia fritti. The same traditional use has been recorded throughout much of Italy, in Spain, Croatia, Belarus, Czech Republic, Slovakia, Hungary, Romania and Bosnia-Herzogovina. Similar uses are recorded in Asia, including northern China, where the flowers are washed, mixed with an equal quantity of flour, steamed for around 20 minutes, seasoned and served warm.

Coastal Wattle

Acacia sophorae (= *A. longifolia* var. *sophorae*)

Description: Low coastal shrub, lower branches often growing through the sand, creamy-yellow flowers borne in fluffy 'fingers' Jul–Oct. Seedpods narrow and twisted.

Where: Very common along some coasts, especially in sand dunes – see map.

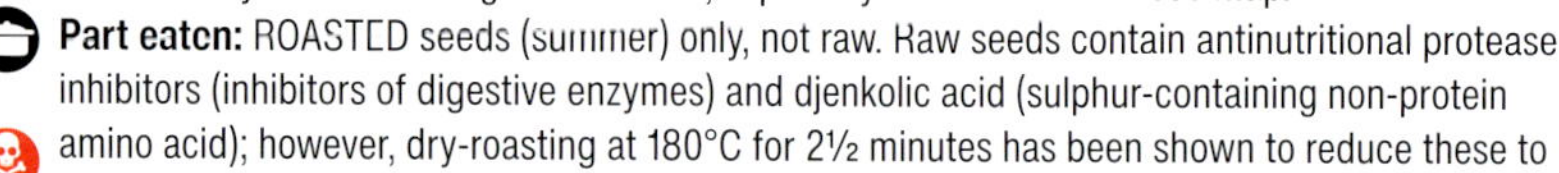

Part eaten: ROASTED seeds (summer) only, not raw. Raw seeds contain antinutritional protease inhibitors (inhibitors of digestive enzymes) and djenkolic acid (sulphur-containing non-protein amino acid); however, dry-roasting at 180°C for 2½ minutes has been shown to reduce these to safe levels (Adiamo, Boughton, Hegarty).

Nutritional value: Lightly roasted seeds are rich in crude protein, oleic acid (a monounsaturated fat thought to be responsible for the health benefit of olive oil), and minerals, especially potassium, calcium and iron (Adiamo). Wattle seed has been shown to have a low glycaemic index (RIRDC).

Use: The common name derives from the former use of the thin branches of wattles in the 'wattle and daub' construction of early colonial houses in Australia. There are more than 1000 kinds of *Acacia*, most of which – including this one – are native to Australia, where the seeds of many have long been used as food by Aboriginal Australians. The ripening bean-like pods of this coastal species were traditionally harvested and roasted by the indigenous inhabitants of Tasmania, then the seeds picked out and eaten. Wattle seeds were also traditionally ground into a flour using stones, the flour then mixed with water to make cakes that would be roasted. (See opposite for the recipe of a modern version!) A single tree can produce a phenomenal quantity of seeds, making this coastal species a potentially important source of food. Admittedly, the strong flavour, oily consistency and gritty texture of wattle flour is not for all, but it is significant that these seeds are among those that have been adopted by the Australian bushfood industry – primarily as a flavour enhancer.

Local relatives: Longleaf wattle (**Sydney golden wattle**, *A. longifolia*) seeds contain a similar amount of djenkolic acid, which is likewise reduced by roasting (Adiamo); these were eaten by the indigenous inhabitants of SE Australia, as were the seeds of the less common **Cootamundra wattle** (*A. baileyana*), which are known to be particularly low in djenkolic acid (Adiamo). See appendix (page 159) for edibility details of other wattles, including the so-called **brush wattle**.

Not to be confused with . . .

the seeds of **laburnum** (*Laburnum anagyroides*). All parts of this yellow-flowered, deciduous tree are considered poisonous, but especially the seeds and unripe seedpods. Symptoms of poisoning include nausea, persistent vomiting, abdominal pain and occasionally death.

laburnum seeds (toxic)

Recipe: Wattle seed bliss balls

Dry-roast the seeds of coastal wattle at 180°C for 2½ minutes.
Then grind the seeds to make a flour.
Place one cupful of roasted wattle seed flour in a food processor with:
½ cup soaked dates with 2 dessertspoons coconut cream and 2½ heaped dessertspoons peanut butter.
(If you have a sweet tooth, you can add 2 teaspoons honey or golden syrup.)
Mix these ingredients together well and roll into balls.
Dry-roast some desiccated coconut, and melt some dark chocolate (say 6 squares).
Roll the balls in the melted chocolate, then in the roasted coconut.
Voilà: your wattle seed bliss balls are ready to serve!

roasted wattle seed flour

wattle seed bliss balls

Pine Family

[Pinaceae]

Resinous, evergreen, cone-bearing trees with needle-like leaves. Includes **stone pine** (*Pinus pinea* of the Mediterranean region – opposite) and **piñon** (*P. edulis* and related pines from SW North America) that are valued for their edible nuts; and the European **larch** (*Larix decidua*, found wild in colder parts of New Zealand) whose gum is chewed by children in Hungary, Slovakia and Switzerland, and whose buds are used in the alpine regions of northern Italy as flavouring for liqueurs and grappa.

Pine

Pinus species

radiata pine seeds

unhulled

hulled

Description: Fast-growing evergreen trees, bearing needles and cones.

Where: Widespread, from the coast to almost 1500 m altitude.

Part eaten: Seeds (autumn), young male pollen cones (spring).

Nutritional value: Pine nuts are a good source of energy, protein, manganese, phosphorus, zinc, iron, and vitamins E, K, B1, B2 and B3 (USDA). The inner bark of the common **lodgepole pine** (*P. contorta*) contains 1.2% sugars (Yanovsky).

Use: The seeds of all pine species are edible, but just 18 or so produce seeds large and tasty enough to bc considered worthwhile, for the turpentine flavour of some is too strong. Pine seeds have served as a traditional food from the Mediterranean to the Himalayas, and beyond to Korea, China, Japan and western North America. The practice of harvesting seeds from wild pines for food dates back more than 12,000 years. This is known from a Late Stone Age archaeological cave site at Grotte des Pigeons in Morocco, where **maritime pine** (*P. pinaster*) seed scales were found that date to 15–12.6 thousand years ago. Fallen cones are often empty – either because the seeds have rotted or because they have already been released – so ripe cones are usually collected directly from the tree (in autumn). The cones are then left to dry in the sun or roasted on the edge of a campfire until the delicate, flake-like, winged seeds are ready to be shaken or beaten out. The thin seed husks are then cracked open and the seeds eaten as is, roasted or ground into flour. The *US Army Guide* notes that the young male pollen cones that grow in spring can be eaten boiled or baked. In Libya and Spain these are traditionally eaten raw, while the Ojibwa people of eastern Canada eat them stewed with meat. Pine pollen itself can also be used and is sold in the markets of South Korea in the form of a cookie. The inner bark of various pines, collected in spring, was traditionally eaten raw or cooked by native Americans; in Sweden, this inner layer of bark was kiln dried, ground into flour, mixed with a small amount of oatmeal and made into thin cakes.

Local relatives: Common wild edible pines include **radiata pine** (*P. radiata*, with shortish, slender needles, typically in clusters of three) whose tiny seeds were collected as food from plantation trees in Basque Country, Spain; **lodgepole pine** (*P. contorta*, short needles in pairs), whose fresh innermost bark was stripped off and eaten by several tribal groups of western North America; **maritime pine** (*P. pinaster*, stout needles in pairs), mentioned above; **ponderosa pine** (*P. ponderosa*, with long, rigid, dull-green needles in bunches of three) whose inner bark and seeds were harvested by the indigenous inhabitants of western North America, and **bishop pine** (*P. muricata*, two needles per bunch) whose small seeds (just 6 mm) were traditionally eaten by the Pomo people of California.

Stone Pine

Pinus pinea

Description: A coniferous evergreen tree up to 25 m or more with long, flexible needle-like leaves in bunches of two.

Where: Cultivated fairly commonly on a small scale from Canterbury north, and only very occasionally found in the wild.

Part eaten: Seeds (autumn).

Nutritional value: Seeds rich in protein, fat, vitamins B1 and B2, potassium, phosphorus, magnesium and linoleic acid, with appreciable amounts of zinc and iron and a high energy value (Nergiz).

Use: A native of the Mediterranean region, where archaeological remains of cones, seeds and charcoal of this pine in the Nerja Caves in southern Spain reveal that the nuts have been used as food for at least 6000 years. Nowadays the seeds or nuts are harvested from both wild and cultivated stands in Spain, Portugal, Italy, Turkey and China. Of these, Spain is the main producer with around 75% of global production. The nuts are eaten raw or roasted and used in breads, candies, sauces, cakes and in various vegetable and meat dishes, or blended with basil, garlic, olive oil and Parmesan to make pesto, or ground into pine nut butter. The traditional method of harvesting involves detaching the mature cones from the branch with the aid of an iron hook atop a long pole, or by climbing the trees; but nowadays a mechanical trunk shaker is used. The nut itself is a creamy white kernel covered by a thin brown film inside a hard woody shell, arranged within the pine cone. The industrial cracking process involves soaking the nuts a little to reduce breakage of the kernels, then compressing them between two rolling cylinders. Otherwise, you can just crack them open with your teeth.

Plantain Family

[Plantaginaceae]

This family includes popular garden plants such as **snapdragons** (page 158), and well-known edible plants such as **psyllium** (*Plantago ovata* and *P. psyllium*) – grown commercially for its seeds; native members such as **koromiko** (*Hebe*), whose leaf buds have served as a medicine against dysentery; and an important poisonous plant, **foxglove** (*Digitalis purpurea*, page 162), source of digoxin, a medication used to treat various heart conditions.

Scrambling Speedwell

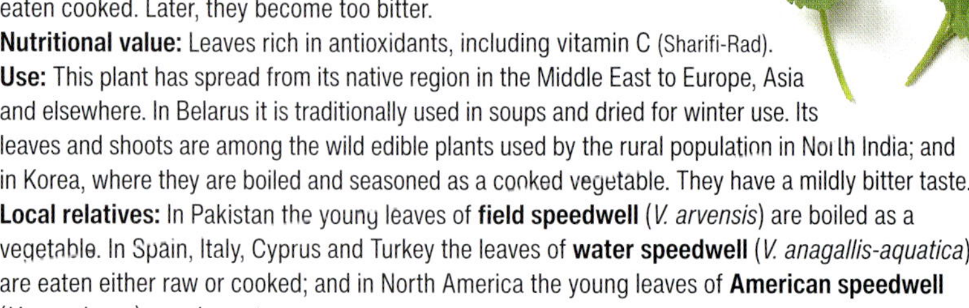

Veronica persica

Description: Low, sprawling plant with sky-blue flowers (all year).
Where: Very common throughout.
Part eaten: Young leaves in spring, usually eaten cooked. Later, they become too bitter.
Nutritional value: Leaves rich in antioxidants, including vitamin C (Sharifi-Rad).
Use: This plant has spread from its native region in the Middle East to Europe, Asia and elsewhere. In Belarus it is traditionally used in soups and dried for winter use. Its leaves and shoots are among the wild edible plants used by the rural population in North India; and in Korea, where they are boiled and seasoned as a cooked vegetable. They have a mildly bitter taste.
Local relatives: In Pakistan the young leaves of **field speedwell** (*V. arvensis*) are boiled as a vegetable. In Spain, Italy, Cyprus and Turkey the leaves of **water speedwell** (*V. anagallis-aquatica*) are eaten either raw or cooked; and in North America the young leaves of **American speedwell** (*V. americana*) are also eaten.

Broad-leaved Plantain / Kopakopa ▶

Plantago major

Description: Large leaves with stringy lengthwise veins. Long flower spikes Jul–Apr.
Where: Very common throughout.
Part eaten: Tender young leaves, before they become too stringy – usually cooked.
Nutritional value: Tender leaves rich in vitamin A (Zennie), magnesium, manganese and vitamin C, often also potassium, calcium, iron and copper, yet low in oxalic acid (Sánchez-Mata).
Use: Native to Eurasia and parts of Africa. In the Mediterranean countries of Spain, Italy, Slovenia, Croatia, Greece, Turkey and Lebanon the tender leaves are collected in spring and served as a vegetable, sometimes raw in salads but more often cooked, in soups for example. Its use as a cooked vegetable extends north into Russia, Belarus and Estonia and east through North India to China. In China, according to the *Chinese Materia Medica*, the plant and seeds were both formerly eaten, and occasionally still are; it adds that 'the seeds are mucilaginous, and have a sweetish, cooling taste'. Tibetans eat the plant boiled or stir-fried. One plant can produce a lot of seeds: up to 36,000 or more. When wet, these become sticky. This enables them to travel the world on people's footwear. Indeed, when the plant reached North America the indigenous population called it 'Englishman's foot' as a mark of where the roaming white man trod. Several tribes went on to adopt the plant as a new vegetable. It reached New Zealand around 1832.
Local relatives: Two other common plantains have a similarly extensive history of use as food: **narrow-leaved plantain** (*P. lanceolata*) and the less-common **buck's horn plantain** (*P. coronopus*).

narrow-leaved plantain
Plantago lanceolata
broad-leaved
plantain / kopakopa
Plantago major
buck's horn plantain
Plantago coronopus

Potato Family

[Solanaceae]

Also known as the **nightshade** family. Members have five-petalled flowers. Includes the highly toxic **deadly nightshade** (page 162), **mandrake**, **henbane** and various kinds of *Datura*, and others that are highly addictive, e.g. **tobacco**. Edible members include **tomato**, **potato**, **bell pepper (capsicum)**, **cayenne pepper**, **chilli peppers**, **tamarillo**, **pepino**, **Cape gooseberry** and **naranjilla** (*Solanum quitoense*) – all of which are from South America; the **eggplant** of Asia; and the native New Zealand **poroporo**.

Black Nightshade / Raupeti

Solanum nigrum

unripe green berries (toxic)

Description: White flowers with yellow centre and small fruit (7-10 mm), unlike the very rare but highly toxic **deadly nightshade** (*Atropa bella-donna*) which has much larger fruit (12 mm+) – see page 162.

Where: Abundant throughout.

Part eaten: Young leaves when boiled for 5 minutes to reduce antinutrients, including phytic acid and oxalic acid (Essack); and fully ripe black berries (all year, but especially Apr). Unripe green berries taste acrid and are mildly toxic due to solanine (Burrows, Connor, Slaughter).

Nutritional value: Ripe berries rich in iron, calcium, vitamins B, C and carotene (Edmonds). Leaves rich in vitamin C, magnesium, iron, potassium and copper (Wehmeyer).

Use: A native of North Africa and Eurasia, where the young leaves and fully ripe black fruits are widely used as food. Within the Mediterranean region their popularity appears to be greatest in Turkey, where young shoots and leaves are sold in the markets of İzmir and often boiled with zucchinis or served with lemon, garlic and olive oil. Further east, in Anatolia, the fruits are also eaten and the leaves sliced thinly and added to a mixture of yoghurt, water, chopped cucumber, crushed garlic, salt, a sprinkling of olive oil and crumbled mint. Across much of Asia, too, there are many records of the young shoots and leaves being cooked as a vegetable and ripe berries being enjoyed raw or cooked, as observed in Pakistan, India, Nepal, Korea and China. Nowadays the plant can also be found bundled up for sale in the markets of Papua New Guinea. With the spread of this plant, the cooked leaves and ripe fruits are now also enjoyed in Ethiopia, Kenya, Tanzania, Zimbabwe and South Africa. For much of the Western world, the most popular part is the ripe berries, eaten raw or in pies and jams. But remember that the berries must be soft and black and fully ripe. If any taste acrid, spit them out; they are not yet ripe! When the plant reached New Zealand in 1853, Māori did not differentiate between this species and the very similar native **small-flowered nightshade** (**raupeti**, **remuroa**, **pōporo**, **poroporo**, *S. americanum*), so the leaves and ripe fruit of both were eaten. Despite its culinary history, the New Zealand National Poisons Centre receives many enquiries about this plant, most often with regard to young children mistaking the green berries for peas, combined with the surprisingly common misconception that this common plant is in fact 'deadly nightshade', a far more dangerous, but fortunately very rare plant (page 162).

Local relatives: The ripe fruit, cooked leaves and shoots of **red-berried nightshade** (*S. villosum*) are eaten in Ethiopia, Kenya, Uganda and Tanzania, but it is important that these not be confused with the poisonous egg-shaped berries of the far more common **bittersweet** (*S. dulcamara*).

Wild Tomato

Solanum lycopersicum
(= *Lycopersicon esculentum*)

Description: Bruised leaves and stems have a characteristic smell. Yellow flowers (all year). Fruit on wild plants usually small, often yellow.
Where: Cultivated, and commonly wild.
Part eaten: Ripe fruit (Jan–Apr).
Nutritional value: Raw fruit rich in vitamins C and A (USDA) and lycopene (Lim), which may have health benefits.
Use: A native of Peru that originally bore only small currant- to cherry-size berries. There is no evidence that tomatoes were ever a food of the Incas – no trace of them in ancient graves nor depictions on their pottery; however, by the early 16th century the cherry tomato had reached Mexico, where it was evidently cultivated. Their name for it was 'tomatl', a name that came with them and the Spanish to Europe. From there the plant was brought to New Zealand, and by 1864 wild plants were springing up here. The ripe fruit is popular raw in salads and also cooked. Unripe green fruit is also occasionally used to make pickle, sauce, chutney or jam.

Tamarillo

Solanum betaceum (= *Cyphomandra betacea*)

Description: Small, soft-wooded tree. Flowers all year, fruits mostly in winter.
Where: Cultivated in frost-free areas, but often found in the wild nearby.
Part eaten: Ripe fruit, minus the thin, bitter-tasting skin (May–Aug).
Nutritional value: Rich in vitamins A, B6, C and E, iron (Ruskin 1989) and potassium (Prohens).
Use: A native of tropical South America, where the tree was originally cultivated by the Incas in gardens high on the mountainsides. It remains popular in this region, where it is known by various local names. The plant reached New Zealand from India in 1891, where the fruit was initially known as **tree tomato**. It received its present pseudo-Spanish commercial name 'tamarillo' in 1967, and began spreading into the wild here around 1983. The fruit is at its best when it becomes soft and sweet on the tree, and then the pulp is eaten either raw or cooked. It is very versatile – great in curries or in sandwiches, cakes, fruit or vegetable salads, sauces, relishes, chutneys, jellies, jams or desserts. The fruit is usually cut in half and the flesh scooped out with a teaspoon, but it can also be dipped briefly in hot water allowing the bitter skin to be peeled off easily. In South America the whole fruit (including the skin) is often enjoyed as a blended juice with milk, ice and sugar.

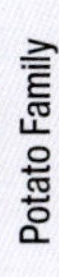

Wild Potato / Rīwai

Solanum tuberosum

Description: White or pink flowers with yellow centre (Nov–Apr).
Where: Can be found almost anywhere frequented by people.
Part eaten: Underground part. But avoid eating potatoes that have turned green (on exposure to light) or have sprouted, as these contain the poisons solanine and chaconine.
Nutritional value: Rich in vitamins C and B6 and potassium (USDA).
Use: A native of the Andes of South America, where starch granules on archaeological remains of human teeth reveal that the tubers have served as food for at least 6000 years. Over that time a selection process has resulted in thousands of distinct types, in a variety of shapes with different-coloured skin and flesh. In the late 16th century the Spanish brought potatoes to Europe, from where they were distributed to become one of the world's most important crops. When Cook and de Surville brought potatoes to New Zealand in 1769, Māori were quick to see their advantages over kūmara: higher yield, easier to store, and more cold-tolerant. By 1820 Māori had developed several named varieties of their own, many of them bred by collecting seeds from the fruit, and giving them new names – **rīwai**, **hīwai**, **huiwaiwaka**, **kapana**, **mahetau**, **parareka**, **parate**, **taewa**, **taewha**, **taiawa**, **taiwha**, **kōtīpō**, **urenika**, **uwhi**, **karuparera**, **peruperu** and **purupuru**. By 1853, potato plants had spread into the wild here.

Cape Gooseberry / Kūpara

Physalis peruviana

Description: Golden fruit within a papery husk (all year). Not to be confused with **apple of Peru**, which is not worth eating (opposite).
Where: Cultivated, and wild in warmer areas, especially in the North Island.
Part eaten: RIPE golden-yellow fruit (all year, but especially Jan–Mar). Unripe fruit tastes acrid and is mildly poisonous, due to solanine glycoalkaloids (Nelson).
Nutritional value: Fruit rich in potassium and vitamins C, A, B1 and B3 (Ruskin 1989, USDA).
Use: A fruit of the Incas, native to Bolivia and Brazil, found nowadays in local markets from Venezuela to Chile, where the fruits are often stewed with honey and eaten as dessert. By 1807, settlers at the Cape of Good Hope in South Africa were growing them – hence the common name – from where the plant was taken to Australasia and several of the Pacific islands. By 1842 it had reached New Zealand, where the ripe yellow fruits were eagerly sought by Māori under the transliterated name **kūpara**. Seeds were taken to India, too, where the fruit is nowadays also collected from the wild. When ripe, the fruit is enjoyed raw in both vegetable and fruit salads, but is also eaten cooked, canned, in jams, sauces or chutneys, and dried – either in the sun or freeze-dried – to make what has been described as 'a very agreeable raisin'. Some have gone as far as to coat these 'raisins' with chocolate.

Cape gooseberry lookalikes

Cape gooseberry should not be confused with **apple of Peru** (*Nicandra physalodes*, top left), whose fruit is not worth eating and which has even proven mildly toxic to grazing stock in Africa (Muthee). Other similar-looking plants include **tomatillo** (*Physalis philadelphica*, top right), which is much less common than Cape gooseberry but no less edible, and **ground cherry** (*Physalis pubescens*, below), which is even less common. The ripe fruit of both – tomatillo and ground cherry – are traditionally eaten in the Americas and are cultivated on a small scale here in New Zealand.

Potato Family

Lily of the Valley Vine

Salpichroa origanifolia

Description: Sprawling, weak-stemmed vine with tender leaves and white bell-shaped flowers – like lily of the valley – (all year); and small, white to pale yellow fruit, 10–15 mm.

Where: Very common among hedges and in neglected land in milder areas of the North Island.

Part eaten: Ripe fruit (autumn mostly).

Use: A native of South America, including Argentina, where the ripe fruit is traditionally collected by the rural inhabitants of the central and northern regions for consuming either raw as a sweet snack, or stewed as a compote. The ripe fruit also has milk-clotting properties and hence has potential for cheese-making. (No food use is recorded for the leaves.)

small fruit (10–15 mm)

Pepino

Solanum muricatum

Description: Grows as a low bush. Also known as **pepino dulce** or **pepino melon**.

Where: Grown in frost-free areas for its fruit, but spreads readily into the wild, appearing in building refuse and in imported nursery soil.

Part eaten: Ripe fruit, when slightly soft with a delicate aroma (summer and autumn).

Nutritional value: Fruit rich in vitamin C and a fair source of vitamin A (Ruskin 1989).

Use: A native of South America (Colombia, Ecuador and Peru), since introduced for its fruit to Morocco, Spain, Israel, Kenya, California and New Zealand. Although some prefer to peel off the thin skin, it is not really necessary. The fruit tastes rather like a honeydew melon. The taste is mild, but I can recommend them in fruit salad.

Protea Family

[Proteaceae]

Besides **proteas**, **banksias** and **grevilleas**, this family includes a few food plants, including **macadamia** and the **Chilean hazel tree** (*Gevuina avellana* of southern Chile and Argentina, cultivated commercially for its edible nuts), and the native **rewarewa**, whose nectar was traditionally collected for food by Māori.

Macadamia

Macadamia integrifolia & *tetraphylla*

Description: Evergreen tree to 15 m, bearing a hard-shelled nut contained within a fleshy husk.

Where: Planted for its edible nuts, sometimes as a street tree. Wild trees now becoming common from Tauranga north.

Part eaten: Kernel of the nut (Apr–Jun). Note, however, that these are toxic to dogs.

Nutritional value: Raw nut rich in vitamins B1, B2, B3, B5 and B6 and in manganese, magnesium, iron, phosphorus, monounsaturated fatty acids and protein (USDA).

Use: A native of SE Queensland and NE New South Wales. Also known as the **Queensland nut**, kindal kindal, boombera, jindilli, bauple, gyndl – the latter being some of the names given by Aboriginal Australians, who have valued the tree highly for its edible nut for thousands of years. This is known from archaeological evidence of early stone technology and plant processing tools used to crack the nuts and grind the kernels that can be dated to about 3500 years ago. And yet there is no evidence that the tree was actually cultivated there until 1858, and it was not until 1875 that it was grown in New Zealand, with self-seeded trees being first recorded in the wild here in 1977. Even now, few people notice the wild trees and fewer still take the trouble to make use of the nuts, perhaps deterred by the challenge of getting past the incredibly hard shell. A standard nutcracker is rarely strong enough; however, a rock or hammer will do the job, or – as was traditional in Australia – a suitably hollowed stone anvil and hammer stone. Rats – with their enviable jaws and sharp teeth – love them too, so it is best to harvest the nuts early while they are on the tree and still enclosed by the soft green husk. No need to battle with separating these husks; just let them dry and they will split open naturally. Remove the hard contents and leave to dry a little until the soft edible nut within the shell shrinks, allowing it to separate easily. The next job of cracking open the hard shell makes for a pleasant evening fireside occupation, so long as you have the right tool (see photo). The nut is edible raw, but is tastier (sweeter) when roasted and can be used in a great variety of dishes. I'm eating one as I write.

Purslane Family

[Portulacaceae]

Members of this family typically have fleshy leaves. Best known is a succulent garden flower known as **moss rose** (*Portulaca grandiflora*). Edible members include **Pacific pigweed** (*P. lutea*), an important source of wild greens on many of the Pacific islands; and **chickenweed** (*P. quadrifida*), a popular small-leaved pot-herb of India and Africa.

Purslane

Portulaca oleracea

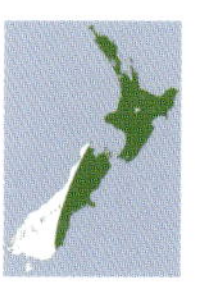

flower

seed capsule

Description: Sprawling plant with reddish stems and succulent leaves up to 2 cm. Small yellow flowers (Nov–Mar) followed by a small capsule with a lid, containing lots of tiny black seeds.
Where: Common throughout, especially North Island.
Part eaten: Tiny seeds (Nov–Apr). Tender leaves and stems (summer), best boiled due to high oxalate content (Sánchez-Mata).
Nutritional value: Tender leaves high in potassium, magnesium, iron, copper, manganese and vitamins C, A and E (Sánchez-Mata). Seeds rich in energy, protein, fat and carbohydrate (Brand-Miller). Leaves and seeds are one of the richest vegetable sources of omega-3 (Rashed, Uddin).
Use: The native region of this plant includes Africa and southern Europe, and extends east through to Pakistan and beyond. Through the writings of Theophrastus, Pliny the Elder and Dioscorides, its use as a vegetable can be traced more than 2000 years back to the ancient Greeks and Romans. In the late 17th century English diarist John Evelyn declared that its leaves and young stalks are, 'generally entertain'd in all our *Sallets*, mingled with the hotter Herbs: 'Tis likewise familiarly eaten alone with *Oyl* and *Vinegar*; but with Moderation' – as per above note re oxalates. Indeed, the leaves and stems have been, and still are, eaten in most Mediterranean countries either raw or cooked in soups, omelettes and vegetable pies. This is true at least in Portugal, Spain, France, Italy, Slovenia, Croatia, Albania, Greece, Cyprus, Turkey, Lebanon, Jordan, Palestine, Egypt, Tunisia and Morocco. Much the same is true right down through most of Africa, where the plant can sometimes be found in local markets, and also in Pakistan, India, Korea and China. As a vegetable the taste is mild, slightly sour with a mucilaginous texture. Less well known are the tiny seeds, which in Africa and India are often mixed with cereals in porridge, bread or cake. In India they are packaged for sale as **kulfa** seeds. The plant is evidently native to North America and Australia, for the seeds were similarly used by the the indigenous inhabitants. Aboriginal Australians would pull up the plants, throw them in heaps on sheets of bark or skin and let the seeds fall out, then sweep them up a few days later into a pile like a heap of black sand. The seeds were then ground on a large flat stone with a smaller hand-held one, then mixed with water to produce a coarse paste that could be shaped into small cakes and baked in hot ashes. A single plant may produce 52,300 seeds, which amounts in weight to around 6.8 g – with more than 1.3 g protein, equivalent in protein to a generous tablespoon of wheat flour.

seeds

Rose Family

[Rosaceae]

This family consists largely of woody shrubs and trees, many of which are armed with thorns, spines or prickles, typically with five-petalled flowers. Included are many popular fruits, such as **apple**, **quince**, **pear**, **peach**, **apricot**, **plum**, **cherry**, **blackberry**, **raspberry**, **loquat** and **strawberry**. With the exception of **sweet almond**, it is inadvisable to eat their seeds in large quantities due to the presence of cyanogenic glycosides – a risk reduced partly by cooking, soaking, drying and fermentation. If the raw fruit is to be juiced, it is wise to remove the seeds first. Native members of the family include **tātarāmoa** (**bush lawyer**, *Rubus* species), whose fruits were traditionally eaten by Māori; and **piripiri** (*Acaena anserinifolia*), whose leaves are used as tea.

Wild Roses

Rosa species

Description: Deciduous thorny shrub. Large flowers, pink to white.

Where: Abundant throughout.

Part eaten: Petals (Nov–Jan), and rosehips (Feb–May), but only after the irritating hairs coating the inside are removed.

Nutritional value: Fruit of the commonest wild species (**sweet briar**) is exceedingly rich in vitamin C (Uggla) and an excellent source of calcium (Damascos).

homemade rose petal liqueur

rosehip

Use: Roses are native to most of the Northern Hemisphere and their culinary use enjoys a similarly wide distribution. From seed remains in an archaeological cave site at Santa Maira, Spain, the use of rosehips as food can be traced back some 10,000 years. As botanist Pierpoint Johnson explained in 1862, 'The fruit of the Dog Rose, or the "Hip" as it is often called, has long been used to form a conserve with sugar [and] an infusion of the crushed fruit in hot water forms an agreeable cooling drink. In some parts of Europe the "Hips" are collected, and sold in the markets for the purpose of mixing with wine. They are often eaten raw by children, and are not unwholesome, but care should be taken to remove all the bristle-like hairs that surround the seeds, as, if swallowed, they produce sickness, and if they lodge in the throat may occasion much more serious injury.' To remove these, I generally use my thumbnail to scrape them away. The flower petals are also used – in salads, jams and jellies, and as a flavouring in 'Turkish delight' – and are dried, too, to scatter over Indian and Middle Eastern dishes. In our own kitchen we place fresh petals in a jar and layer them with a sprinkle of sugar, then leave the mixture for several days to allow a delightfully scented syrup to develop. Strain this and, with time, it becomes a liqueur (pictured).

Local relatives: By far the most common species here is the **sweet briar** (*R. rubiginosa*), which is used as above; also the less-common **dog rose** (*R. canina*), **burnet rose** (*R. pimpinellifolia*) and **rugosa rose** (*R. rugosa*) – pictured.

Blackberry

Rubus fruticosus agg.

Description: Thorny scrambling shrub with large white or pink flowers and black fruits.

Where: Abundant throughout.

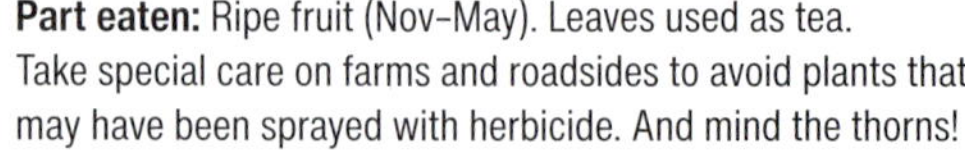

Part eaten: Ripe fruit (Nov–May). Leaves used as tea.

Take special care on farms and roadsides to avoid plants that may have been sprayed with herbicide. And mind the thorns!

Nutritional value: Raw fruit rich in vitamins C and K and manganese (USDA). Fresh leaves rich in vitamin C (Jones).

Use: A native of Europe, where the fruit has long been enjoyed as food, as evidenced by masses of seeds excavated from the early Neolithic settlements of Chevdar and Kazanlŭk in Bulgaria, which date back more than 6000 years. The fruit, when soft and fully ripe, is sweet and is often eaten fresh; it is also a popular ingredient in desserts, jams, yoghurt, fruit pies, crumbles and wine. Children in particular often enjoy collecting them. Large quantities are grown commercially in Mexico and the USA, where the leaves are also dried and sold as tea, largely for their antioxidant content.

Local relatives: The fruit of the very similar **cut-leaved blackberry** (*R. laciniatus*, right) of Europe is used in the same way, as are those of the far less-common Asian **Himalaya blackberry** (*R. rugosus*), which is collected from the wild in the Indian Himalayas and is now grown in New Zealand under a new name: **keriberry**.

Wild Raspberry

Rubus idaeus

Description: Shrub with weak prickles. Flowers white.

Where: In scattered localities throughout, sometimes forming dense thickets.

Part eaten: Ripe fruit (Jan–Mar). Leaves used for tea.

Nutritional value: Raw fruit rich in vitamin C and manganese (USDA).

Use: A native of the Northern Hemisphere, including North America, where the fruit was traditionally collected by indigenous peoples; and Denmark, where archaeological evidence from a late-Mesolithic coastal settlement reveals consumption of the fruit by humans more than 6000 years ago. The plant was not brought into cultivation until about 500 years ago in Europe, where the tradition of collecting the wild fruit survives. Although often eaten fresh, they are also used as a dessert, in purées, preserves, juice, jam, jelly, wine and spirits, canned or freeze-dried. The leaves are dried and used as tea, largely by pregnant women to ease labour – in the last trimester only.

Local relatives: The ripe fruit of **yellow Himalayan raspberry** (*R. ellipticus*) – occasionally found around Auckland – is enjoyed in Pakistan, Nepal, Sikkim and India.

Strawberry-raspberry

Rubus rosifolius (= *R. rosaefolius*)

Description: A prickly sub-shrub with white flowers, also known as **roseleaf bramble**.

Where: In semi-shade in scrub and open forest.

Part eaten: Fruits Oct–Jan.

Nutritional value: Fruits relatively rich in vitamins E and C (Francis) and in antioxidants generally (Bowen-Forbes).

Use: A native of Asia, including the temperate Himalayas where the fruit is collected from the wild as food by the Memba and Apatani tribes of Arunachal Pradesh in NE India. The plant is nowadays also found across much of Africa, where the fruits are offered for sale almost year-round in Ugandan markets. In my experience the fruit is generally sour and not particularly tasty; however, in many of these places they are eaten either as is or made into drinks and preserves.

Japanese Wineberry

Rubus phoenicolasius

Description: Prickly scrambling shrub with small fruits Dec–Apr.

Where: Cultivated for its fruit, and now reasonably common in the wild, particularly in the North Island.

Part eaten: Ripe fruit (Dec–Apr).

Nutritional value: Wild fruit contains more α- and β-carotene than those of cultivars (Imanishi). Fruit rich in anthocyanins (Veberic), with medium levels of sugars, mainly glucose and sucrose (Mikulic-Petkovsek).

Use: The wild fruit is traditionally eaten in the plant's native region of China, Japan and Korea. It was introduced from Japan to Europe in the 1870s; in 1890 to the USA; and reached New Zealand around 1922. In all three regions the plant has escaped cultivation to become established along roadsides and in open scrubland. The fruit is eaten raw, or as a dessert, and in jams and jellies.

Indian Strawberry

Potentilla indica
(= *Duchesnea* = *Fragaria*)

Description: Mat-forming, with yellow flowers (Jul–Apr).

Where: Grown in gardens as groundcover and as an ornamental, but now commonly wild in damp, shady places.

Part eaten: Ripe fruit (Oct–July).

Nutritional value: Fruit is rich in minerals (Bajracharya) and considerably richer in antioxidants than other strawberry species, sugar content about the same and vitamin C content considerably lower (Vasilisin). Leaves rich in vitamin C (Zennie).

Use: The native region of this strawberry extends from Afghanistan to Japan, including India where the ripe fruit is particularly popular with children in the northern states of Jammu and Kashmir, Assam, Arunachal Pradesh and Mizoram. Their popularity extends north to Nepal and east to China, where they are eaten by Tibetans in the Shangri-La region and by the Yi people of Liangshan, and to Jeju Island off the south coast of South Korea. The fruit is small and insipid due to a lack of acidity, yet they have been used lately also in Europe for garnishing cakes and pastries.

Woodland Strawberry

Fragaria vesca (= *Potentilla*)

Description: Also known as **alpine strawberry**. Low-growing plant with white flowers (Sep–Apr) and small fruit.

Where: Roadsides, damp banks and forest clearings to 1000 m.

Part eaten: Leaves, and fruit (Nov–Apr).

Nutritional value: Fruit and leaves rich in vitamin C (Cerne, Jones).

Use: A native of Eurasia, and of North America where the fruit has long been enjoyed by indigenous inhabitants. Similarly, in England, Spain, Italy, Estonia, Belarus, Czech Republic, Slovakia, Hungary, Romania, Croatia, Bosnia, Albania, Bulgaria and Turkey the fruits continue to be collected from the wild, often eaten raw and occasionally made into jam by adding sugar and boiling for around 30 minutes. The fruit is very small, but superior in flavour to the Indian strawberry (above) and garden strawberry. Over much of Europe the spring leaves are also cooked as a pot-herb or used as an ingredient in soups.

Local relatives: Although the **garden strawberry** (*F.* x *ananassa*) also occurs wild in New Zealand, it is generally found only in and around gardens.

Salad Burnet

Sanguisorba minor

Description: Short plant with greyish leaves and pinkish flowers (Oct–Apr).

Where: Dry grassy places in scattered localities, especially in limestone country.

Part eaten: Tender stems and leaves in spring. (Later, they darken and become too bitter.)

Nutritional value: Leaves especially rich in antioxidants (Vanzani), including vitamins A, E and C (Ranfa), and rich in magnesium (Sánchez-Mata).

Use: A native of the Mediterranean and Europe, where the plant's value as a salad herb is commemorated in 16th-century verse by Italian naturalist Costanzo Felici: '*L'insalata non è né buona né bella, se in essa non entra la pimpinella*' – loosely translated as 'the salad is neither good nor beautiful, if the burnet (la pimpinella) is not included'. Here in New Zealand this 'good and beautiful' plant is valued more as forage for livestock, earning it the local name of **sheep's burnet**. When crushed, the leaves smell slightly of cucumber, and are best eaten raw or added only at the end of cooking or as a garnish. The young leaves are still collected from the wild in Britain, Spain, Italy, Slovakia, Bosnia and Turkey, and are nowadays cultivated in the USA and New Zealand as a form of microgreens.

Wild Loquat

Eriobotrya japonica (= *Rhaphiolepis bibas*)

Description: Evergreen tree to 8 m with yellow fruit 3–5 cm.

Where: Widely planted in the warmer north, where its seeds are spread by kererū and other birds, and humans, so that it is now common in the wild.

Part eaten: Flesh of the fruit (Oct–Dec). Don't chew the seeds, though, as these contain amygdalin and prunasin (Tanaka 2020).

Nutritional value: Raw fruit rich in vitamin A, yet surprisingly low in vitamin C (USDA).

Use: The trees have long been cultivated for their fruit in their native China, whence they were introduced to Japan by Buddhist monks during the Tang dynasty (618–907). Loquats are nowadays cultivated in the Mediterranean region, South Africa, South America, California, India and Australia, and by home gardeners in New Zealand too. The fruit tastes like a cooked apple with a hint of apricot, and is available these days in cans, and used to make fruit drinks, jam and a light wine.

Wild Apple

Malus domestica

Description: Deciduous tree. Flowers white or pink. Fruits usually smaller than cultivated apples; crab apples even smaller.

Where: Common near railway lines, roadsides and tracks, picnic sites, abandoned orchards and gardens.

Part eaten: Flowers (Oct-Nov) and fruit (Mar-Jun). Seeds best not eaten in large quantities as they contain cyanogenic glycosides, e.g. amygdalin and prunasin (Senica).

Nutritional value: Fruit a reasonably good source of vitamin C (USDA).

Use: Apples here in New Zealand are descended from a cultivated hybrid from Eurasia that began spreading into the wild in 1872. According to archaeological evidence from a Mesolithic coastal settlement in Denmark, similar fruit was eaten by European hunter-gatherer communities as early as 4000 BC. Varieties bearing smaller fruits are sometimes referred to as **crab apples**. These can be quite tart, but I regularly use them to liven up fruit and savoury salads, and also in cooking as a winter substitute for tomatoes. Crab apples are also great sliced and dried (right) – serving as a great ingredient of 'trail mix' – or in pickles, jams, jellies and pies. The apple blossoms can also be used, as a garnish in salads and fruit dishes. Wherever you find wild apples, they are worth using. They proved particularly useful in the 1990s, during the siege of Sarajevo, when they were eaten fresh or pickled or made into apple vinegar and apple brandy; the dried skin of the fruit was also used with the leaves to make a simple beverage.

crab apple
fresh and d

Wild Pear

Pyrus communis

Description: Deciduous tree with white flowers (Sep-Oct).

Where: In scattered places throughout, often along roadsides and around old gardens and orchards.

Part eaten: Fruit (Mar-Apr). Seeds best not eaten in large quantities, due to the presence of amygdalin, a cyanogenic glycoside (Senica).

Nutritional value: Raw fruit a minor source of vitamin C (USDA).

Use: This tree's native region stretches from Europe to northern Iraq, including Turkey, where pears are still collected from the wild and eaten fresh or made into jam; and Dalmatia and SW Herzegovina, where the wild fruit was particularly appreciated during the Second World War. Ripe pears are enjoyed raw or dried or baked in pies, pastries, etc., and grilled with grated chocolate. Highly recommended!

Quince

Cydonia oblonga (= *C. vulgaris* = *Pyrus cydonia*)

Description: Deciduous tree with pink flowers.

Where: Common in neglected gardens, also wild.

Part eaten: Fruit (Feb–Apr), usually cooked, and flowers (Oct). Seeds best not eaten in large quantities, due to cyanogenic glycosides, including amygdalin and prunasin (Sabir).

Nutritional value: Raw fruit rich in vitamin C (USDA).

Use: A native of the Middle East that later reached the Mediterranean region, where it was valued by the Romans. Most varieties of the fruit are too hard, astringent or sour to eat raw, so are generally baked or stewed or used to make jam, quince paste or jelly. Their intense fragrance and flavour combines well with apple in fruit pies.

Local relatives: Chinese or **Japanese quince** (*Chaenomeles speciosa*), cultivated mostly for its showy flowers, is also found wild. Its cooked fruit is used in a similar way in the Hengduan Mountain region of China's western Yunnan.

Wild Peach

Prunus persica

Description: Deciduous tree with pink flowers (Aug–Oct).

Where: Found throughout, near gardens, orchards, paths and roads; more so in the north.

Part eaten: Ripe fruit (Dec–Mar). Due to prunasin and amygdalin in the seeds, these should not be eaten in large quantities (Senica).

Nutritional value: Raw fruit a reasonable source of vitamin C (USDA).

Use: A native of northern China, where archaeological evidence reveals that the fruit has been collected from the wild for some 8000 years and cultivated for at least 4000 years. From China it was taken to Japan and westward through Asia to the Mediterranean around 300 BC. The ripe fruit is enjoyed fresh, but also cooked, dried, made into jelly, jam, juice, wine and peach brandy.

Wild Plum

Prunus domestica

Description: Deciduous tree, sometimes thorny, with white flowers.

Where: Common along tracks and roadsides and near settlements.

Part eaten: Fruits (Jan–Feb) and flowers (Aug–Sep). Not the seeds, though, due to cyanogenic glycosides, including amygdalin and prunasin (Sultana, Senica).

Nutritional value: Raw fruit a reasonable source of vitamin C (USDA).

Use: The wild plums found in New Zealand are descended from a hybrid between the Eurasian sloe and the cherry plum (see page 140). The ripe fruit is eaten fresh, dried, or made into jam, desserts, sauce, juice or wine. In Estonia, the flowers are also used in infusions.

Sweet Cherry

Prunus avium (= *Cerasus*)

Description: Also known as **bird cherry**. Deciduous tree with small, dark-red fruit 8–17 mm.

Where: Widely grown, particularly in Central Otago and Canterbury, now also wild.

Part eaten: Flowers (Sep–Nov) and ripe fruit (Nov–Feb). The bony seeds should not be ground up and eaten due to the presence of cyanogenic glycosides, e.g. amygdalin and prunasin (Senica).

Nutritional value: Raw fruit a reasonable source of vitamin C (USDA).

Use: Native to North Africa and Europe through to Afghanistan, where the fruit is still collected from wild trees and eaten raw, made into jam, dried or used to distil a kind of fruit brandy, which is particularly popular in Spain, Hungary and Romania. In Italy some of the country's top chefs are nowadays using the flowers as a garnish.

Local relatives: The fruit of the very common **Japanese hill cherry** (*P. serrulata*) and **Taiwan cherry** (*P. campanulata*) are unfortunately too small and astringent to be worth eating. The so-called **sour cherry** or **pie cherry** (*P. cerasus*) and **St Lucie cherry** or **mahaleb cherry** (*P. mahaleb*) are both widely used in Europe, and the **black cherry** or **rum cherry** (*P. serotina*) is a traditional food of indigenous Americans; however, all three species are much less common in New Zealand.

Cherry Plum

Prunus cerasifera (= *Cerasus myrobalanos*)

Description: Also known as **Myrobalan plum**. Deciduous tree with spiny branchlets. Fruit 1.7–3 cm, yellow to orange-red or scarlet, sometimes dark crimson.

Where: Widely cultivated, but also common wild, particularly along the eastern side of the South Island.

Part eaten: Fruits (Nov–Jan). Seeds should not be ground up and eaten, due to the presence of amygdalin (Petrevska).

Nutritional value: Fresh fruit rich in citric acid and vitamin C (Celik).

Use: A native of Eurasia. In rural Italy the fruit is traditionally eaten fresh off the tree; likewise in Belarus, where the fruit is also made into jam. The fruit is widely appreciated in Bulgaria and neighbouring North Macedonia, where it is eaten raw, in soups and jam, marmalade and compote. In Macedonia and East Georgia the fruit is also used for making alcoholic beverages, including brandy and vodka.

Rowan

Sorbus aucuparia (= *Pyrus*)

Description: Small deciduous tree or shrub with white flowers (Oct–Nov) and red fruits (Jan–Apr).

Where: Widely grown and common in the wild, particularly in the South Island.

Part eaten: Ripe fruit, collected after the first frost, when they are sweeter; usually cooked, as they can be slightly toxic raw due to trace amounts of bitter-tasting parasorbic acid, which is transformed by heat to sorbic acid (Janick).

Nutritional value: Wild fruit rich in vitamins C, A and K, yet very low in sodium (Sánchez-Mata).

Use: A native of Eurasia, where archaeological evidence from Denmark suggests that the fruit was eaten as far back as 4000 BC. Although the bitter taste of the raw fruit limits their use, they have been traditionally eaten this way as a snack in Spain, Bosnia, Russia, Belarus, Latvia and Estonia. More commonly the fruit is stirred briefly in boiling water or left for about 10 hours in diluted vinegar. The pectin-rich fruit can then be made into jelly, pressed to make juice, or fermented to make a wine or liqueur. In hard times the dried fruit has also been ground into a meal and used as an ingredient of bread. A breakthrough came in 1810, when shepherds in what is now the Czech Republic discovered a sport bearing non-bitter berries, which led to some countries cultivating the fruit on a commercial scale.

Local relatives: The **service tree** (or **sorb tree**, *S. domestica*), whose overripe fruit is also eaten, is occasionally planted in New Zealand but is not yet known in the wild.

Hawthorn

Crataegus monogyna

Description: Thorny deciduous shrub or small tree. Flowers sweet-scented, white or cream. Red fruits up to 1 cm.

Where: Very common throughout. A hedge plant spread by birds.

Part eaten: Thin flesh of ripe fruit in autumn (May), flowers (Oct–Nov), young shoots and leaves (spring).

Nutritional value: Fruit rich in sugars, antioxidants, dietary fibre, calcium and vitamin A, often also potassium, magnesium, copper, manganese and vitamins C and E, yet low in sodium (Sánchez-Mata). Flowers rich in vitamin C (Barros 2011), as are the fresh leaves (Jones).

Use: A native of Europe, where archaeological evidence suggests that the fruit was eaten as far back as 4000 BC. Despite the rather mealy taste and large seed, this is commonly eaten raw around the Mediterranean – in Portugal, Spain, Italy, Croatia, Bosnia-Herzegovina, Cyprus, Turkey, Tunisia and Morocco; and further north – in Russia, Britain, Poland, Slovakia, Hungary, Bulgaria and Moldova. In many of these countries the fruit is used for making jam and liqueurs, too. In Slovenia the fruits are macerated in brandy. The fruit has been used for making vinegar and wine, and – during times of famine in Hungary and Austria – even dried, ground and mixed with flour to make bread. In many of these countries the raw flowers, young shoots and leaves are eaten in spring or brewed to make herbal teas.

Local relatives: In China, entire orchards are devoted to supplying the edible fruit of the **Chinese hawthorn** (*C. pinnatifida*), a tree that is occasionally planted here too, though not yet known in the wild.

Sedges

[Cyperaceae]

These are grass-like plants whose stems typically have a triangular cross-section. Members include **papyrus** (*Cyperus papyrus*), from whose stem one of the first types of paper was made; and others that are cultivated for food, such as **Chinese water chestnut** (*Eleocharis dulcis*) and **chufa** (*C. esculentus*) – below. Native members include **kukuraho (pūrua grass**, *Bolboschoenus fluviatilis*), whose tuberous roots were traditionally eaten by Māori.

Yellow Nut Grass

Cyperus esculentus

Description: Also known as **yellow nut sedge**, as this is not really a grass but a sedge (with a triangular stem).

Where: A troublesome weed in gardens.

Part eaten: Nut-like tubers at the end of long spindly rhizomes (raw or cooked). Best in moderation, as the plant (like rye) is occasionally subject to ergot, a fungal toxin.

Nutritional value: Raw tubers high in starch and fats, a good source of fibre and amino acids, and rich in phosphorus, calcium, iron, potassium, zinc, magnesium and copper (Arafat, Ekeanyanwu).

Use: This sedge is native to the warmer regions of Europe, Africa, Asia and the Americas, where its edible tubers – known as **chufa**, **tiger nuts**, **Zulu nuts** or **earth almonds** – are collected from the wild and eaten raw, fried, baked, roasted, or ground into flour, or made into a drink known as horchata de chufa. The plant is also deliberately cultivated as a food supply in southern Europe, Asia and Africa, despite being widely acknowledged nowadays as one of the world's worst weeds. Indeed, the plant has a venerable history dating to at least 5000–4000 BC, when it earned the distinction of being one of the most ancient domesticated foodstuffs of ancient Egypt. The plant remains relevant in Egypt today, where a panel of 20 judges found that when chufa tuber is coated with chocolate, the taste and nutritive value was superior to that of commercial peanut coated with chocolate.

Local relatives: Tubers of the equally common **nut grass** (**purple nut sedge**, *C. rotundus* – with tubers borne intermittently along the length of the rhizomes) are a traditional food of the Paiute people of Utah, and are cooked and eaten in Bosnia-Herzegovina and in Ethiopia. However, the commonest introduced species in New Zealand, **umbrella sedge** (*C. eragrostis*), bears no such tubers – edible or otherwise.

dried **tiger nuts** or **chufa** for sale

Sumac Family

[Anacardiaceae]

Sumac is best known as a reddish-purple powder from the ground fruit of **Syrian sumac** (*Rhus coriaria*), used in Middle Eastern cuisine to add a tart, lemony taste to salads or meat. Other important members of the family include **pistachio**, **cashew**, **mango** and the **mombin** fruit tree of tropical America. All are trees or shrubs with tiny flowers, many of which produce a resinous or milky sap containing urushiol, which can be highly irritating on contact with the skin. This oil may be distributed throughout the leaves, stems, roots and immature fruits, as in **poison ivy** (*Toxicodendron* species); or concentrated in just one part, as in the fruit wall of the cashew and pistachio, both of which are rendered edible by roasting – even though an unfortunate few may still be allergic to them.

Staghorn Sumac

Rhus typhina

Description: Deciduous shrub or small tree with tiny, greenish flowers. The forking branches and velvety stems are reminiscent of stag antlers, hence the common name.

Where: A common garden plant, particularly in the South Island, spreading freely into the wild along roadsides, etc., by suckering.

Part eaten: Ripe fruit (Feb–May) steeped in water to make a drink. The leaves should NOT be eaten due to a high concentration of tannin and plant acids (Murray).

Nutritional value: The fruit is rich in magnesium, phosphorus, sodium and iron, and contains more ash, protein, unsaturated fatty acids (especially oleic acid), and fibre than the Syrian sumac of commerce, but less potassium, calcium and vitamins. The sour flavour of the fruit is from malic acid (Kossah).

Use: A native of eastern North America, where several indigenous tribes traditionally used various methods to make a drink from the berries. The Algonquin of Quebec steeped them in water and sweetened this liquid in recent times with sugar to make a kind of lemonade. The Ojibwa people from the same region made a similar drink from the fresh or dried berries but sweetened it with maple sugar, and also dried the seed heads for winter use, as did the Menominee of Wisconsin and Michigan. A 2009 pharmacological study comparing the constituents of this sumac with the so-called Syrian sumac of the Mediterranean recommended both as useful sources of ingredients for the food industry.

Local relatives: The **Peruvian pepper tree** (*Schinus molle*) and **Brazilian pepper tree** (*S. terebinthifolia*) both occur wild in New Zealand, bearing pink-red berries that are sometimes mixed with commercial peppercorns for colour. However, ingestion of large amounts may result in severe digestive tract irritation (Burrows).

Verbena Family

[Verbenaceae]

Members of this family typically have square stems and aromatic leaves arranged in opposite pairs. Well-known members include **lemon verbena** (*Aloysia citrodora*), which is grown for its lemon-flavoured leaves, used to brew a herbal tea and to flavour various dishes.

ripe fruit

green fruit (toxic)

Lantana

Lantana camara

Description: Aromatic shrub to about 2 m high, with square stems and hairy leaves, flowering all year. Clumps of small black berries, each about the size of a peppercorn.

Where: Originally grown as an ornamental garden plant. Seeds are readily spread by birds so has become common along roadsides, particularly north of Tauranga. Now banned from sale, propagation and distribution.

Part eaten: Ripe fruit (all year), but only when black. NOT the unripe green fruits or leaves, which are poisonous, causing irritation of the digestive tract (Burrows).

Nutritional value: Ripe fruits rich in vitamin B3, potassium and iron, with moderate amounts of vitamin C, magnesium and calcium (Herzog).

Use: Native to Central and South America. The plant was introduced from Brazil to Europe in the 17th century, and thence to India in 1809, where the ripe fruit now serves as a common snack for rural children and farm labourers throughout the Indian subcontinent, from Nepal right through to the Western Ghats and Kotagiri Hills in southern India. By around 1858 the plant had reached Africa, where children and adults of Ethiopia, southern Africa and Uganda now gather the fruit from the wild. For example, in the village of Zougoussi in central Côte d'Ivoire 40–80% of the children eat the fruit and do so virtually throughout the year. In the USA the ripe fruit is sometimes offered for sale in San Diego by the company Specialty Produce for consumption either raw or for making into jams and jellies. But do remember: unripe fruit is poisonous.

Violet Family

[Violaceae]

A family best known for its decorative members that are often planted in the flower garden, including **pansies** and **violets**. The flowers of many have a long history of culinary use in Europe and the Middle East to flavour and decorate various dishes, to make syrup or to eat candied as a sweet. Some are used as a source for scents in the perfume industry. The family also includes shrubs, vines or small trees, including New Zealand's native **māhoe (whiteywood)**, whose flowers are likewise sweetly scented.

Wild Violet

Viola odorata

Description: Heart-shaped leaves. Blue-purple flowers, strongly and sweetly scented.
Where: Common garden escape throughout.
Part eaten: Young leaves (minus stems), and flower petals (mostly Jul–Oct).
Nutritional value: Leaves rich in magnesium, potassium and calcium (Lim), vitamin C and carotene, though the flowers themselves have no special nutritional value (Grlić).
Use: Native to Morocco through to Kazakhstan, including most of Europe, where we know from the Roman author Pliny the Elder that the flowers have been valued for their scent and colour for at least 2000 years. Not until the medieval period was the plant grown in kitchen gardens, it seems, when its young leaves and flowers were used in salads. A 15th-century English dessert recipe describes cooking the 'Flourys of Vyolet' with almond milk, rice flour and honey, while a 17th-century sherbet made of violet flowers in the Ottoman Empire is recorded as the favourite drink of Sultan Mehmet IV. Nowadays the petals are more commonly used to adorn salads, cakes and the like, as practised by some of the top chefs of Italy, a country where the leaves are also traditionally used – in vegetable soups.
Local relatives: Similar uses have been recorded for the flowers of the less-common **field pansy** (*V. arvensis*), **garden pansy** (*V.* x *wittrockiana*), **dog violet** (*V. riviniana*) and **wild pansy** (*V. tricolor*, above left).

Walnut Family

[Juglandaceae]

Besides several species of edible **walnut** (*Juglans* species), this family includes several kinds of **hickory** (*Carya* species), some of which also provide edible nuts – e.g. the North American **pecan** (*C. illinoinensis*).

Walnut

Juglans regia

Description: Deciduous tree. Nuts on wild trees usually smaller, with thicker shells.

Where: Wild in regions of early European settlement, particularly around Wellington, Christchurch and Otago.

Part eaten: Kernel of fresh nut (Mar–May). Also unripe fruit pickled in vinegar – picked late Dec before the shell has started to harden. TIP: Test with a skewer.

Nutritional value: Nuts especially rich in unsaturated fats and minerals, including potassium, magnesium, phosphorus, calcium, iron and zinc and vitamins B1, B6 and B9 (USDA). Also rich in polyphenols, which may have health benefits (Heinrich).

Use: Native to a region extending from Turkey through to the Himalayas, including Iran, where pollen and charcoal evidence from lakes and peat bogs suggests that the tree was first domesticated in this region some 4500 years ago. The brain-like shaped kernel of the nut is commonly eaten raw, but also roasted or used in cakes and breads. If you find the fresh nuts too bitter, try removing the paper-thin skin; if this does not help, the nut may be rancid and no longer fit for eating. In Italy and France an edible oil is traditionally pressed from the nuts for use as flavouring, in salad dressings and cooking. In England and Hungary, at least, the young green, unripe fruit is pickled in vinegar and eaten. In Italy and Poland unripe green walnuts are steeped in alcohol to make a liqueur.

Local relatives: In northern New Zealand, the more common species is the **Japanese walnut** (*J. ailantifolia*, right), whose nuts are available for sale in the markets of northern Japan; note however that these are generally far harder to open.

nuts – hulled and unhulled

unripe walnut fruit

Japanese walnut

Water Plantain Family

[Alismataceae]

Members of this family have three-petalled flowers and are typically aquatic. Included are the **duck potato** (*Sagittaria* species) of North America, whose rhizomes are traditionally eaten by several indigenous tribes and sold in Californian markets as a wild vegetable; **Chinese arrowhead** (*S. trifolia*), which is cultivated as a food crop in parts of Asia; and **sawah lettuce** (*Limnocharis flava*), whose leaves and young flowering stalks are used in Asia in soups or mixed vegetable dishes.

Water Plantain

Alisma plantago-aquatica

Description: Leaves heart-shaped with a pointed tip, clustered at the base of the plant. Small, pale lilac flowers (Oct–Feb).

Where: In muddy ponds and slow-flowing water. CAUTION: It is very important to avoid potentially polluted areas (like storm water run-off), as the plant is a known accumulator of heavy metals, including lead (Rumyantseva).

Part eaten: Rhizomes, cooked as this removes the bitter taste and the risk of parasites.

Nutritional value: Rhizome rich in starch (Grlić).

Use: A native of Africa and Eurasia; the rhizome is traditionally cooked and eaten in Hungary, Bosnia, Croatia, the Indian Himalayas (where it is sometimes sold in markets), Mongolia and China. This underground part of the plant can also be dried and milled into flour to make bread and porridge, or baked as a substitute for potatoes. The *US Army Survival Manual* recommends them as an emergency food – after boiling or soaking them in water to remove the bitter taste.

APPENDIX: OTHER PLANTS OF INTEREST

Of the more than 1000 edible wild plant species known in New Zealand, it is practicable to feature only the most common and important ones. The following additional plants are listed here either because they are less common, or because no confirmation could be found of an established traditional culinary use, or their nutritional value is otherwise questionable.

Akebia (*Akebia quinata*), also commonly known as **chocolate vine** from the scent of its flowers. This climber is a native of China and Japan, where its sausage-shaped fruit is eaten raw. Although wild in New Zealand, it rarely produces fruit here.

Alexanders (*Smyrnium olusatrum*). This relative of celery is a recent escape from cultivation, so is not yet common here; however, in its native Mediterranean region its stems and young leaves are used as a vegetable.

Alyssum (*Lobularia maritima*). A white-flowered member of the cress family, common near the coast, recommended by recent writers as a pungent addition to salads. No traditional culinary use is recorded from the plant's native Mediterranean region.

Angelica (*Angelica* species). The **Portuguese angelica** (*A. pachycarpa*), an ornamental garden plant, is common in the wild here but has no known traditional culinary use. The true **garden angelica** (*A. archangelica*), whose leaves, stems and roots are traditionally used as food in Europe, is not known to grow wild here in New Zealand.

Araucaria (*Araucaria* species) – pine-like trees native to New Guinea, Australia and South America. These include the **monkey puzzle** (*A. araucana*) and **Paraná pine** (*A. angustifolia* or **candelabra tree**), whose seeds are a traditional food of the Mapuche of South America, and **bunya bunya** (*A. bidwillii*) whose seeds are a traditional food of Aboriginal Australians. Though present in New Zealand none of these trees is common, in contrast with the common **Norfolk Island pine** (*A. heterophylla*). Like the bunya bunya and monkey puzzle, this tree bears large, edible pine-like seeds. Its male and female cones are often borne on separate trees, and high up; however, each female cone can contain 80–200 seeds (Patil).

Arum, Italian (*Arum italicum*) – may be confused with other lily species but for its dark green leaves with creamy mid-rib and veins. A survey conducted in Croatia (quoted in Grlić) found that more than 30% of the households along the coast resorted to eating the rhizomes during the Second World War, a traditional usage recorded from neighbouring Bosnia and Herzegovina, where they are made into porridge and bread. These cannot be eaten raw, though, due to calcium oxalate raphides (Connor).

Arum Lily (or **calla lily**, *Zantedeschia aethiopica*) – a very common plant in swampy areas about which the National Poisons Centre receives many enquiries (Slaughter). It is a native of South Africa, where the young leaves and stems are traditionally used by the Xhosa, Fingo and Sotho people as a vegetable – but only after cooking, as microscopic calcium oxalate crystals in the raw plant can cause a painful burning sensation of the lips and mouth and swelling of the throat.

Barnyard Grass (*Echinochloa crus-galli*) – a common grass here. In Europe the seeds were used as food from at least the 12th century, and also more recently – often to eke out grain supplies in times of famine.

Beech, European (*Fagus sylvatica*) – occasionally wild here, mostly near planted trees. Although the seeds and new leaves have been used as food in many European countries, this has often resulted in irritation of the digestive tract. Toxin unknown (Burrows).

Begonia, Bedding (*Begonia semperflorens-cultorum*) – a cultivated hybrid sometimes wild near settlements. Its flowers are marketed as food in Korea but are eaten sparingly due to high oxalic acid content (Laferriere).

Bindweeds (*Calystegia* and *Convolvulus* species). Besides the native bindweeds, the main introduced ones here are the very common **large bindweed** (*Calystegia silvatica* subsp. *disjuncta*) of SW Europe and NW Africa (for which I find no record of traditional use as food), and **field bindweed** (*Convolvulus arvensis*), whose young leaves are cooked and eaten in southern Europe but probably not in large quantities, due to known purgative properties (Schultheiss, Burrows).

Boneseed (*Chrysanthemoides monilifera*) – a very common bush with yellow, daisy-like flowers. Although the ripe fruit is eaten by many contemporary Khoe-San descendants of South Africa's Cape South Coast, it consists primarily of a large, bone-hard seed, on which the layer of edible flesh is very thin.

Boxthorn (*Lycium ferocissimum*) – an African member of the nightshade family, very common as a hedge plant and along the coast. Its orange-red fruit is reputedly eaten by the people of Transkei, but have been suspected on more than one occasion of poisoning humans and pigs there, triggering symptoms typical of narcotic poisoning (Bizimana).

Broom (*Cytisus scoparius*). Although the flowers and flower buds of this very common shrub have been used in herbal teas, they contain low levels of toxic alkaloids. In one case in California, four boys who ate the flowers subsequently developed nausea and vomiting (Burrows). In Spain the flowers of the similar-looking **Spanish broom** (*Spartium junceum*) are collected in spring to make a liqueur and other beverages, yet eating the flowers themselves has led to at least three cases of poisoning (Riccardi), and at least 68 cases of poisoning have resulted from confusing its hard, dark green shoots with those of wild asparagus (Colombo).

Broomrape (*Orobanche* species). Although no reports were found of traditional food use of our local species, *O. minor*, the stems of others (*O. crenata* and *O. californica*) have been boiled and eaten as a kind of asparagus – despite a propensity among this family of semi-parasitic plants for them to interact with their host plants to produce toxins (Burrows).

Bullwort (*Ammi majus*) – a white-flowered member of the carrot family that is fairly rare in New Zealand. Its young stems and leaves are used as food in the plant's native Mediterranean region, but contact with the seeds, in particular, can cause photodermatitis.

Buttercups (*Ranunculus* species). Besides the **creeping buttercup** (*R. repens*, page 31), several other buttercup species have been eaten, but always cooked. This caveat is especially true of our common **celery-leaved buttercup** (*R. sceleratus*) which happens to be one of the more toxic species, especially when flowering, when it may contain up to 2.5% protoanemonin (Burrows), which can cause dermatitis, burning and itching of the skin, a rash and blisters. In Friuli, NE Italy, its leaves are collected in spring and generally boiled together with a traditional mixture of wild herbs, then sautéed with butter or lard and garlic.

Calla Lily – see **Arum Lily**

Camellia (*Camellia* species). The common ornamental species is *C. japonica*, which rarely grows wild here; its juicy petals are traditionally eaten as a vegetable in Korea and Japan. The species used to produce common tea is *C. sinensis*, which is not commonly encountered in New Zealand.

Canary Grass (*Phalaris canariensis*) – not common. Although it is true that the seeds of a hairless cultivar of this grass provide a safe human food, the same is not true of wild plants due to the irritating nature of fine hairs attached to the hulls. These hairs can sometimes occur as a contaminant in wheat flour used in baking, incidences of which have been linked to cancer of the oesophagus (Magnuson, Abdel-Aal).

Cape Ivy (*Senecio angulatus*) – a common scrambling, yellow-flowered vine, native to South Africa, where the leaves have reportedly been used as spinach; however, they are known to contain toxic pyrrolizidine alkaloids (Burrows).

Centaury (*Centaurium erythraea*) – a very common herb with pink-lilac flowers. The leaves have been eaten raw in Hungary and Italy but taste exceedingly bitter. In Russia they are used to flavour vermouth; however, high doses of related *Centaurium* species have proven toxic to goats (Burrows).

Chamomile (*Chamaemelum nobile*). Packaged chamomile tea is generally derived from the dried flowers of this plant or from those of **German chamomile** (*Matricaria recutita*), neither of which is common here in the wild.

Chamomile, Rayless (**pineapple weed**, *Matricaria discoidea*). The flowerheads of this common, pineapple-scented chamomile were occasionally chewed by indigenous North Americans, and evidently used to prepare a pale golden tea, and as perfume.

Chamomile, Stinking (*Anthemis cotula*). This is reasonably common in the North Island and parts of the South Island. It smells and tastes quite different from the culinary chamomile and is an occasional contaminant in herbal teas, which can irritate the skin and mucous membranes (Burrows).

Charlock (*Sinapis arvensis = Mutarda = Rhamphospermum*). This mustard relative is a native of Europe, North Africa and SW Asia, where the young leaves and flower buds are widely used as food – usually cooked; however, it is not common here.

Chervil (*Anthriscus cerefolium*) – a parsley-like plant whose leaves are used in Europe to flavour salads and soups; however, the plant is not yet common in the wild here. It should not be confused with the highly poisonous **hemlock** (page 44).

Chickweed, Mouse-ear (*Cerastium* species). These velvety-leaved chickweeds are rarely used as food; however, the young shoots and leaves of *C. glomeratum* have been used as a vegetable in parts of Uttarakhand, North India, and those of *C. fontanum* as a vegetable (and as forage) in rural Pakistan.

Cocksfoot (*Dactylis glomerata*) – a very common grass here whose inner stalk is occasionally eaten as a snack in Belarus, Hungary and Spain.

Columbine (*Aquilegia vulgaris*) – a purple-flowered garden plant that is common in the wild. In northern Spain and Belarus these flowers are sucked for their nectar, but the plant itself is potentially poisonous (Murray).

Comfrey (*Symphytum officinale*) – a native of Europe, where the leaves (and to a lesser extent the roots) were formerly used as a vegetable. Both are now known to contain toxic pyrrolizidine alkaloids; however, neither is likely to lead to poisoning unless eaten regularly over long periods (Murray) or by children, who are particularly vulnerable (WHO). Alkaloid concentrations are highest in the roots (1000–8000 ppm); concentrations in the leaves can (under some conditions) be less than 100 ppm (Burrows). Of greater concern is the frequency with which comfrey leaves have been confused with those of the highly poisonous **foxglove** (Wu) (page 162).

Cotoneaster (*Cotoneaster* species). No traditional food use is recorded for the common, larger-leaved cotoneasters; however, members of tribal farming communities from Ladakh to northern Nepal eat the ripe fruit of the much rarer **small-leaved cotoneaster** (*C. microphyllus*) raw as a snack or preserved as jam and jelly. Although these are known to contain prunasin and amygdalin, the content is not high enough to be of concern (Kisel).

Couch Grass (*Elytrigia repens*). The rhizomes of this very common weedy grass have been used in Sweden, Slovakia and Poland as famine food.

Cow Parsley (*Anthriscus sylvestris*) – a parsley-like plant whose leaves are sometimes eaten in

Europe. It has become reasonably common around Christchurch, but is easily confused with the highly poisonous **hemlock** (page 44).

Crowfoot Grass (*Eleusine indica*) is reasonably common here. In times of famine the small seeds have been used in India, Pakistan and parts of Africa, cooked whole or ground into a flour. In Indonesia the young seedlings are eaten raw or cooked as a side dish with rice.

Daisy, Marguerite (*Argyranthemum frutescens*), a common wild daisy, whose flowers are sometimes eaten even though they can be very bitter.

Dahlia (*Dahlia pinnata*) is a native of Mexico, where it was an important root crop in pre-Columbian times, when it served as an emergency food in case of failure of the maize crop. In parts of Mexico cooked dahlia tubers remain a popular food, sold by street vendors in the larger cities. If they are to be eaten raw they are harvested in spring, but if destined for baking or storage the tubers should be gathered at the end of the growing season – at other times they are apt to taste too bitter. At their best they contain around 10% inulin, also citric and malic acids (Whitley). In Mexico the flower petals, too, evidently have a long history of traditional culinary use (Lara-Cortés). In New Zealand the common garden dahlia, which is a hybrid (*Dahlia coccinea* × *D. pinnata*), is found in the wild largely as a garden discard.

Evening Primrose (*Oenothera* species) – plants with large yellow flowers, many of which open in the evening. Although the Cherokee of North America are known to have cooked the leaves of *O. biennis* as greens and boiled its roots as potatoes, very little is known regarding the edibility of the two common species here: *O. glazioviana* (a large-flowered hybrid) or its fragrant cousin that thrives in sand (*O. stricta*).

Feverfew (*Tanacetum parthenium*) – a common daisy-like plant. Its essential oil is deemed safe in small doses, but possibly not so in large doses (Lechkova).

Fir, Douglas (*Pseudotsuga menziesii*). This native of western North America is common in places here. Its crushed foliage smells of orange and its sweet gum was formerly chewed by the indigenous inhabitants of the region.

Fir, Giant (*Abies grandis*). A much less common tree in New Zealand than Douglas fir, this is another native of western North America, where its gum was likewise formerly chewed by the indigenous inhabitants of British Columbia.

Firethorn, Orange (*Pyracantha angustifolia*) – a common hedging plant that is readily spread by birds. A native of China, where the pectin-rich fruit is made into jam and liqueur. Although rich in vitamin C, sugar, potassium, calcium, iron, zinc and copper (Wang 2018), the seeds may contain small quantities of hydrogen cyanide so should not be eaten (Chari).

Fireweed, Brazilian (*Erechtites valerianifolius*) – a reasonably common purple-flowered weed north of Hamilton. The young tops are consumed as a leafy vegetable in Indonesia, Malaysia and Assam, either raw or steamed with rice, and the leaves recommended in Brazil either raw in salads, sautéed or in soups, omelettes and other dishes. However, the plant is known to store toxic pyrrolizidine alkaloids (Mukherjee).

Flax (*Linum* species). These delicate plants are quite unrelated to **harakeke**, the native **New Zealand flax** (*Phormium tenax*), despite both being excellent sources of fibre. The best known of them, the so-called **common flax** or **linseed** (*L. usitatissimum*), which provides edible 'flax seed', linseed oil, and the fibre from which linen is made, is not common in New Zealand. Here, the three common species are **rauhuia** (the native **New Zealand linen flax**, *L. monogynum*), **pale flax** (*L. bienne*) and **purging flax** (*L. catharticum*), none of which have traditional uses as food.

Fleabane (*Conyza* or *Erigeron* species). The common fleabanes here are *E. bonariensis*, *E. canadensis* and *E. sumatrensis*, all of which are native to the Americas. Although a minor food use is recorded for the **Canadian fleabane** (*E. canadensis*) by the Miwok of northern California, this plant has caused intoxication in lambs and cattle (Burrows); its traditional use is primarily medicinal.

Forget-me-not (*Myosotis* species) – common blue-flowered garden plants in the borage family that spread freely, especially in shady places. In Italy the new shoots and leaves are included in some traditional cooked spring herb mixes: however, the plant is potentially toxic to the liver due to pyrrolizidine alkaloids, which occur in virtually every species of this family (Kristanc).

Fuchsia, Hardy (*Fuchsia magellanica*) – a common garden plant found in scattered localities. In Chile and Argentina its berries are a traditional source of food.

Fumitory (*Fumaria* species) – pink-flowered herbs of the poppy family. The leaves of *F. officinalis* have been eaten raw or cooked in Turkey, but the really common species here is **scrambling fumitory** (*F. muralis*) for which no ethnographic evidence of edibility is found. There is also some evidence that the genus is mildly toxic (Burrows).

Ginger, Wild (*Hedychium* species). **Kahili ginger** (*H. gardnerianum*) is a very widespread and troublesome weed in the North Island. This and **yellow ginger** (*H. flavescens*) are both ornamental gingers, neither of which has any culinary use.

Goat's Rue (*Galega officinalis*) – a vetch-like plant common between Palmerston North and Wellington. The young shoots have been used as a vegetable in England, Bosnia, Croatia and Turkey, but older plants are mildly toxic (Burrows).

Grasses. Individual grasses listed by name elsewhere in this appendix include: barnyard grass, cocksfoot, couch grass, crowfoot grass, Himalayan fairy grass, Indian doab, Kentucky bluegrass, Manchurian wild rice, meadow foxtail, oats, tall oat grass, palm grass, quaking grass, ratstail, rough bristle grass, summer grass, sweet grasses.

Ground Ivy (*Glechoma hederacea*) – a purplish-flowered member of the mint family, commonly grown as groundcover but also wild. In Eastern Europe the leaves have been used as flavouring, but they are toxic in large quantities and may also stimulate the uterus to contract and induce abortion (Simkova); toxin unknown, possibly glechomanolide or sapogenin (Burrows).

Groundsels (*Senecio* species). **Common groundsel** (*S. vulgaris*) is a very common member of the daisy family, with small yellow flowers. In the Czech Republic and throughout much of Turkey its leaves are boiled and eaten, which is inadvisable as the plant is known to contain toxic pyrrolizidine alkaloids (Burrows). A very common species on beaches is **purple groundsel** (*S. elegans*), with daisy-like flowers with pink-purple petals and a yellow centre. Although its leaves have reportedly been used as spinach in South Africa, *Senecio* in general are known to contain toxic pyrrolizidine alkaloids (Burrows).

Hawkweed, Mouse-ear (*Pilosella officinarum*) – a common dandelion-like plant in high country; a native of Europe, where the plant's traditional use is primarily medicinal – as a diuretic.

Hawthorn, Indian (*Rhaphiolepis indica*). A native of SE Asia, this shrub is common in the northern North Island – both planted and wild. In southern China the purplish-black fruit is gathered by wood collectors and eaten cooked, but they are too sour and astringent to eat raw.

Hemp (*Cannabis sativa*). Found wild in New Zealand in scattered localities, but not common. Three strains reflect three uses of the plant: (1) fibre, (2) seeds for food and oil, and (3) resin production for hallucinogenic, sedative, analgesic or anti-inflammatory purposes. Most wild plants are likely to be the latter and hence unsuitable for food.

Henbit (*Lamium amplexicaule*). This reasonably common member of the mint family is a native of Eurasia and North Africa. In Croatia, Turkey, Pakistan, North India and Korea the leaves are reportedly used as a vegetable; however, neurological effects have been noted in sheep; toxicant unknown (Burrows).

Herb Robert (*Geranium robertianum*) – a very common pink-flowered plant that is native to much of the Northern Hemisphere, where it has not been recorded as a traditional food, probably due to the plant's unpleasant taste and smell.

Himalayan Balsam (*Impatiens glandulifera*) – a tall pink-flowered garden escape common in wet areas, and native to the Himalayas where the seeds are eaten raw; however, the flowers, crushed leaves and stems contain the naphthoquinone lawsone (naphthalenic acid), which may cause mild to moderate irritation of the digestive tract (Burrows). The plant is also a known hyperaccumulator of cadmium (Coakley).

Himalayan Fairy Grass (*Miscanthus nepalensis*) – very conspicuous along roadsides in northern North Island. In the Darjeeling region of the Himalayas the immature flower spikes are chewed by the Nepalese while trekking.

Holly (*Ilex aquifolium*) – very common shrub throughout New Zealand. In Albania the dried leaves have been used as herbal tea, but the whole plant, including the leaves, contains an array of potential toxins; the main risk, though, is to children eating the fruit (Burrows).

Honey Locust (*Gleditsia triacanthos*) – a thorny deciduous tree, reasonably common from Christchurch north. It bears creamish pea-like flowers and large pods 15–20 cm long. North American Cherokee ate the sweet raw pulp between the seeds and also made a drink from this.

Horse Chestnut (*Aesculus hippocastanum* pages 26, 163) – a deciduous tree of the Balkans, widely planted here and occasionally wild. The leaves, flowers and seeds all contain the toxic glycoside esculin (Hardin), but in times of famine in the Czech Republic the dried seeds were ground into flour, and in Estonia were traditionally used as a coffee substitute and in jam. Preparation generally involved long leaching of the seeds in water or with wood ash, or slow roasting to remove harsh and bitter flavours and reduce the toxicity (Foca). None of this is recommended, though, as fatalities from the nuts are not unknown (Connor); or, more commonly, mild to moderate neurological symptoms (Burrows). Not to be confused with **sweet chestnut** – page 26.

Horseweed – see **Fleabane**

Hydrangea (*Hydrangea macrophylla*). The dried fermented leaves of var. *thunbergii* are used in Japan to produce a sweet tea, amacha, that is traditionally consumed at Hanamatsuri, a religious festival celebrating the birth of the Buddha. The sweet component is phyllodulcin, which is 600–800 times as sweet as sucrose (Suzuki). However, consumption of *Hydrangea* leaves and buds can occasionally cause digestive tract disturbance (Burrows).

Hydrocotyle, or **marsh pennywort** (*Hydrocotyle umbellata*) – an aquatic plant of the Americas (from Minnesota to Chile), recently introduced to Asia as an aquarium plant and spreading in New Zealand since 2005, mostly around Auckland. There is only very limited ethnographic evidence of its traditional use as greens – by the Cahuilla people of southern California.

Ice-cream Bean (*Inga* species). With more than 280 species of *Inga* trees and shrubs in Central and South America, there may be several kinds in New Zealand, where trees have been self-seeding in warmer areas since 2007. In South America the sweet, white cottony pulp of the ripe large seedpod is popular as a snack. The seeds themselves are usually spat out.

Indian Doab (*Cynodon dactylon*) – a common grass here. Rhizomes have been collected in winter in Spain as a famine food, ground into flour to make bread, or sometimes eaten raw as a snack.

Ivy-leaved Toadflax (*Cymbalaria muralis*) – a common, small-leaved trailing plant on walls. Pierpoint Johnson (1862) writes that this plant is 'eaten in southern Europe as a salad, and is a good anti-scorbutic; its taste is not unlike that of cress'. Although Johnson is correct about the plant being native to southern Europe, I find no independent confirmation of any traditional culinary use. I also find Johnson's claim hard to reconcile with my own experience: the leaves are too acrid to be of use in salads, even when young.

Jasmine (*Jasminum* species). In China the petals of **sambac jasmine** (*Jasminum sambac*) are briefly added to tea to add fragrance, then sifted out before packing in airtight boxes. However, sambac jasmine is not found in New Zealand, and the common wild species here (*J. polyanthum*) is not known to have a comparable traditional use.

Jellybeans (*Disphyma clavellatum*) – a coastal ice plant found in the southern South Island and technically native as it is understood to be a recent self-introduction to New Zealand from Australia. No traditional use is recorded.

Kentucky Bluegrass (*Poa pratensis*). In Belarus and Hungary the stems and young shoots of this grass are chewed by children.

Lettuce, Acrid (*Lactuca virosa*) – a native of Europe and NW Africa, similar to the **prickly lettuce** (*L. serriola*, page 58) but with upper leaves horizontal, dark red midribs and stem. Although the young leaves have been eaten in salads, they are generally too bitter and have mildly sedative properties. Eaten to excess the plant can even be poisonous (Besharat, Burrows, De Smet).

Lime or **Linden** (*Tilia cordata*) – a deciduous tree from Europe, where the flowers, delicate leaves and inner bark are eaten fresh. In Russia the flowers are used for flavouring wine, liquor, cognac and as a popular herbal tea. Though fairly common in New Zealand, trees are less common in the wild.

Linaria, Purple (*Linaria purpurea*, also known as **purple toadflax**) – very common purple-flowered plant native to Italy, where no food use is recorded. Besides tasting acrid, there is a potential risk from quinazoline alkaloids and flavonoid glycosides (Burrows). Not recommended.

Linseed – see **Flax**

Liquidambar (*Liquidambar styraciflua*). Trees found in New Zealand are mostly planted, occasionally wild. This deciduous tree is a native of the Americas. The hardened gum was used by Cherokee as a chewing gum.

Lobelia (*Lobelia erinus*) – a scrambling, blue-flowered garden escape native to South Africa, where the leaves are reportedly used as a pot-herb. Although no adverse reaction is reported for this species, all parts of other species of *Lobelia* are known to contain toxic substances (Murray).

Loosestrife (*Lythrum* species). In the Calabria region of Italy the young shoots of **purple loosestrife** (*L. salicaria*) are served as a boiled vegetable or in salads; older leaves taste too bitter. However, the more common species in New Zealand is **hyssop loosestrife** (*L. hyssopifolia*), which has caused poisoning in sheep (Lancaster).

Lupins (*Lupinus* species). Although lupins have been valued since ancient times for fodder, food and as soil-builders, the seeds of many are toxic. In New Zealand, by far the most common wild ones are two American species (neither of which are known to have been traditionally used as food there): the yellow-flowered **tree lupin** (*L. arboreus*), in which the toxic alkaloids are known to be unpredictable, with large variations (Adler); and the **Russell lupin** (*L. polyphyllus*) whose seeds are considered non-edible due to poisoning in animals and people (Burrows, Pilegaard). The species most commonly used as a green manure is **blue lupin** (*L. angustifolius*), which occurs wild here only rarely; it is from the Mediterranean, where its domestication was initiated in the early 20th century, leading to the development of the first fully domesticated cultivar with low alkaloid content (Hane).

Maidenhair Tree (*Ginkgo biloba*) – commonly planted and found wild here only rarely. This is a native of China, where the peeled nuts are cooked and eaten – but in moderation only, due to the toxin 4-O-methylpyridoxine (Burrows). Local Chinese can be seen eagerly gathering the fallen fruits in Auckland's Cornwall Park.

Male Fern (*Dryopteris filix-mas*) – a very common Northern Hemisphere fern. Its rhizome is eaten as mush or bread in Bosnia, and the young shoots are used as a vegetable in North India; however, the plant is known to contain thiaminase, an enzyme that destroys vitamin B1 (thiamine). Cooking may render the thiaminase inactive enough to prevent thiamine deficiency (Kumar 2010), but caution is nevertheless advised.

Mallow, Californian (*Malva assurgentiflora*) is not particularly common in New Zealand. Although no traditional use as human food is recorded in its native region of California, the leaves and twigs are eaten by sheep and cattle.

Mallow, Creeping (*Modiola caroliniana*). This is a very common South American red-flowered mallow with no known food use. Consumption in large quantities by goats, cattle and sheep has resulted in neurological disease. Toxin unknown (Burrows).

Manchurian Wild Rice (*Zizania latifolia*). The very young shoots of this giant aquatic grass are eaten as a vegetable in China, Japan and Korea. It is not common in New Zealand, where the plant is known for blocking drains around Dargaville and is declared a pest.

Marram Grass (*Calamagrostis arenaria = Ammophila*) – a common plant of sand dunes here. An English translation of the *Flora of the USSR* claims that 'the rhizomes are used for food in Iceland', but I find no independent confirmation of this or any other use by humans as food; only for thatch, basket making, sand-dune stabilisation and as fodder for grazing animals.

Mayten (*Maytenus boaria*) – a South American evergreen tree with fairly inconspicuous greenish flowers and small red fruit, that has recently become a common pest in native bush and scrub. It was used medicinally in South America by the Mapuche. Although there is no evidence that the seeds were traditionally eaten, European colonists did extract an oil from them, similar to linseed oil, that is rich in omega-6 and omega-9 fatty acids (Ginocchio).

Meadow Foxtail (*Alopecurus pratensis*). The stem of this not uncommon Eurasian grass is chewed in Hungary.

Medick, Black (*Medicago lupulina*) – a yellow-flowered native of North Africa and Eurasia that is now common here. In China the young stems and leaves are reputedly eaten fresh or stir-fried; however, experimental evidence reveals that saponins are present in sufficiently high concentrations to be toxic to monogastric animals, including humans (Górski). Its raw seeds should not constitute a major part of the diet, due to the presence of canavanine (Bell).

Mercury (*Mercurialis annua*) – an uncommon Mediterranean native with inconspicuous flowers. Despite records from Turkey, Bosnia, France, Germany and Italy of the traditional use of cooked leaves as a vegetable or in soups, plants remain toxic even when boiled. Toxins unknown (Burrows).

Monkey Musk (*Erythranthe guttata = Mimulus guttatus*) – a common, yellow-flowered streamside plant. This is a native of western North America, where the leaves were occasionally eaten, both raw and cooked, by the indigenous peoples of northern California.

Mullein, Woolly (*Verbascum thapsus*) – a tall, yellow-flowered native of Europe and western Asia that is common in New Zealand in stony ground. A decoction or infusion of the flowers, and to a lesser extent of the leaves, is traditionally used as a medicine after the irritating hairs have been first strained out with muslin. Due to the elusive nature of these branched hairs, consumption in large quantities is inadvisable (Turker).

Mustard, Indian (*Brassica juncea*) – a popular edible green from Asia, also known as **mizuna** or **mustard lettuce**. Although this self-seeds readily here, it is rarely found far from gardens. The plant is a strong accumulator of toxic heavy metals, including cadmium, lead and mercury, so take special care to avoid collecting from polluted sites (Kumar 2011).

Navelwort (*Umbilicus rupestris*, **dandy** or **wall pennywort**). This small, fleshy plant with greenish flowers is not common except in rock walls around Wellington and Christchurch. It is a native of Western Europe where reports of its traditional use as food are sparse; however, the leaves were eaten raw by the Romans and still are used in Sicily. Toxicological analysis confirms that the leaves are safe to eat either raw or cooked (Iyda).

Norfolk Island Pine – see **Araucaria**

Oat Grass, Tall (*Arrhenatherum elatius*) – a common grass from the Northern Hemisphere. In Hungary the stem is chewed by children.

Oats (*Avena* species). In southern China the seeds of **wild oat** (*A. fatua*) are collected as food, dried, smashed and fried. This and the **common oat** (*A. sativa*) of cultivation both grow wild in New Zealand.

Onion Grass (*Romulea rosea*, or **rosy sandcrocus**) – a small and reasonably common pink-flowered garden escape. Although corms of plants in this family (Iridaceae) are generally toxic, the unripe seed capsules of this grass-like plant are evidently popular among the Khoe-San children of South Africa.

Palm Grass (*Setaria palmifolia*) – a tall Asian grass with palm-like leaves, domesticated in the islands of New Guinea for its thickened young shoots and stem hearts, which serve as a vegetable. Grown in New Zealand as an ornamental plant but fairly common now in the wild, mostly north of Hamilton.

Parsley Piert (*Aphanes arvensis = Alchemilla*) – a low, parsley-like member of the rose family, which herbalist Nicholas Culpeper recommended in 1653 as 'a very good sallad herb [and] very wholesome'; however, its use does not seem to have caught on in Europe or elsewhere, most likely because of the plant's astringent taste.

Parsnip, Wild (*Pastinaca sativa*). Although the roots of wild specimens are generally too stringy to be worth eating, there are a few records from Europe of these being gathered for use in soups. During the siege of Sarajevo the root and young shoots were collected for use as a vegetable.

Pea, Everlasting (*Lathyrus latifolius*) – a climbing plant with purplish-pink flowers. The seeds of this common roadside species are toxic, particularly so with excessive and prolonged consumption (Burrows) causing lathyrism, and the poison is not destroyed by heat. Young shoots, on the other hand, are eaten as a cooked vegetable in Bosnia and Herzegovina.

Pea, Sweet (*Lathyrus odoratus*) – an attractive garden climber that occasionally grows wild. The seeds are toxic in large quantities (Murray) causing lathyrism, and the poison is not destroyed by heat. Nevertheless, in Sicily these are boiled and eaten – presumably only in small quantities. In Italy and Korea the bitter-tasting flowers are also eaten.

Pea, Tangier (*Lathyrus tingitanus*). This is another common climber here. Its seeds are likewise understood to be toxic, having caused skeletal changes in rats that are typical of lathyrism (Lewis 1948).

Periwinkle (*Vinca major*) – a native of the Mediterranean region. Although the *Cambridge World History of Food* states that the seeds of this common purple-flowered groundcover have 'served humans as food, especially during times of hardship', I find no corroborating ethnographic evidence for this. The plant is also known to contain numerous alkaloids, and the genus is noted for causing digestive disturbance and being neurotoxic (Burrows).

Pineapple Weed – see **Chamomile, Rayless**

Pokeweed (*Phytolacca americana*) – not to be confused with the far more common **inkweed** (page 163). This is a native of North America, where the leaves have been cooked as a pot-herb and the berries used to make jellies; however, as we now know, cooking does not reliably destroy the toxins (De Smet).

Poplar (*Populus* species) – deciduous trees of the Northern Hemisphere. In spring, indigenous inhabitants of North America scraped the edible tissue from inside the bark of **necklace poplar** (*P. deltoides*), cooked this or dried it and pounded it into flour. Similar uses of poplar cambium are recorded from Europe.

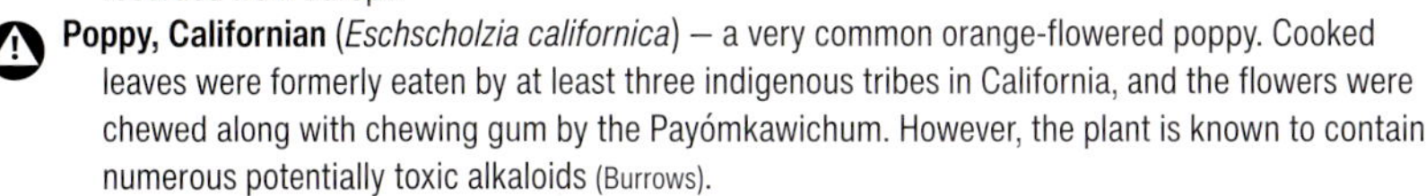

Poppy, Californian (*Eschscholzia californica*) – a very common orange-flowered poppy. Cooked leaves were formerly eaten by at least three indigenous tribes in California, and the flowers were chewed along with chewing gum by the Payómkawichum. However, the plant is known to contain numerous potentially toxic alkaloids (Burrows).

Poppy, Field (*Papaver rhoeas*). In its native Mediterranean region the young leaves and shoots, flower petals and seeds are traditionally eaten. This is not without risk, though: in Turkey, at least, this practice has led to several people being hospitalised with seizures, confusion, etc., suggesting that this plant or a local subspecies of it is problematic (Günaydın, Koçak).

Poppy, Long-headed (*Papaver dubium*). Across much of Turkey the young shoots and leaves of this Eurasian poppy are eaten, both raw and cooked. As the latex of *Papaver* in general can be mildly toxic, caution is advised (Murray).

Poppy, Opium (*Papaver somniferum*). Seeds of this Eurasian poppy are commonly sprinkled on breads and cakes, etc. However, the dried sap of the same plant is the source of opium (a narcotic drug), which can occasionally contaminate the surface of the seeds during harvesting, especially if the capsule happens to get crushed during the extraction process (Burrows).

Purpletop (*Verbena bonariensis* & *V. incompta*). These common, almost identical purple-flowered plants are both native to South America, where no traditional food use is recorded.

Quaking Grass, Large (*Briza maxima*) – a common and attractive coastal plant from southern Europe. In Bosnia and Herzegovina, the seeds are cooked to make porridge and bread. In Spain, the tender spikelets, gathered in spring, are eaten raw as a snack.

Queen of the Night (*Cestrum nocturnum*) – an evergreen woody shrub with cream flowers that emit a strong scent at night. The plant has proven toxic to livestock; however, the cooked leaves are consumed in Mexico (the plant's native region), where the boiled water is discarded.

Rape (*Brassica napus*, also known as **oilseed rape**) – both wild and cultivated – is a native of Europe, where the leaves and young tender leafy shoots are eaten as a vegetable.

Ratstail (*Sporobolus africanus*) – a reasonably common grass here. In times of famine in Ethiopia, its seeds are ground and baked as bread.

Rough Bristle Grass (*Setaria verticillata*). The small seeds of this grass are gathered as food in Africa and India, but need to be parched to remove the bristly husk.

Saltwort (*Salsola kali*) – a sprawling succulent plant of shingle, sand and gravel, often near beaches. In Italy, the young shoots are boiled in traditional vegetable mixtures. However, the plant is high in oxalates, and is not common here.

Scarlet Pimpernel (*Lysimachia arvensis* = *Anagallis*) – a very common red-flowered garden weed. In Turkey the leaves are cooked and eaten. However, the plant contains a triterpenoid saponin that has proven toxic to mice. In humans, there may be headache, trembling and temporary rheumatic pains (Burrows).

Seaweeds, Introduced – see **Wakame**. (Native species are covered in *A Field Guide to the Native Edible Plants of New Zealand.*)

Silk Tree (*Albizia julibrissin*) – a pink-flowered deciduous tree. The wattle-like leaves are recommended as fodder for livestock. According to the *Chinese Materia Medica* they have also served in China as human food; however, even those few small young leaves I have eaten – both raw and thoroughly cooked – leave an unpleasantly acrid aftertaste. The seeds are known to be toxic (Burrows).

Silverweed (*Argentina* species = *Potentilla*). The so-called **common silverweed** (*A. anserina*) is a very rare and recent yellow-flowered arrival from the Northern Hemisphere, whose roots were previously cultivated as a food crop. No traditional culinary use is known for the far more common endemic **New Zealand silverweed** (*A. anserinoides*).

Snapdragon (*Antirrhinum majus*) – a native of SW Europe, widely cultivated as an ornamental plant and now common wild here in New Zealand. From the early 19th century it was cultivated in Russia and Iran for the production of an edible oil from its seeds, which recent analysis shows to be superior in antioxidant content (and in several other respects) to extra virgin olive oil (Ramadan).

Snowflake (*Leucojum aestivum*). In Bosnia and Croatia the cooked bulbs of this plant have been eaten, but probably only as a last resort as it contains several toxic alkaloids: lycorine, lycorenine and galanthamine (Burrows).

Spruce, Sitka (*Picea* species). A native of western North America, where several indigenous tribes collected the gum for chewing. Members of the Kitasoo cooked the inner bark, too, and sometimes dried it for later use as food.

St John's Wort (*Hypericum perforatum*) – a very common weed with yellow flowers, native to Eurasia and North Africa. In Europe the flowers have long been used to brew a herbal tea (often to ease symptoms of depression); however, adverse effects have occasionally resulted from interactions with other drugs (Burrows).

St Paul's Wort, Common (*Sigesbeckia orientalis*) – a yellow-flowered weed of the daisy family, occasionally found in the northern North Island. According to the 16th-century *Chinese Materia Medica* the leaves have been used 'as food after boiling, which removes the bad odor and taste and produces a mucilaginous pot-herb'. Chemical analysis suggests that this plant should be used only in moderation (Nwaogu).

Stock, Hoary (*Matthiola incana*) – a common garden plant with pink-purple flowers, now common on coastal cliffs and banks. This member of the cabbage family is native to a small region – from Spain to Greece – where the seedpods have reportedly been eaten in times of famine.

Stonecrop (*Sedum acre*) – a very common mat-like, yellow-flowered succulent, native to Europe, Greenland and North Africa. Its acrid stems and leaves have occasionally been used in salads or as a spice; however, these contain the piperidine alkaloids sediene and sediendione, which may potentially cause birth defects (Burrows). Also appropriately known as **biting stonecrop**.

Summer Grass (*Digitaria sanguinalis*) – a common grass here from Eurasia. In Europe, from eastern Germany to Ukraine, the seeds are sometimes still ground into flour.

Sweet Grass, Floating (*Glyceria fluitans*) – a common grass of ditches, riverbanks and ponds. In Europe its seeds were used as food in prehistoric times, a use that continued in Belarus at least until the late 1940s.

Sweet Grass, Reed (*Glyceria maxima*) – a common grass of swamps, pools, edges of slow-flowing streams. Its seeds are small, but in times of famine in Hungary they have been ground into flour.

Sweet Pea – see **Pea**

Tansy (*Tanacetum vulgare*). Widely cultivated and occasionally wild. Young leaves and flowers are occasionally eaten raw or cooked in Europe; however, an essential oil in them may contain the neurotoxic thujone (De Smet) and there are several instances of fatal overdoses of the tea or oil (Burrows).

Tradescantia (*Tradescantia* species) are native to North and South America, where traditional food use is recorded for some species. Consumption of others has resulted in reddened eyes, mouth, lips and tongue, with excess salivation (Burrows). Our common local species (**wandering Willie**, *T. fluminensis*) is used in rural areas of SE Brazil as forage for rabbits and in Argentina as a medicinal plant. Several people have experimented with eating it raw and cooked and have reported no ill effects (Alves); however, it commonly causes allergic reactions on the skin of dogs and occasionally in people (Dugdale).

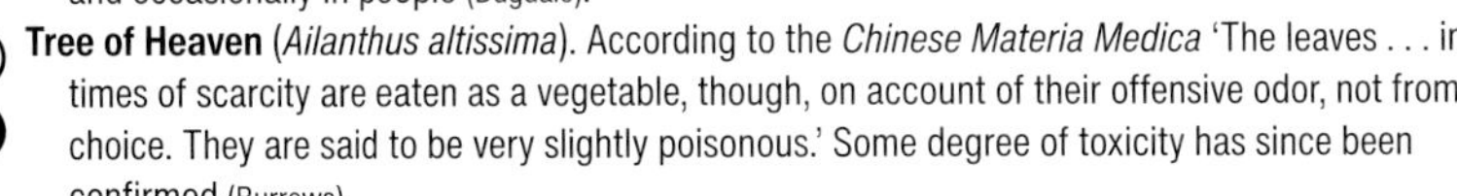

Tree of Heaven (*Ailanthus altissima*). According to the *Chinese Materia Medica* 'The leaves . . . in times of scarcity are eaten as a vegetable, though, on account of their offensive odor, not from choice. They are said to be very slightly poisonous.' Some degree of toxicity has since been confirmed (Burrows).

Tutsan (*Hypericum androsaemum*, **shrubby St John's wort**) – a common yellow-flowered shrub. The attractive red to black berries are not known to be toxic, but are certainly unpalatable.

Vervain (*Verbena officinalis*) – a reasonably common tall, mauve-flowered plant with a square stem. Although young leaves are sometimes parboiled as a vegetable and the flowering top brewed as a herbal tea, evidence suggests that its use during pregnancy is not safe (Fateh).

Vetch (*Vicia sativa*) – a very common sprawling, purple-flowered member of the pea family. Untreated seeds cannot be considered suitable for human consumption due to high levels of β-cyanoalanine and its γ-glutamyl derivative (Tate, Connor). While soaking, cooking and discarding the cooking water does reduce the toxins, it does not eliminate them (Tate). In the Czech Republic, Pakistan and China its young leaves are cooked and eaten as a vegetable.

Wakame Seaweed (*Undaria pinnatifida*). This large, golden-brown, crinkly and somewhat slimy seaweed is a native of NE Asia and Russia. In Japan it is a traditional food. Some time before 1987 it was accidentally introduced to New Zealand, where it has become a pest.

Water Lily (*Nymphaea alba*). This white-flowered water lily is a native of Europe and NW Africa to the Himalayas, where the rhizomes have been cooked as a vegetable. However, they contain an alkaloid (nupharin), rendering them mildly poisonous (Irvine).

Wattle, Brush (*Paraserianthes lophantha = Albizia = Acacia*) – a very common evergreen shrub or small tree with feathery leaves and cream-coloured, brush-like flowers. Seeds are a traditional food of Aboriginal Australians (Brand-Miller, pers comm 2023), and are exceedingly rich in protein, dietary fibre, potassium, magnesium, calcium, iron, zinc and copper, low in sodium, and a good source of energy and carbohydrate (Brand 1985). They do, however, contain 1–2% djenkolic acid (Connor), a compound that can be reduced to safe levels by roasting (Boughton).

Wattles (*Acacia* species). In recent times, wattle flowers have been cooked and eaten. This is not recorded as a traditional use among Aboriginal Australians, who did however consume the rather tasteless wattle gum, a substance that was later collected by early European settlers as a source of gum arabic, used in confectionery, etc. Examples commonly found in New Zealand include **silver wattle**, **black wattle** and **green wattle** (*A. dealbata*, *A. mearnsii* and *A. decurrens*, all also sometimes known as '**mimosa**'), whose gum can be mixed with water and sweetened to make a jelly.

Willow, White (*Salix alba*), a medium to large deciduous tree common along riverbanks and around ponds. Although the bitter-tasting inner bark has been dried and powdered in northern Europe in times of famine for making bread, it contains salicylates and an unusually large – and potentially harmful – amount of tannin (8–20%) (Highfield).

Willowherb (*Epilobium* species). Herbs with small, four-petalled pink flowers. The leaves of some have been used overseas as a vegetable; however, little is known concerning the most common introduced species here (*E. ciliatum*).

Wonder Tree (*Idesia polycarpa*) – a deciduous tree from China and Japan commonly cultivated in the warmer north of New Zealand for its bright red berries, which provide colour throughout the winter. Also common wild. Several books (e.g. Sturtevant, Tanaka 1976, Kunkel, Mansfeld) and websites claim that the fruit is edible (raw or cooked). I tried one and found this claim hard – if not impossible – to reconcile with the fruit's intensely bitter, disagreeable taste, and with the lack of ethnographic evidence from either China or Japan. I was eventually able to trace the error back to 1867 when the tree was first introduced to the USA and Europe at the Paris Exhibition, where it was proudly billed as 'a new fruit tree'. The mix-up was naturally discovered, but the claim was by then already in print. History goes full circle, for the fruit (both pulp and seed) are nowadays being investigated as a source of biodiesel fuel, and a high-grade edible oil – once a process is developed for removing the bitter compounds. Subchronic toxicity tests provided the all-clear for this potential food use as recently as 2024 (Zeng).

Wood Sorrel (*Oxalis*). This name has been applied loosely here to the entire Oxalidaceae family; however, the original **wood sorrel** (*O. acetosella*) of temperate Eurasian woodlands and shady places is not known to be present in New Zealand.

Wormwood (*Artemisia absinthium*) – a tall herb with silvery foliage, native to temperate Eurasia and North Africa; cultivated here in New Zealand and occasionally wild. Across much of Europe the leaves and flowers are used, generally for making tea or liqueur, but also as a bitter seasoning. Slight toxicity in high doses, as noted by the World Health Organization (De Smet).

Woundworts (*Stachys* species) are members of the mint family. The commonest species here is **hedge woundwort** (*S. sylvatica*), whose leaves have a strong and unpleasant smell and taste with no recorded traditional culinary use, although an infusion of leaves is used medicinally in Iran, Turkey, Serbia, Italy and Kosovo (Gören, Tomou). A slightly less common relative (**staggerweed**, *S. arvensis*) is best known for causing neurological problems in sheep. The most innocuous species found in New Zealand is **marsh woundwort** (*S. palustris*), whose tubers are eaten in Europe; however, this is quite rare here.

Yellow Archangel (*Lamium galeobdolon*) – a very common, yellow-flowered member of the mint family. Although the flowers are reportedly sucked for nectar in northern Spain, and the flowers themselves eaten as a snack by children in Hungary, these have been found to contain potentially toxic compounds (Egebjerg).

Yew (*Taxus baccata*) – an evergreen tree planted here and commonly wild, especially in the South Island. A native of North Africa and Europe, where the red part of the fruit (aril) is sometimes eaten; however, the seeds (and leaves) contain toxic taxines. If the seed is chewed and swallowed in quantity, the outcome can even be fatal (Burrows, Murray).

Yucca (*Yucca* species), all of which are native to North and Central America, where the indigenous inhabitants ate the flowers and fruit of several kinds.

POISONOUS PLANTS

In the event of a suspected poisoning, the National Poisons Centre advice is to quickly remove any remaining plant material and rinse the mouth; do not try to make the person vomit or give food or liquid (unless advised to). If practicable, take a sample of the plant and phone the **Poisons Centre** on **0800 764 766** (24 hours a day, 7 days a week) for further specific information. That said, in New Zealand, cases of serious poisoning are rare (Slaughter).

Agapanthus (*Agapanthus* species) – sticky acrid sap irritating to the mouth, eyes and skin (Anywar); and rhizomes purgative (Slaughter).

Apple of Sodom (*Solanum linnaeanum*), which is common north of Hamilton – fruits taste awful and are poisonous.

Arum Lilies (*Arum italicum* and *Zantedeschia aethiopica*) – see page 21.

Bittersweet (*Solanum dulcamara*), which is more common in the South Island – all parts poisonous, particularly unripe berries and leaves.

Castor Oil Plant (*Ricinus communis*), which is more common in the North Island. Seeds poisonous, but these are so hard to chew and swallow that most cases recover.

Cherry Laurel (*Prunus laurocerasus*) – all parts, particularly seeds and leaves, mildly toxic.

Daffodils (*Narcissus* species) – bulbs poisonous.

Daphne (*Daphne* species) – all parts toxic, but primarily the acrid-tasting fruit, which can be fatal to a child.

Deadly Nightshade (*Atropa bella-donna*). Although all parts are highly poisonous (three berries sufficient to kill a child), this plant is – at the time of writing – exceedingly rare in New Zealand and there are no known instances of poisoning here. Unlike **black nightshade** (page 126), the fruit is large (12 mm+) and black, and not borne in clusters.

Euphorbia (*Euphorbia* species) are toxic and the milky sap is potentially very irritating, especially to the eyes.

Foxglove (*Digitalis purpurea*) – all parts poisonous. Eaten in large quantities can lead to vomiting, purging, giddiness, confused vision, slow pulse, convulsions, and even death.

Hemlock (*Conium maculatum*) – all parts poisonous, particularly root and seeds; tastes and smells unpleasant.

Horse Chestnut (*Aesculus hippocastanum*) – children have been poisoned by eating the seeds, or making 'tea' from the leaves and twigs.

Hydrangea (*Hydrangea macrophylla*) – leaves and buds can cause digestive tract disturbance.

Inkweed (*Phytolacca octandra*) – the most toxic part is the roots; consumption of the bitter-tasting black berries is likely to cause diarrhoea. Not to be confused with the far rarer **pokeweed** (page 156).

Iris (*Iris* species) – bulb and rhizomes purgative.

Jerusalem Cherry (*Solanum pseudocapsicum*) – all parts are poisonous; however, the ripe fruit present the most risk due to their attractiveness to children.

Karaka (*Corynocarpus laevigatus*) – raw kernels are highly toxic, leading to convulsions and paralysis.

Kōwhai (*Sophora* species) – all parts poisonous, especially seeds.

Laburnum (*Laburnum anagyroides*) – all parts poisonous, including the flowers, but especially the seeds and unripe seedpods. Indeed, if eaten in large quantities, can be fatal.

Lily of the Valley (*Convallaria majalis*) – all parts toxic.

Melia (*Melia azedarach*), also known as **Persian lilac** or **Chinaberry** – leaves and fruit toxic.

Moth Plant (*Araujia sericifera*) – leaves and stems can cause digestive and neurological problems; fruit only mildly toxic.

Oleander (*Nerium oleander*) – tastes unpleasant; whole plant very toxic, including the leaves, bark, flowers and fruit. A small quantity of fresh leaf can kill an adult. Avoid chewing on twigs or using the branches as skewers.

Privet (*Ligustrum* species) – fruit mildly toxic, causing vomiting and diarrhoea.

Rhododendron, Azalea (*Rhododendron* species) – whole plant, including the nectar and honey made from it, moderately toxic, potentially causing severe digestive distress; leaves unpalatable and unlikely to be eaten.

with distinctive green spots on the petals

Snowflake (*Leucojum aestivum*) – bulbs (and to lesser extent the leaves) mildly toxic, with a similar poison profile to daffodils.

Thorn Apple (*Datura stramonium*) – all parts poisonous, particularly the seeds and leaves; just 4–5 grams can be fatal to a child.

Tutu (*Coriaria* species) – except for the juice of the petals, all parts (including seeds) very poisonous, potentially leading to convulsions and death.

Woolly Nightshade (*Solanum mauritianum*) – all parts mildly poisonous, especially unripe berries, which contain the same toxic alkaloids as green potatoes. Crushed leaves smell of kerosene.

Acknowledgements

'It takes a village to raise a child,' they say, and the same might well be said of many books; in this case, a global village that has involved every continent except Antarctica, where researchers have been painstakingly gathering generations of experience of local foraging practices and traditional methods of food preparation. The overall endeavour has engaged communities from diverse cultures sharing their ancestral knowledge with local researchers, who have been cataloguing and cross-checking these reports for accuracy. Meanwhile, chemists have been conducting nutritional, anti-nutritional and toxicity tests on the plants concerned. Closer to home, the relevance of all this to Aotearoa has involved many friends and experts – too many to name – who have helped over the 50 years that I have been learning about New Zealand's edible wild plants.

Photo credits

Plant photos by Andrew Crowe, except: harvesting prickly pear (Loula George); horsetail roots (Trevor James); *G. dissectum* (Mike Wilcox); and from Wikimedia Commons: amaranth candy (Julio R. Flores Andrade); *Alternanthera* flower (R. H. Mohlenbrock/ USDA-NRCS Plants Database); ripe *Monstera* fruit (B.navez); taro corms (Yongxinge); enset corm (IITA) and flower (Rillke); Darwin's barberry flowers (Lin linao) and fruit (Anne Burgess); birch trees (Speifensender); *Canna* rhizomes (Fpalli); pondweed flowers (JMK); *Silene* flower inset (Vinayaraj); spurrey plant (Kenraiz), flowers (Rasbak) and seeds (Stefan. lefnaer); chickweed flowers (Kaldari); *Arenaria* (Matt Lavin); mukhwas (Martyvis); gooseberry (Jonline); edible chrysanthemum (MathKnight-at-TAU); sunflower seeds (Kaldari); salsify flower (Stephen Lea) and root (Simon Speed); variegated thistle leaves (Valerie75) and flower (Zeynel Cebeci); day lily root (Gilles Ayotte); elderberry fruit (Agnieszka Kwiecień – Nova); polypody (H. Zell); horsetail plant (MPF); mulberry leaf (Ayda D) and fruit (DS28); storksbill (Lamiot); *Pelargonium* (Forest & Kim Starr); dolma (Benoît Prieur); *Arbutus* (Fabienkhan); buckwheat seeds (Soebe); cornbind plant (Olivier Pichard) and seeds (Stefan.lefnaer); wireweed (Dalgial); tiger lily bulbs (Walter Grassroot); *Anredera* in flower (John Tann); Basella plantation (Judgefloro); Turk's cap (William Farr); bladder hibiscus (Bogdan); sycamore seeds (Frank Vincentz) and tree (Matthieu Sontag); horehound (Eugene Zelenko); wild sage leaf (Harry Rose) and flowers (AnemoneProjectors); *Clerodendrum* (Katherine Wagner-Reiss); monkey apple (Melburnian); cider gum (Wouter Hagens); tree nettle (Steve Kerr); dwarf nettle (Alexis); mountain pawpaw tree (Michael Hermann and cropsforthefuture.org); passionflower (Dr. Avishai Teicher); banana passionfruit habit (Forest and Kim Starr); *Wisteria* seeds (Steve Hurst) and flowers (3268zauber); alfalfa sprouts (Thesupermat); stone pine seeds (Pacman); Salpichroa fruit (Gabriela Ruellan); purslane flower (Didier Descouens) and seed capsule (Loasa); sweet cherry (Andrikkos); cherry plum (An-d); yellow nut grass tubers (Tamorlan); sumac (Webaware); *Viola odorata* flowers (Fritz Geller-Grimm); Alisma flower (Bff); apple of Sodom (Forest & Kim Starr); bittersweet (H. Zell); daphne (Miya); deadly nightshade fruit (Kurt Stüber) and flower (Robert Flogaus-Faust); Jerusalem cherry (fir0002); laburnum seeds (Ercé) and flowers (Katrin Schneider); *Convallaria* (H. Zell).

From Adobe stock images (stock.adobe.com): Indian mallow (Manjunatha S/Wirestock), trailing abutilon (Ichuang), Turk's cap (Wagner Campelo), hollyhock (Michael), *Arum italicum* (lidian neeleman), *Zantedeschia aethiopica* (guentermanaus).

Selected references

To produce an accessible and portable field guide that can effectively double as an authoritative source book has naturally involved some compromise. For this reason, you will find no distracting inline referencing in the text for the traditional uses of the plants; instead you will find these listed geographically here by continent: Africa, Americas, Asia, Australasia, Europe and those with a global overview. Inline referencing – in highly abbreviated form by the surname of the first author only – is reserved for the more technical aspects of the book, directing you to the corresponding two sections of selected references: nutritional assessments (page 177) and toxicity studies (page 181).

Africa

Ethnobotanical studies consulted from Morocco, Libya and Egypt in the north, through Côte d'Ivoire, Cameroon, Ethiopia, Uganda, Kenya and Tanzania, to Namibia, Zimbabwe, Swaziland and South Africa.

Addis, G., et al. 2005. Ethnobotanical study of edible wild plants in some selected districts of Ethiopia. *Hum Ecol* 33.1: 83-118.

Agea, J. G., et al. 2011. Contribution of wild and semi-wild food plants to overall household diet in Bunyoro-Kitara Kingdom, Uganda. *Agric Res J* 6.4: 134-44.

Arkcoll, D. 1997. 'Some useful wild plants from Southern Africa'. *New Crops, New Products* 1: 171-76. RIRDC, Canberra.

Balemie, K. and Kebebew, F. 2006. Ethnobotanical study of wild edible plants in Derashe and Kucha Districts, South Ethiopia. *J Ethnobiol Ethnomed* 2.53: 1-9.

Daba, T. and Shigeta, M. 2016. Enset (*Ensete ventricosum*) production in Ethiopia: its nutritional and socio-cultural values. *Agric Food Sci Res* 3.2: 66-74.

De Vynck, J. C., et al. 2016. Indigenous edible plant use by contemporary Khoe-San descendants of South Africa's Cape South Coast. *S Afr J Bot* 102: 60-69.

Dweba, T. P. and Mearns, M. A. 2011. Conserving indigenous knowledge as the key to the current and future use of traditional vegetables. *Int J Inf Manage* 31.6: 564-71.

FAO. 1988. *Traditional Food Plants: A resource book for promoting the exploitation and consumption of food plants in arid, semi-arid, and sub-humid lands of Eastern Africa*. FAO, Rome.

Flyman, M. V. and Afolayan, A. J. 2006. The suitability of wild vegetables for alleviating human dietary deficiencies. *S Afr J Bot* 72.4: 492-97.

Forskål, P. 1775. *Flora Ægyptiaco-Arabica, sive Descriptiones Plantarum, quas per Ægyptum Inferiorem et Arabiam Felicem Detexit*. Hauniæ.

Fox, F. W. and Young, M. E. N. 1982. *Food from the Veld: Edible wild plants of southern Africa*. Delta, JBurg.

Goodman, S. M. and Hobbs, J. J. 1988. The ethnobotany of the Egyptian Eastern Desert: a comparison of common plant usage between two culturally distinct Bedouin groups. *J Ethnopharmacol* 23.1: 73-89.

Grubben, G. J. H. and Denton, O. A. (eds), 2004. *Plant Resources of Tropical Africa 2. Vegetables*. PROTA, Wageningen.

Jansen van Rensburg, W. S., et al. 2007. African leafy vegetables in South Africa. *Water SA* 33.3: 317-26.

Lulekal, E., et al. 2011. Wild edible plants in Ethiopia: a review on their potential to combat food insecurity. *Afrika Focus* 24.2: 71-121.

Lyimo, M., et al. 2003. Identification and nutrient composition of indigenous vegetables of Tanzania. *Plant Foods Hum Nutr* 58.1: 85-92.

Mahklouf, M. 2019. Ethnobotanical study of edible wild plants in Libya. *Eur J Ecol* 5.2: 30-40.

Maroyi, A. 2013. Use of weeds as traditional vegetables in Shurugwi District, Zimbabwe. *J Ethnobiol Ethnomed* 9.60: 1-10.

Maroyi, A. 2014. Not just minor wild edible forest products: consumption of pteridophytes in sub-Saharan Africa. *J Ethnobiol Ethnomed* 10.78: 1-9.

Meragiaw, M., et al. 2015. Indigenous knowledge (IK) of wild edible plants (WEPs) and impacts of resettlement in Delanta, Northern Ethiopia. *Res Rev: J Herb Sci* 5.3: 8-26.

Mercy, N. A., et al. 2016. Survey of wild vegetables in the Lebialem highlands of South Western Cameroon. *J Plant Sci* 4.6: 172-84.

Morales, J. 2018. The contribution of botanical macro-remains to the study of wild plant consumption during the Later Stone Age and the Neolithic of north-western Africa. *J Archaeol Sci Rep* 22: 401-12.

Moteetee, A. and Van Wyk, B. E. 2006. Sesotho names for exotic and indigenous edible plants in southern Africa. *Bothalia* 36.1: 25-32.

Moteetee, A., et al. 2019. A review of the ethnobotany of the Basotho of Lesotho and the Free State Province of South Africa (South Sotho). *S Afr J Bot* 122: 21-56.

Naciri, Kaoutar, et al. 2022. Ethnobotanical knowledge of wild food plants in Khenifra, a province in the Middle Atlas region of Morocco. *GSC Adv Res Rev* 13.2: 180-200.

Nortje, J. M. and Van Wyk, B. E. 2019. Useful plants of Namaqualand, South Africa: A checklist and analysis. *S Afr J Bot* 122: 120-35.

Ntuli, N. R., et al. 2012. Traditional vegetables of northern KwaZulu-Natal, South Africa. *Afr J Agric Res* 7.45: 6027-34.

Ogle, B. M. and Grivetti, L. E. 1985. Legacy of the chameleon: Edible wild plants in the Kingdom of Swaziland, Southern Africa. *Ecol Food Nutr* 17.1: 1-30.

Pemberton, R. W. 2000. Waterblommetjie (*Aponogeton distachyos*, Aponogetonaceae), a recently domesticated aquatic food crop in Cape South Africa with unusual origins. *Econ Bot* 54.2: 144–49.

Pijls, L., et al. 1995. Cultivation, preparation and consumption of ensete (*Ensete ventricosum*) in Ethiopia. *J Sci Food Agric* 67.1: 1–11.

Powell, B., et al. 2014. Wild leafy vegetable use and knowledge across multiple sites in Morocco? *J Ethnobiol Ethnomed* 10.34: 1–11.

Rose, E. F. and Guillarmod, A. J. 1974. Plants gathered as foodstuffs by the Transkeian peoples. *S Afr Med J* 48: 1688–90.

Ruskin, F. R. (ed). 2006. *Lost Crops of Africa*. 3 vols. Nat Acad Press, Washington DC.

Shackleton, S. E., et al. 1998. Use and trading of wild edible herbs in the central lowveld savanna region, South Africa. *Econ Bot* 52.3: 251–59.

Szuman, K. and Lall, N. 2020. '*Zantedeschia aethiopica*'. Ch 46 in *Underexplored Medicinal Plants from Sub-Saharan Africa*. Acad Press.

Tanji, A. and Nassif, F. 1995. Edible weeds in Morocco. *Weed Technol* 9.3: 617–20.

Van Damme, P., et al. 1922. Plant uses by the Topnaar of the Sesfontein area (Namib Desert). *Afrika Focus* 8.3–4: 253–81.

Van Wyk, B.-E. 2011. The potential of South African plants in the development of new food and beverage products. *S Afr J Bot* 77.4: 857–68.

Yemata, G. 2020. *Ensete ventricosum*: a multipurpose crop against hunger in Ethiopia. *Sci World J* 2020. 1–10.

Americas

North, South and Central America, with a focus on the indigenous inhabitants of the region, from Alaska and Canada through Mexico, Peru and Brazil, to Chile and Argentina (including Patagonia).

Ager, T. A. and Ager, L. P. 1980. Ethnobotany of the Eskimos of Nelson Island, Alaska. *Arctic Anthropol* 17.1: 26–48.

Alba, T. M., et al. 2020. Ethnobotany, ecology, pharmacology, and chemistry of *Anredera cordifolia* (Basellaceae): a review. *Rodriguésia* 71: 01042019.

Alves, T. D. C. 2020. *Plantas alimentícias não convencionais (PANC) da Travessia Teresópolis-Petrópolis, Serra dos Órgãos, RJ.* Dissertação de Mestrado, Universidade Federal Rural do Rio de Janeiro.

Angier, B. 1974. *Field Guide to Edible Wild Plants*. Stackpole, PA.

Arnason, T., et al. 1981. Use of plants for food and medicine by native peoples of eastern Canada. *Canad J Bot* 59.11: 2189–325.

Austin, D. F. 2004. *Florida Ethnobotany*. CRC Press, FL.

Barrett, S. A. and Gifford, E. W. 1933. *Miwok Material Culture*. Yosemite Nat Hist Assn.

Bautista-Cruz, A., et al. 2011. The traditional medicinal and food uses of four plants in Oaxaca, Mexico. *J Med Plants Res* 5.15: 3404–11.

Bohs, L., 1989. Ethnobotany of the genus *Cyphomandra* (Solanaceae). *Econ Bot* 43.2: 143–63.

Brill, S. and Dean, E. 1994. *Identifying and Harvesting Edible and Medicinal Plants in Wild (and not so wild) Places*. HarperCollins, NY.

Carpenter, T. M. and Steggerda, M. 1939. The food of the present-day Navajo Indians of New Mexico and Arizona. *J Nutr* 18.3: 297–305.

Carrasco, B., et al. 2009. Genetic structure of highland papayas (*Vasconcellea pubescens* (Lenné et C. Koch) Badillo) cultivated along a geographic gradient in Chile as revealed by Inter Simple Sequence Repeats (ISSR). *Genet Resour Crop Evol* 56.3: 331–37.

Chamorro, M. F. and Ladio, A. 2020. Native and exotic plants with edible fleshy fruits utilized in Patagonia and their role as sources of local functional foods. *BMC Complement Med Ther* 20: 1–16.

Core, E. L. 1967. Ethnobotany of the southern Appalachian Aborigines. *Econ Bot* 21.3: 198–214.

Corrêa, M. P., et al. 1926. *Dicionário das Plantas Úteis do Brasil e das Exóticas Cultivadas*. Vol 1. Imprensa Nacional, Rio de Janeiro.

Coville, F. V. 1895. Some additions to our vegetable dietary. *USDA Yearbook*. pp 205–14.

Crowhurst, A. 1972. *The Weed Cookbook*. Lancer, NY.

Daly, A. B. 2014. *Narrating changing foodways: wild edible plant knowledge and traditional food systems in Mapuche lands of the Andean Temperate Forests, Chile.* Thesis, UBC.

de Mösbach, E. W. 1992. *Botánica Indígena de Chile*. Museo Chileno de Arte Precolombino.

Díaz-Betancourt, M., et al. 1999. Weeds as a source for human consumption. A comparison between tropical and temperate Latin America. *Rev Biol Trop* 47.3: 329–38.

Domico, T. 1979. *Wild Harvest: Edible Plants of the Pacific Northwest*. Hancock House, BC.

dos Reis, M. S., et al. 2014. Landscapes with Araucaria in South America. *Ecol Soc* 19.2:43.

Duarte, O. and Paull, R. 2015. *Exotic Fruits and Nuts of the New World*. CABI, Wallingford.

Elias, T. S. and Dykeman, P. A. 2009. *Edible Wild Plants: A North American Field Guide*. Sterling, NY.

Fernald, M. L. and Kinsey, A. C. 1958. *Edible Wild Plants of Eastern North America*. Harper, NY.

Fernández, A. and Martínez, G. J. 2019. Las plantas en la alimentación de pobladores rurales de los ambientes serranos de La Calera (Dpto. Colón, Córdoba, Argentina): Una perspectiva etnobotánica diacrónica. *Bonplandia* 28.1: 43–69.

Francis, J. K. (ed). 2004. *Wildland Shrubs of the United States and Its Territories: Thamnic Descriptions 1.* USDA.

Freitus, J., 2005. *Wild Jams and Jellies: Delicious Recipes Using 75 Wild Edibles*. Stackpole Books, PA.

Gabriel, I. 1975. *Herb Identifier and Handbook*. Sterling, NY.

Gifford, E. W. 1967. *Ethnographic notes on the Southwestern Pomo*. Uni California Press.

Harrington, H. D. 1967. *Edible Native Plants of the Rocky Mountains*. UNMP, Albuquerque.

Jacob, M. C. M. and Albuquerque, U. P. (eds). 2021. *Local Food Plants of Brazil*. Springer.
Kermath, B. M., et al. 1992. *Food Plants in the Americas*. Kermath, Bennett & Pulsipher, USA.
Kujawska, M. and Łuczaj, Ł. 2015. Wild edible plants used by the Polish community in Misiones, Argentina. *Hum Ecol* 43.6: 855–69.
Kujawska, M. and Pieroni, A. 2015. Plants used as food and medicine by Polish migrants in Misiones, Argentina. *Ecol Food Nutr* 54.3: 255–79.
Ladio, A. H. 2001. The maintenance of wild edible plant gathering in a Mapuche community of Patagonia. *Econ Bot* 55.2: 243–54.
Ladio, A. H. and Lozada, M. 2000. Edible wild plant use in a Mapuche community of northwestern Patagonia. *Hum Ecol* 28: 53–71.
Ladio, A. H. and Lozada, M. 2003. Comparison of wild edible plant diversity and foraging strategies in two aboriginal communities of northwestern Patagonia. *Biodivers Conserv* 12: 937–51.
Ladio, A. H. and Lozada, M. 2004. Patterns of use and knowledge of wild edible plants in distinct ecological environments: a case study of a Mapuche community from northwestern Patagonia. *Biodivers Conserv* 13: 1153–73.
Leitão, F., et al. 2014. Medicinal plants traded in the open-air markets in the State of Rio de Janeiro, Brazil: an overview on their botanical diversity and toxicological potential. *Rev Bras Farmacogn* 24.2: 225–47.
Lira, R., et al. (eds). 2016. *Ethnobotany of Mexico*. Springer.
Medsger, O. P. 1939. *Edible Wild Plants*. Macmillan, NY.
Ministério da Saúde (Brasil). 2015. *Alimentos Regionais Brasileiros*. Brasilia.
Moerman, D. E. 1998. *Native American Ethnobotany*. Timber Press, Portland.
Morton, J. F. 1963. Principal wild food plants of the United States excluding Alaska and Hawai`i. *Econ Bot* 17.4: 319–30.
Norton, C. H. 2019. *Inuit ethnobotany in the North American Subarctic and Arctic*. Thesis, Université de Montréal.
Palmieri, V. S., et al. 2022. Wild edible plants of the Central Mountains in Argentina. *Rodriguésia* 73: 1–14.
Paniagua-Zambrana, N. Y., et al. 2020. *Ethnobotany of the Andes*. Springer.
Passos, M. A. B. 2023. Plantas Alimentícias Não Convencionais (PANC) no estado do Maranhão, Brasil. *Revista Foco* 16.3: 1–40.
Petzold 2006 – see under **Nutritional Assessments**.
Reagan, A. B. 1934. Plants used by the Hoh and Quileute Indians. *Trans Kans Acad Sci* 37: 55–70.
Ruskin, F. R. (ed). 1989. *Lost Crops of the Incas*. Nat Acad Press, Washington DC.
Sartori, V. C., et al. 2020. *Plantas Alimentícias Não Convencionais*. Educs.
Sauer, J. D. 1969. Identity of archaeologic grain amaranths from the valley of Tehuacan, Puebla, Mexico. *Am Antiq* 34.1: 80–81.
Scarpa, G. F. 2009. Wild food plants used by the indigenous peoples of the South American Gran Chaco: a general synopsis and intercultural comparison. *J Appl Bot Food Qual* 83.1: 90–101.
Shoji, K. 2023. Starch grains on human teeth as evidence for 4000 BCE potato consumption at the Cruz Verde site, northern coast of Peru. *Archaeol Sci Rep* 51: 104152.
Smith, N. 2023. *Amazon Fruits: An Ethnobotanical Journey*. Springer.
Sparkman, Philip S. 1908. The culture of the Luiseno Indians. *UCPAAE* 8.4: 187–234.
Starfield, B. 2000. Is US health really the best in the world? *J Am Med Assn* 284.4: 483–85.
Yanovsky, E. 1936. *Food Plants of the North American Indians*. USDA Misc Pub 237.

Asia

Turkey, Georgia, Syria, Israel and Palestine through Iran, Pakistan, India, Nepal, China to Korea, Japan, Indonesia and New Guinea.

Abbas, Z., et al. 2016. Ethnobotany of the Balti community, Tormik valley, Karakorum range, Baltistan, Pakistan. *J Ethnobiol Ethnomed* 12: 1–16.
Abbasi, A. M., et al. 2013. Ethnobotanical appraisal and cultural values of medicinally important wild edible vegetables of Lesser Himalayas-Pakistan. *J Ethnobiol Ethnomed* 9.66: 1–13.
Abbasi, A. M., et al. 2015. *Wild Edible Vegetables of Lesser Himalayas 1*. Springer.
Acharya, K. P. and Acharya, R. 2010. Eating from the wild: Indigenous knowledge on wild edible plants in Parroha VDC of Rupandehi district, Central Nepal. *Int J Soc Forestry* 3.1: 28–48.
Adnan, et al. 2023. The diversity and traditional knowledge of wild edible vegetables in Aceh, Indonesia. *Ethnobot Res Appl* 26: 1–16.
Agarwal, R. and Chandra, V. 2019. Diversity of wild edible plants in the Mandal-Chopta forest, Uttarakhand. *J Med Plants Stud* 7: 89–92.
Ahmad, K. and Pieroni, A. 2016. Folk knowledge of wild food plants among the tribal communities of Thakht-e-Sulaiman Hills, NW Pakistan. *J Ethnobiol Ethnomed* 12.1: 1–15.
Ajaib, M., et al. 2014. Ethnobotanical studies of herbs of Agra Valley ParaChinar, Upper Kurram Agency, Pakistan. *Int J Biol Biotech* 11.1: 71–83.
Akan, H., et al. 2013. An ethnobotanical research of the Kalecik mountain area (Şanlıurfa, South-East Anatolia). *Biodivers Conserv* 6: 84–90.
Ali-Shtayeh, M. S., et al. 2008. Traditional knowledge of wild edible plants used in Palestine (NW Bank): a comparative study. *J Ethnobiol Ethnomed* 4.1: 1–13.
Angami, A., et al. 2006. Status and potential of wild edible plants of Arunachal Pradesh. *Indian J Tradit Knowl* 5.4: 541–50.
Arı, S., et al. 2015. Ethnobotanical survey of plants used in Afyonkarahisar-Turkey. *J Ethnobiol Ethnomed* 11.84: 1–15.
Arinathan, V., et al. 2007. Wild edibles used by Palliyars of

the western Ghats, Tamil Nadu. *Indian J Tradit Knowl* 6.1: 163–68.
Bandyopadhyay, S. and Sobhan, K. M. 2009. Wild edible plants of Koch Bihar district, West Bengal. *Nat Prod Radiance* 8.1: 64–72.
Baranov, A. I. 1967. Wild vegetables of the Chinese in Manchuria. *Econ Bot* 21.2: 140–55.
Barua, U., et al. 2007. Wild edible plants of Majuli island and Darrang districts of Assam. *Indian J Tradit Knowl* 6.1: 191–94.
Bhalla, S. and Chand, T. 2007. Traditional foods and beverages of Himachal Pradesh. *Indian J Tradit Knowl* 6.1: 17–24.
Bhattarai, S., et al. 2009. Wild edible plants used by the people of Manang district, central Nepal. *Ecol Food Nutr* 48.1: 1–20.
Bhujel, D., et al. 2018. Wild edible plants used by ethnic communities in Kalimpong district of West Bengal, India. *NeBIO* 9.4: 314–26.
Biswas, K. and Das, A. P. 2011. 'Documentation of wild leafy vegetables from the tribal dominated parts of Malda District of Paschimbanga, India'. In *Recent Studies in Biodiversity and Traditional Knowledge in India*. pp 301–06.
Burkill, I. H. 1935. *A Dictionary of the Economic Products of the Malay Peninsula*. 2 vols. Crown Agents for the Colonies, London.
Bussmann, R. W., et al. 2017. Ethnobotany of Samtskhe-Javakheti, Sakartvelo (Republic of Georgia), Caucasus. *Indian J Tradit Knowl* 16.1: 7–24.
Cakir, E. A. 2017. Traditional knowledge of wild edible plants of Igdir Province (East Anatolia, Turkey). *Acta Soc Bot Pol* 86.4: 1–20.
Chotimah, H. E., et al. 2013. Ethnobotanical study and nutrient content of local vegetables consumed in Central Kalimantan, Indonesia. *Biodiversitas* 14.2: 106–11.
Dai, L., et al. 2014. Fruit quality of 12 provenances of *Idesia polycarpa* in China. *J Food Agric Environ* 12.2: 802–07.
Dangwal, L. R., et al. 2014. Exploration of wild edible plants used by Gujjar and Bakerwal tribes of District Rajouri (J&K), India. *J Appl Nat Sci* 6.1: 164–69.
Deka, N. and Devi, N. 2015. Aquatic angiosperm of BTC area, Assam, with reference to their traditional uses. *Asian J Plant Sci Res* 5.5: 9–13.
Denham, T. 2011. Early agriculture and plant domestication in New Guinea and Island Southeast Asia. *Curr Anthropol* 52 (S4): S379–95.
Denham, T. 2018. *Tracing Early Agriculture in the Highlands of New Guinea*. Routledge.
Dhar, A. K. and Dhar, R. S. 2000. Culinary and potherbs of Jammu and Kashmir. *J Herbs Spices Med Plants* 7.3: 7–18.
Djamali, M., et al. 2010. Notes on arboricultural and agricultural practices in ancient Iran based on new pollen evidence. *Paléorient* 36.2: 175–88.
Dogan, Y. 2012. Traditionally used wild edible greens in the Aegean Region of Turkey. *Acta Soc Bot Pol* 81.4: 329–42.
Dogan, Y., et al. 2004. The use of wild edible plants in western and central Anatolia (Turkey). *Econ Bot* 58.4: 684–90.
Dogan, Y., et al. 2013. Wild edible plants sold in the local markets of Izmir, Turkey. *Pak J Bot* 45.S1: 177–84.
Dutta, U. 2012. Wild vegetables collected by the local communities from the Chlrang Reserved Forest of BTAD, Assam. *Int J Sci Adv Technol* 2.4: 116–25.
Eksik, C. and Akan, H. 2023. Contributions to edible plants for human consumption in Mardin Province. *AKU J Sci Eng* 23: 555–75.
Eradze, N., et al. 2024. Edible and medicinal plants in some communities of Dusheti municipality (East Georgia, Caucasus). *World J Adv Res Rev* 22.1: 1014–22.
Ertuğ, F. 2000. An ethnobotanical study in central Anatolia (Turkey). *Econ Bot* 54.2: 155–82
Ertuğ, F. 2004. Wild edible plants of the Bodrum area (Muğla, Turkey). *Turk J Bot* 28.1–2: 161–74.
Esiyok, D., et al. 2004. Herbs as a food source in Turkey. *Asian Pac J Cancer Prev* 5.3: 334–39.
Essig, F. B. and Dong, Y. F. 1987. The many uses of *Trachycarpus fortunei* (Arecaceae) in China. *Econ Bot* 41.3: 411–17.
Fan, L., et al. 2020. Analysis of heavy metal content in edible honeysuckle (*Lonicera japonica* Thunb.) from China and health risk assessment. *J Environ Sci Health B* 55.10: 921–28.
Farooq, A. 2021. Wild edible plants used by rural population in District Poonch, J&K, India. *Asian J Med Sci* 2.6: 491–7.
Firat, M. and Azirat, A. 2016. Edible *Allium* L. species that are sold as fresh vegetables in public bazaars of Hakkâri province and its surroundings in Turkey. *Acta Biologica Turcica* 29.1: 14–19.
Fuller, D., et al. 2004. Early plant domestications in southern India: some preliminary archaeobotanical results. *Veg Hist Archaeobot* 13.2: 115–29.
Geng, Y., et al. 2016. Traditional knowledge and its transmission of wild edibles used by the Naxi in Baidi Village, northwest Yunnan province. *J Ethnobiol Ethnomed* 12.10: 1–21.
Guo, H. B., et al. 2007. *Zizania latifolia* Turcz. cultivated in China. *Genet Resour Crop Evol* 54.6: 1211–17.
Gupta, Y. C., et al. 2018. Edible flowers. *Proc Nat Conference on Floriculture for Rural and Urban Prosperity in the Scenario of Climate Change*, Pakyong, India.
Gürdal, B. and Kültür, S. 2014. The edible and miscellaneous useful plants in Marmaris (Southwest Turkey). *J Fac Pharm İstanbul* 44.1: 69–78.
Hamayun, M., et al. 2007. Studies on traditional knowledge of medicinal herbs of Swat Kohistan, District Swat, Pakistan. *J Herbs Spices Med Plants* 12.4: 11–28.
Hanif, U., et al. 2013. Ethnobotanical studies on some wild plants of head Qadirabad and adjoining areas, Pakistan. *Int J Phytomedicine* 5.3: 373–77.
Hinnawi, N. S. A. 2010. *An Ethnobotanical Study of Wild Edible Plants in the Northern West Bank 'Palestine'*.

Diss, An-Najah Nat Uni.
Hu, S. 2005. *Food Plants of China*. Chin Uni Press, HK.
Huang, H. and Ferguson, A. R. 2001. Kiwifruit in China. *N Z J Crop Hortic Sci* 29.1: 1-14.
Jain, A., et al. 2011. Dietary use and conservation concern of edible wetland plants at Indo-Burma hotspot: a case study from northeast India. *J Ethnobiol Ethnomed* 7.29: 1-17.
Ju, Y., et al. 2013. Eating from the wild: diversity of wild edible plants used by Tibetans in Shangri-la region, Yunnan, China. *J Ethnobiol Ethnomed* 9.28: 1-22.
Kadioglu, Z., et al. 2020. Wild edible plant species used in the Ağrı province, eastern Turkey. *Anales Jard Bot Madrid* 77. 2: 1-14.
Kang, Y., et al. 2012. Wild food plants and wild edible fungi of Heihe valley (Qinling Mountains, Shaanxi, Central China): Herbophilia and indifference to fruits and mushrooms. *Acta Soc Bot Pol* 81.4: 405-13.
Kang, Y., et al. 2013. Wild food plants and wild edible fungi in two valleys of the Qinling Mountains (Shaanxi, Central China). *J Ethnobiol Ethnomed* 9.26: 1-19.
Kar, A., et al. 2013. Wild edible plant resources used by the Mizos of Mizoram, India. *KUSET* 9.1: 106-26.
Kargıoğlu, M., et al. 2010. Traditional uses of wild plants in the middle Aegean region of Turkey. *Hum Ecol* 38.3: 429-50.
Kaval, İ., et al. 2015. Survey of wild food plants for human consumption in Geçitli (Hakkari, Turkey). *Indian J Tradit Knowl* 14.2: 183-90.
Kayang, H. 2007. Tribal knowledge on wild edible plants of Meghalaya, Northeast India. *Indian J Tradit Knowl* 6.1: 177-81.
Khan, M. and Hussain, S. 2014. Diversity of wild edible plants and flowering phenology of District Poonch (J&K) in the Northwest Himalaya. *Indian J Sci Res* 9.1: 32-38.
Khare, C. P. 2008. *Indian Medicinal Plants: An Illustrated Dictionary*. Springer.
Kim, H. and Song, M.-J. 2013. Ethnobotanical analysis for traditional knowledge of wild edible plants in North Jeolla Province (Korea). *Genet Resour Crop Evol* 60.4: 1571-85.
Kislev, M.E., et al. 1992. Epipalaeolithic (19,000 BP) cereal and fruit diet at Ohalo II, Sea of Galilee, Israel. *Rev Palaeobot Palynol* 73.1-4: 161-66.
Kislev, M. E., et al. 2006. Early domesticated fig in the Jordan Valley. *Science* 312: 1372-74.
Kızılarslan, Ç. 2012. An ethnobotanical study of the useful and edible plants of İzmit. *Marmara Pharm J* 16: 194-200.
Koçyiğit, M. F. and Özhatay, N. F. 2009. The wild edible and miscellaneous useful plants in Yalova province (northwest Turkey). *J Fac Pharm İstanbul* 40: 19-29.
Kültür, Ş. 2008. An ethnobotanical study of Kırklareli (Turkey). *Phytol Balc* 14.2: 279-89.
Liu, F.-H., et al. 2017. Ethnobotanical research on origin, cultivation, distribution and utilization of hemp (***Cannabis sativa*** L.) in China. *Indian J Tradit Knowl* 16.2: 235-42.
Lu, C. L. and Li, X. F. 2019. A review of *Oenanthe javanica* (Blume) DC. as traditional medicinal plant and its therapeutic potential. *eCAM* 6495819: 1-17.
Margaritis, E. 2013. Distinguishing exploitation, domestication, cultivation and production: the olive in the third millennium Aegean. *Antiquity* 87.337: 746-57.
Mayer-Chissick, U. and Lev, E. 2014. 'Wild edible plants in Israel tradition versus cultivation'. In *Medicinal and Aromatic Plants of the Middle-East*. Springer.
Mir, M. Y. 2014. Documentation and ethnobotanical survey of wild edible plants used by the tribals of Kupwara, J&K, India. *Int J Herb Med* 2.4: 11-18.
Mozhui, R., et al. 2011. Wild edible fruits used by the tribals of Dimapur district of Nagaland, India. *Pleione* 5.1: 56-64.
Mükemre, M., et al. 2016. Survey of wild food plants for human consumption in villages of Çatak (Van-Turkey). *Indian J Tradit Knowl* 15.2: 183-91.
Narayanan, M. K. and Kumar, N. A. 2007. Gendered knowledge and changing trends in utilization of wild edible greens in Western Ghats, India. *Indian J Tradit Knowl* 6.1: 204-16.
Negi, P. S. and Subramani, S. P. 2015. Wild edible plant genetic resources for sustainable food security and livelihood of Kinnaur district, Himachal Pradesh, India. *Int J Conserv Sci* 6.4: 657-68.
Nōkai, D. N. 1895. *Useful Plants of Japan Described and Illustrated*. Ag Soc Japan, Tokyo.
Ochse, J. J. and van den Brink, R. C. B. 1977. *Vegetables of the Dutch East Indies*. ANU Press, Canberra.
Ong, H. G., et al. 2016. Ethnobotany of the wild edible plants gathered in Ulleung Island, South Korea. *Genet Resour Crop Evol* 63.3: 409-27.
Özbucak, T. B., et al. 2006. The contribution of wild edible plants to human nutrition in the Black Sea region of Turkey. *Ethnobot Leafl* 10: 98-103.
Panda, S. and Thami, J. K. 2022. An ethnomedicinal field survey report on traditionally used plants by the Nepalese of Alubari Jungle Busty in Darjeeling Himalaya as potential immunity booster and fever-related herbal drugs. *Indian J Tradit Knowl* 21.1: 157-67.
Park, Y. J., et al. 2005. Kinds and characteristics of edible flowers marketed as food material in Korea. *Korean J Community Living Sci* 16.4: 47-57.
Parmar, C. and Kaushal, M. K. 1982. *Wild Fruits of the Sub-Himalayan Region*. Kalyani, New Delhi.
Patiri, B. and Borah, A. 2007. *Wild Edible Plants of Assam*. Geetakhi, Guwahati.
Pemberton, R. W. and Lee, N. S. 1996. Wild food plants in South Korea; market presence, new crops, and exports to the United States. *Econ Bot* 50.1: 57-70.
Polat, R., et al. 2015. Survey of wild food plants for human consumption in Elazığ (Turkey). *Indian J Tradit Knowl* 1.1: 69-75.
Porterfield, W. M. 1951. The principal Chinese vegetable foods and food plants of Chinatown markets. *Econ Bot* 5.1: 3-37.
Potts, D. T. 2018. Arboriculture in ancient Iran: Walnut (*Juglans regia*), plane (*Platanus orientalis*) and the 'Radde dictum'. *DABIR* 6: 101-9.

Radha, B., et al. 2013. Wild edible plant resources of the Lohba range of Kedarnath forest division (KFD), Garhwal Himalaya, India. *Int Res J Biol Sci* 2.11: 65–73.
Rana, J. C., et al. 2012. Genetic resources of wild edible plants and their uses among tribal communities of cold arid region of India. *Genet Resour Crop Evol* 59.1: 135–49.
Rawat, D. S. and Kharwal, A. D. 2014. Ethnobotanical studies of weed flora in Shivalik Hills, Himachal Pradesh, India. *Int J Adv Res* 2.5: 218.
Reddy, K. N., et al. 2007. Traditional knowledge on wild food plants in Andhra Pradesh. *Indian J Tradit Knowl* 6.1: 223–29.
Rekka, R. and Kumar, S. S. 2014. Ethnobotanical notes on wild edible plants used by Malayali tribals of Yercaud hills, Eastern Ghats, Salem District, Tamil Nadu. *Int J Herb Med* 2.1: 39–42.
Rethy, P., et al. 2010. Ethnobotanical studies of Dehang-Debang Biosphere Reserve of Arunachal Pradesh with special reference to Memba tribe. *Indian J Tradit Knowl* 9.1: 61–67.
Roy, B., et al. 1998. *Plants for Human Consumption in India*. Bot Survey of India, Calcutta.
Salvi, J. and Katewa, S. S. 2016. Documentation of folk knowledge on underutilized wild edible plants of Southern Rajasthan. *Indian J Nat Prod Resour* 7.2: 169–75.
Saqib, Z. and Sultan, A. 2005. Ethnobotany of Palas Valley, Pakistan. *Ethnobot Leafl* 1: 28.
Sasi, R., et al. 2011. Wild edible plant diversity of Kotagiri Hills – a part of Nilgiri Biosphere Reserve, Southern India. *J Research Biol* 2: 80–87.
Şenkardeş, İ. and Tuzlaci, E. 2016. Wild edible plants of southern part of Nevsehir in Turkey. *Marmara Pharm J* 20: 34–43.
Sharma, B. C. 2012. Wild vascular plants traditionally used as vegetables in Darjeeling hills, India. *Pleione* 6.1: 186–94.
Sher, Z., et al. 2014. Traditional knowledge on plant resources of Ashezai and Salarzai valleys, District Buner, Pakistan. *Afr J Plant Sci* 8.1: 42–53.
Shimoda, M. and Yamasaki, N. 2016. '*Fallopia japonica* (Japanese Knotweed) in Japan: Why is it not a pest for Japanese people?' In *Vegetation Structure and Function at Multiple Spatial, Temporal and Conceptual Scales*. Springer.
Singh, B., et al. 2012. Wild edible plants used by Garo tribes of Nokrek Biosphere Reserve in Meghalaya, India. *Indian J Tradit Knowl* 11: 166–71.
Singh, B., et al. 2016. Ethnobotany, traditional knowledge, and diversity of wild edible plants and fungi: A case study in the Bandipora District of Kashmir Himalaya, India. *J Herbs Spices Med Plants* 22.3: 247–78.
Singh, B., et al. 2019. Assessing ethnic traditional knowledge, biology and chemistry of Lepidium didymum L., lesser-known wild plants of Western Himalaya. *Proc Natl Acad Sci India Sect B Biol Sci* 89: 1087–94.
Singh, H. B. and Arora, R. K. 1978. *Wild Edible Plants of India*. ICAR, New Delhi.
Singh, K. D., et al. 2016. Nutraceutical usage of wild edible plants among the Garo tribe of Meghalaya, India. *Int J Sci Environ Technol* 5.5: 2959–65.
Sinha, R. and Lakra, V. 2007. Edible weeds of tribals of Jharkhand, Orissa and West Bengal. *Indian J Tradit Knowl* 6.1: 217–22.
Song, M.-J., et al. 2013. Traditional knowledge of wild edible plants on Jeju Island, Korea. *Indian J Tradit Knowl* 12.2: 177–194.
Srivastava, R. C., et al. 2010. Indigenous biodiversity of Apatani plateau: Learning on biocultural knowledge of Apatani tribe of Arunachal Pradesh for sustainable livelihoods. *Indian J Tradit Knowl* 9: 432–42.
Srivastava, T. N. 1988. Wild edible plants of Jammu & Kashmir State – an ethno-botanical study. *Anc Sci Life* 7.3-4: 201–06.
Stuart, G. A. 1911. *Chinese Materia Medica*. Am Presbyterian Mission, Shanghai.
Sulaiman, Naji, et al. 2022. Food behavior in emergency time: Wild plant use for human nutrition during the conflict in Syria. *Foods* 11.177: 1-15.
Tareen, N. M., et al. 2016. Ethnomedicinal utilization of wild edible vegetables in district Harnai of Balochistan Province-Pakistan. *Pak J Bot* 48.3: 1159–71.
Tharmabalan, R. T. 2023. Identification of wild edible plants used by the Orang Asli, indigenous peoples of the Malay Peninsula. *Front Sustain Food Syst* 7: 1-12.
Wang, J., et al. 2020. An ethnobotanical survey of wild edible plants used by the Yi people of Liangshan Prefecture, Sichuan Province, China. *J Ethnobiol Ethnomed* 16: 1-27.
Watt, G. 2014. *A Dictionary of the Economic Products of India*. CUP.
Yabuno, T. 1987. Japanese barnyard millet (*Echinochloa utilis*, Poaceae) in Japan. *Econ Bot* 41.4: 484–93.
Yang, L., et al. 2015. Cultural uses, ecosystem services, and nutrient profile of flowering quince (*Chaenomeles speciosa*) in the Highlands of Western Yunnan, China. *Econ Bot* 69.3: 273–83.
Yumkham, S. D., et al. 2017. Edible ferns and fern-allies of North East India: a study on potential wild vegetables. *Genet Resour Crop Evol* 64: 467–77.
Zhang, L., et al. 2016. Ethnobotanical study of traditional edible plants used by the Naxi people during droughts. *J Ethnobiol Ethnomed* 12.39: 1-9.
Zheng, Y., et al. 2014. Archaeological evidence for peach (*Prunus persica*) cultivation and domestication in China. *PloS One* 9.9: e106595.
Zhou, L., et al. 2006. 'Chinese Edible Botanicals: Types, Efficacy and Safety'. Ch 98 in *Handbook of Food Science, Technology, and Engineering*. Taylor & Francis.

Australasia

Australia and New Zealand.

Ahmed, A. K. and Johnson, K. A. 2000. Horticultural development of Australian native edible plants. *Aust J Bot* 48.4: 417–26.
Brand-Miller 1993 – see under **Nutritional Assessments**.

Chapman, G. B. 1944. *Health Grows Naturally*. Democracy Pub Co, Wellington.

Colenso, W. 1868. On the botany of the North Island of New Zealand. *Trans NZ Inst* 1: 1-58. In part 3 – essays.

Cribb, A. B. and J. W. 1975. *Wild Food in Australia*. Collins, Sydney. [1987 edn]

Crowe, A. 2004. *A Field Guide to the Native Edible Plants of New Zealand*. Penguin, Auckland.

Ferguson, A. R. 2004. 1904 – the year that kiwifruit (*Actinidia deliciosa*) came to New Zealand. *NZ J Crop Hortic Sci* 32.1: 3-27.

Florin, S. A., et al. 2020. The first Australian plant foods at Madjedbebe, 65,000-53,000 years ago. *Nat Commun* 11.1: 1-8.

House, A. P. N. and Harwood, C. E. (eds). 1992. *Australian dry-zone Acacias for human food: Proceedings of a workshop held at Glen Helen, NT, Australia, 7-10 Aug 1991*. CSIRO Pub.

Isaacs, J. 2002. *Bush Foods*. New Holland, Sydney.

Langlands, P. 2024. *Foraging New Zealand*. Penguin, Auckland.

Lister, P. R., et al. 1996. 'Acacia in Australia: Ethnobotany and potential food crop. In *Progress in New Crops*. ASHS Press, Alexandria, VA.

Maiden, J. H. 1889. *The Useful Native Plants of Australia*. Turner and Henderson, Sydney.

Maslin, B. R., et al. 1998. *Edible Wattle Seeds of Southern Australia: A review of species for use in semi-arid regions*. CSIRO Pub.

Netzel 2007 – see under **Nutritional Assessments**.

Sisson, L. 2023. *Fungi of Aotearoa*. Penguin, Auckland.

Slaughter 2012 – see under **Toxicity Studies**.

Wessell, A. 2022. 'Unsettling the history of macadamia nuts in northern New South Wales'. In *'Going Native?' Settler Colonialism and Food*. Springer.

Williams, C. J. 2012. *Medicinal Plants in Australia 3: Plants, Potions and Poisons*. Rosenberg, NSW.

Europe

Iceland, Norway, Sweden, Denmark, Russia, Estonia, Belarus, Ukraine, Moldova, Spain, France, Great Britain, Belgium, Germany, Switzerland, Poland, Czech Republic, Slovakia, Hungary, Romania, Serbia, Bulgaria, North Macedonia, Albania, Bosnia-Herzegovina, Croatia, Slovenia and Italy.

Abbet, C., et al. 2014. Ethnobotanical survey on wild alpine food plants in Lower and Central Valais (Switzerland). *J Ethnopharmacol* 151.1: 624-34.

Aura, J. E., et al. 2005. Plant economy of hunter-gatherer groups at the end of the last Ice Age: plant macroremains from the cave of Santa Maira (Alacant, Spain) ca. 12000-9000 BP. *Veg Hist Archaeobot* 14: 542-50.

Behre, K.-E. 2008. Collected seeds and fruits from herbs as prehistoric food. *Veg Hist Archaeobot* 17.1: 65-73.

Beiser, R. 2014. *Essbare Wildkräuter und Wildbeeren für Unterwegs*. Kosmos, Stuttgart.

Bianco, V. V. 1992. Usual and specialty vegetable crops in Mediterranean countries. *Acta Hortic* 318: 65-76.

Biscotti, N. and Pieroni, A. 2015. The hidden Mediterranean diet: wild vegetables traditionally gathered and consumed in the Gargano area, Apulia, SE Italy. *Acta Soc Bot Pol* 84.3: 327-38.

Brindza, J., et al. 2016. 'Traditional Foods in Slovakia'. Ch 5 in *Traditional Foods*. Springer.

Cerne, M. 1992. Wild plants from Slovenia used as vegetables. *Acta Hortic* 318: 87-96.

Ciocarlan, N. and Ghendov, V. 2015. Ethnobotanical and ecological studies of wild edible plants from Bugeac Steppe, Republic of Moldova. *J EcoAgriTourism* 11.2: 18-23.

Conran, C. 2004. 'La Ceuillette: Foraging for edible wild plants in Southern France'. In *Wild Food: Proceedings of the Oxford Symposium on Food and Cookery*.

Cornara, L., et al. 2009. Traditional uses of plants in the Eastern Riviera (Liguria, Italy). *J Ethnopharmacol* 125.1: 16-30.

Culpeper, N. 1653. *Culpeper's Complete Herbal*. Kelly, London.

De Natale, A., et al. 2021. An ethnobotanical survey of wild edible plants of Campania (Italy). *Bull Reg Nat Hist* 1.1: 1-122.

Deforce, K., et al. 2009. Iron Age acorns from Boezinge (Belgium): The role of acorn consumption in prehistory. *Archaol Korresp* 12.3: 381-92.

Della, A., et al. 2006. An ethnobotanical survey of wild edible plants of Paphos and Larnaca countryside of Cyprus. *J Ethnobiol Ethnomed* 2.34: 1-9.

Dénes, A., et al. 2012. Wild plants used for food by Hungarian ethnic groups living in the Carpathian Basin. *Acta Soc Bot Pol* 81.4: 381-96.

Di Novella, R., et al. 2013. Traditional plant use in the national park of Cilento and Vallo Di Diano, Campania, Southern, Italy. *J Ethnopharmacol* 145.1: 328-42.

Dolina, K. and Łuczaj, Ł. 2014. Wild food plants used on the Dubrovnik coast (south-eastern Croatia). *Acta Soc Bot Pol* 83.3: 175-81.

Dreon, A. L. and Paoletti, M. G. 2009. The wild food (plants and insects) in Western Friuli local knowledge (Friuli-Venezia Giulia, North Eastern Italy). *Contrib Nat Hist* 12: 461-88.

Evelyn, J. 1699. *Acetaria, a Discourse of Sallets*. B. Tooke, London. 2nd edn 1706.

Geraci, A., et al. 2018. The wild taxa utilized as vegetables in Sicily (Italy): A traditional component of the Mediterranean diet. *J Ethnobiol Ethnomed* 14: 1-27.

Ghirardini, M. P., et al. 2007. The importance of a taste. A comparative study on wild food plant consumption in twenty-one local communities in Italy. *J Ethnobiol Ethnomed* 3.22: 1-14.

González, J. A., et al. 2011. The consumption of wild and semi-domesticated edible plants in the Arribes del Duero (Salamanca-Zamora, Spain). *Genet Resour Crop Evol* 58: 991-1006.

Greig, J. 1983. Plant foods in the past: A review of the evidence from northern Europe. *J Plant Foods* 5: 179-214.

Grieve, M. 1931. *A Modern Herbal*. Jonathan Cape, London.
Grlić, L. 1990. *Enciklopedija Samoniklog Jestivog Bilja*. August Cesarec Zagreb.
Guarrera, P. M. 2003. Food medicine and minor nourishment in the folk traditions of Central Italy (Marche, Abruzzo and Latium). *Fitoterapia* 74.6: 515–44.
Guarrera, P. M. and Savo, V. 2016. Wild food plants used in traditional vegetable mixtures in Italy. *J Ethnopharmacol* 185: 202–34.
Hadjichambis, A. C. H., et al. 2008. Wild and semi-domesticated food plant consumption in seven circum-Mediterranean areas. *Int J Food Sci Nutr* 59.5: 383–414.
Hartwich, C. and Håkanson, G. 1905. Über Glyceria fluitans, ein fast vergessenes einheimisches Getreide. *Z Lebensm-Unters Forsch* 10: 473–78.
Heinrich, M., et al. 2005. Understanding local Mediterranean diets: A multidisciplinary pharmacological and ethnobotanical approach. *Pharmacol Res* 52.4: 353–66.
Janaćković, P., et al. 2019. Traditional knowledge on plant use from Negotin Krajina (Eastern Serbia): An ethnobotanical study. *Indian J Tradit Knowl* 18.1: 25–33.
Johnson, C. P. 1862. *The Useful Plants of Great Britain*. Hardwicke, London.
Kalle, R. and Sõukand, R. 2012. Historical ethnobotanical review of wild edible plants of Estonia (1770s–1960s). *Acta Soc Bot Pol* 81.4: 271–81.
Kalle, R. and Sõukand, R. 2013. Wild plants eaten in childhood: a retrospective of Estonia in the 1970s–1990s. *Bot J Linn* 172.2: 239–53.
Komarov. V. L. (ed). 1963. *Flora of the USSR. Vol. 2*. Israel Program for Scientific Translations.
Kubiak-Martens, L. 1999. The plant food component of the diet at the late Mesolithic (Ertebolle) settlement at Tybrind Vig, Denmark. *Veg Hist Archaeobot* 8: 117–27.
Lentini, F. and Venza, F. 2007. Wild food plants of popular use in Sicily. *J Ethnobiol Ethnomed* 3.15: 1–12.
Licata, M., et al. 2016. A survey of wild plant species for food use in Sicily (Italy) – results of a 3-year study in four Regional Parks. *J Ethnobiol Ethnomed* 12.1: 1–24.
Lightfoot, J. 1777. *Flora Scotica*. 2 vols. B. White, London.
Linnaeus, C. 1811. *Lachesis Lapponica: A Tour in Lapland*. White and Cochrane, London.
Lucchetti, L., et al. 2019. Ethnobotanical uses in the Ancona district (Marche region, Central Italy). *J Ethnobiol Ethnomed* 15.1: 1–33.
Łuczaj, Ł. 2012. Ethnobotanical review of wild edible plants of Slovakia. *Acta Soc Bot Pol* 81.4: 245–55.
Łuczaj, Ł and Kujawska, M. 2012. Botanists and their childhood memories: an underutilized expert source in ethnobotanical research. *Bot J Linn* 168.3: 334–43.
Łuczaj, Ł., et al. 2011. Marsh woundwort, *Stachys palustris* L. (Lamiaceae): an overlooked food plant. *Genet Resour Crop Evol* 58.5: 783–93.
Łuczaj, Ł., et al. 2012. The use and economic value of manna grass (*Glyceria*) in Poland from the middle ages to the twentieth century. *Hum Ecol* 40.5: 721–33.
Łuczaj, Ł., et al. 2012. Wild food plant use in 21st century Europe: the disappearance of old traditions and the search for new cuisines involving wild edibles. *Acta Soc Bot Pol* 81.4: 359–70.
Łuczaj, Ł., et al. 2013. Wild edible plants of Belarus: from Rostafiński's questionnaire of 1883 to the present. *J Ethnobiol Ethnomed* 9.1: 1–17.
Łuczaj, Ł., et al. 2013. Wild food plants used in the villages of the Lake Vrana Nature Park (northern Dalmatia, Croatia). *Acta Soc Bot Pol* 82.4: 275–81.
Łuczaj, Ł., et al. 2013. Wild vegetable mixes sold in the markets of Dalmatia (southern Croatia). *J Ethnobiol Ethnomed* 9: 2: 1–12.
Łuczaj, Ł., et al. 2014. 'Wild Food Plants of Dalmatia (Croatia)'. Ch 8 in *Ethnobotany and Biocultural Diversities in the Balkans*. Springer.
Łuczaj, Ł., et al. 2015. Wild food plants and fungi used by Ukrainians in the western part of the Maramureş region in Romania. *Acta Soc Bot Pol* 84.3: 339–47.
Mabey, R. 1972. *Food For Free*. Collins, Glasgow.
Martínez, F. and Montero, G. 2004. The *Pinus pinea* L. woodlands along the coast of South-western Spain: data for a new geobotanical interpretation. *Plant Ecol* 175: 1–18.
Menendez-Baceta, G., et al. 2012. Wild edible plants traditionally gathered in Gorbeialdea (Biscay, Basque Country). *Genet Resour Crop Evol* 59.7: 1329–47.
Miskoska-Milevska, E., et al. 2020. Traditional uses of wild edible plants in the Republic of North Macedonia. *Phytol Balcan* 26.1: 155–62.
Mithen, S., et al. 2001. Plant use in the Mesolithic: evidence from Staosnaig, Isle of Colonsay, Scotland. *J Archaeol Sci* 28.3: 223–34.
Motti, R., et al. 2020. The contribution of wild edible plants to the Mediterranean diet: An ethnobotanical case study along the coast of Campania (Southern Italy). *Econ Bot* 74: 249–72.
Nebel, S., et al. 2006. Ta chòrta: Wild edible greens used in the Graecanic area in Calabria, Southern Italy. *Appetite* 47.3: 333–42.
Nedelcheva, A. 2013. An ethnobotanical study of wild edible plants in Bulgaria. *Eurasia J BioSci* 7: 77–94.
Ninčević Runjić, T., et al. 2024. Wild edible plants used in Dalmatian Zagora (Croatia). *Plants* 13.1079: 1–16.
Paoletti, M. G., et al. 1995. Pistic, traditional food from western Friuli, NE Italy. *Econ Bot* 49.1: 26–30.
Papež Kristanc, A., et al. 2024. Traditional use of wild edible plants in Slovenia: A field study and an ethnobotanical literature review. *Plants* 13.621: 1–29.
Parada, M., et al. 2011. Ethnobotany of food plants in the Alt Emporda region (Catalonia, Iberian Peninsula). *J Appl Bot Food Qual* 84.1: 11–25.
Pardo-de-Santayana, M., et al. 2005. The gathering and consumption of wild edible plants in the Campoo (Cantabria, Spain). *Int J Food Sci Nutr* 56.7: 529–42.
Pardo-de-Santayana, M., et al. 2010. 'The ethnobotany of Europe, past and present'. In *Ethnobotany in the New Europe: People, Health and Wild Plant Resources*.
Paura, B., et al. 2021. Design a database of Italian vascular alimurgic flora (AlimurgITA): preliminary results. *Plants*

2021.10.743: 1-29.

Paura, B. and Di Marzio, P. 2022. Making a virtue of necessity: The use of wild edible plant species (also toxic) in bread making in times of famine according to Giovanni Targioni Tozzetti (1766). *Biology* 11.285: 1-26.

Pieroni, A. 1999. Gathered wild food plants in the upper valley of the Serchio River (Garfagnana), Central Italy. *Econ Bot* 53.3: 327-41.

Pieroni, A. 2017. Traditional uses of wild food plants, medicinal plants, and domestic remedies in Albanian, Aromanian and Macedonian villages in South-Eastern Albania. *J Herb Med* 9: 81-90.

Pieroni, A., et al. 2002. Ethnopharmacology of liakra: traditional weedy vegetables of the Arbëreshë of the Vulture area in southern Italy. *J Ethnopharmacol* 81.2: 165-85.

Pieroni, A., et al. 2005. Food for two seasons: Culinary uses of non-cultivated local vegetables and mushrooms in a south Italian village. *Int J Food Sci Nutr* 56.4: 245-72.

Pignone, D. and Laghetti, G. 2010. On sweet acorn (*Quercus* spp.) cake tradition in Italian cultural and ethnic islands. *Genet Resour Crop Evol* 57.8: 1261-66.

Ranfa, A., et al. 2014. The importance of traditional uses and nutraceutical aspects of some edible wild plants in human nutrition: the case of Umbria (central Italy). *Plant Biosyst* 148.2: 297-306.

Redžić, S. 2006. Wild edible plants and their traditional use in the human nutrition in Bosnia-Herzegovina. *Ecol Food Nutr* 45.3: 189-232.

Redžić, S. 2010. Use of wild and semi-wild edible plants in nutrition and survival of people in 1430 days of siege of Sarajevo during the war in Bosnia and Herzegovina (1992-1995). *Coll Antropol* 34.2: 551-70.

Redžić, S. and Ferrier, J. 2014. 'The use of wild plants for human nutrition during a war: eastern Bosnia (Western Balkans)'. Ch 9 in *Ethnobotany and Biocultural Diversities in the Balkans*. Springer.

Rigat, M., et al. 2009. Ethnobotany of food plants in the high river Ter valley (Pyrenees, Catalonia, Iberian Peninsula): non-crop food vascular plants and crop food plants with medicinal properties. *Ecol Food Nutr* 48.4: 303-26.

Rivera, D., et al. 2006. 'Gathered Mediterranean food plants – Ethnobotanical investigations and historical development'. In Local Mediterranean Food Plants and Nutraceuticals. *Forum Nutr* 59: 18-74.

Romano, D., et al. 2013. Ethnobotanical uses of Brassicaceae in Sicily. *Acta Hort* 1005: 197-204.

Sánchez-Mata, M. C. and Tardío, J. (eds). 2016. *Mediterranean Wild Edible Plants: Ethnobotany and Food Composition Tables*. Springer.

Sansanelli, S. and Tassoni, A. 2014. Wild food plants traditionally consumed in the area of Bologna (Emilia Romagna region, Italy). *J Ethnobiol Ethnomed* 10.69: 1-11.

Shikov, A. N., et al. 2017. Traditional and current food use of wild plants listed in the Russian Pharmacopoeia. *Front Pharmacol* 8.841: 1-15.

Signorini, A. M., et al. 2009. Plants and traditional knowledge: An ethnobotanical investigation on Monte Ortobene (Nuoro, Sardinia). *J Ethnobiol Ethnomed* 5.6: 1-15.

Simkova, K. and Polesny, Z. 2015. Ethnobotanical review of wild edible plants used in the Czech Republic. *J Appl Bot Food Qual* 88.1: 49-67.

Sõukand, R. and Kalle, R. 2016. *Changes in the Use of Wild Food Plants in Estonia*. Springer.

Stolicná, R. 2016. Possibilities of using wild plants in the traditional culinary culture of Slovakia. *Slovensky Narodopis* 64.2: 241-50.

Stryamets, N., et al. 2015. From economic survival to recreation: contemporary uses of wild food and medicine in rural Sweden, Ukraine and NW Russia. *J Ethnobiol Ethnomed* 11.53: 1-18.

Svanberg, I. 2012. The use of wild plants as food in pre-industrial Sweden. *Acta Soc Bot Pol* 81.4: 317-27.

Svanberg, I. and Egisson, S. 2012. Edible wild plant use in the Faroe Islands and Iceland. *Acta Soc Bot Pol* 81.4: 233-38.

Svanberg, I., et al. 2012. Uses of tree saps in northern and eastern parts of Europe. *Acta Soc Bot Pol* 81.4: 343-57.

Tardío, J., et al. 2005. Wild food plants traditionally used in the province of Madrid, Central Spain. *Econ Bot* 59.2: 122-36.

Tardío, J., et al. 2006. Ethnobotanical review of wild edible plants in Spain. *Bot J Linn* 152.1: 27-71.

Tripodi, G., et al. 2012. *Brassica fruticulosa* Cyr. and *Brassica incana* Ten. (Brassicaceae) as Mediterranean traditional wild vegetables: a valuable source of bioactive compounds. *J Essent Oil Res* 24.6: 539-45.

Ucchesu, M., et al. 2015. Earliest evidence of a primitive cultivar of *Vitis vinifera* L. during the Bronze Age in Sardinia (Italy). *Veg Hist Archaeobot* 24: 587-600.

Vitalini, S., et al. 2013. Traditional knowledge on medicinal and food plants used in Val San Giacomo (Sondrio, Italy) – An alpine ethnobotanical study. *J Ethnopharmacol* 145.2: 517-29.

Wright, C. A. 2001. *Mediterranean Vegetables*. Harvard Common Press, Boston.

Global Perspective

Authoritative international food plant studies; monographs discussing a plant or group of plants, with no specific focus on nutritional analysis or toxicology; and global compendiums of plants simply reputed to be edible.

Airy-Shaw, H. K. 1932. A revision of the genus *Leycesteria*. *Bull Misc Inf* (Roy Bot Gdns, Kew) 4.XXI: 161-76.

Altschul, S. 1973. *Drugs and Foods from Little-Known Plants*. HUP, MA.

Anjo, F. A., et al. 2021. *Acacia mearnsii* gum: A residue as an alternative gum Arabic for food stabilizer. *Food Chem* 344: 128640.

Arafat, S. M., et al. 2009. Chufa tubers (*Cyperus esculentus* L.): As a new source of food. *World Appl Sci J* 7.2: 151-56.

Bainbridge, D. A. 2006. *Acorn Use as Food*. Sierra Nature Prints, CA.

Basden, R. 1966. The occurrence and composition of manna in *Eucalyptus* and *Angophora*. *Proc Linn Soc NSW* 90.2: 152–56.

Bharucha, Z. and Pretty, J. 2010. The roles and values of wild foods in agricultural systems. *Philos Trans R Soc Lond B: Biol Sci* 365.1554: 2913-26.

Bryant, C. 1783. *Flora Diaetetica: or History of Esculent Plants*. B. White, London.

CABI. 2021. '*Spergula arvensis* (L.(1753)), corn spurry'. CABI Compendium datasheet. https://doi.org/10.1079/cabicompendium.50838

Chaurasiya, A., et al. 2021. An updated review on Malabar spinach (*Basella alba* and *Basella rubra*) and their importance. *J Pharmacogn Phytochem* 10.2: 1201–07.

Coon, N. 1974. *The Dictionary of Useful Plants*. Rodale, PA.

Defelice, M. S. 2002. Yellow nutsedge *Cyperus esculentus* L. – snack food of the Gods. *Weed Technol* 16.4: 901–07.

Dennell, R. W. 1976. The economic importance of plant resources represented on archaeological sites. *J Archaeol Sci* 3.3: 229–47.

Department of the Army. 1992. *US Army Survival Manual*. Barnes & Noble, NY.

Department of the Army. 2019. *The Official U.S. Army Illustrated Guide to Edible Wild Plants*. Lyons Press, Guilford, CT.

Donkin, R. A. 1980. *Manna: An Historical Geography*. Springer.

Edwards, S. E., et al. 2015. *Phytopharmacy: An Evidence-Based Guide to Herbal Medicinal Products*. John Wiley, Chichester.

Facciola, S. 1990. *Cornucopia – A Source Book of Edible Plants*. Kampong Pubs.

FAO. 1995. *Dimensions of Need: An Atlas of Food and Agriculture*. FAO, Rome.

Fern, K., et al. Plants for a Future website. https://pfaf.org/

Francisco-Ortega, J. and Zona, S. 2013. Sweet sap from palms, a source of beverages, alcohol, vinegar, syrup, and sugar. *Vieraea* 41: 91–113.

French, B., et al. Food Plants International website. https://foodplantsinternational.com/

Galen – see Grant.

Gerarde, J. 1597. *The Herball or Generall Historie of Plantes*. John Norton, London.

Gören, A. C. 2014. Use of *Stachys* species (mountain tea) as herbal tea and food. *Rec Nat Prod* 8.2: 71–82.

Grant, M. 2002. *Galen on Food and Diet*. Routledge, London.

Groom, Q. J., et al. 2019. The origin of *Oxalis corniculata* L. *PeerJ* 7:e6384.

Guil-Guerrero, J. L. and Torija-Isasa, M. E. 2003. Edible wild plants. *Rec Prog Med Plants* 8: 411–46.

Hanelt, P. 1998. Lesser known or forgotten cruciferous vegetables and their history. *Proc Int Symp Brassicas* 459: 39–46.

Harrison, S. G. 1951. Edible pine kernels. *Kew Bull* 6.3: 371–75.

Haynes, J. and McLaughlin, J. 2000. Edible palms and their uses. *Sheet* MDCE-00-50-1. IFAS, UF, FL.

Howes, F. N. 1949. *Vegetable Gums and Resins*. Chronica Botanica Co, Mass.

Janick, J. and Paull, R. E. (eds). 2008. *The Encyclopedia of Fruit and Nuts*. CABI, Wallingford.

Karg, S. 2012. Oil-rich seeds from prehistoric contexts. *Acta Palaeobot* 52.1: 17–24.

Kiple, K. F. and Ornelas, K. C. (eds). 2000. *The Cambridge World History of Food*. CUP.

Koike, A., et al. 2015. Edible flowers of *Viola tricolor* L. as a new functional food: Antioxidant activity, individual phenolics and effects of gamma and electron-beam irradiation. *Food Chem* 179: 6–14.

Kunkel, G. 1984. *Plants for Human Consumption*. Koeltz Sci Books, Koenigstein.

Lim, T. K. 2012-16. *Edible Medicinal and Non Medicinal Plants*. 12 vols. Springer.

Lin, L., et al. 2009. *Discovering Indigenous Treasures: Promising Indigenous Vegetables from around the World*. AVRDC – The World Vegetable Center.

Lindley, J. and Moore, T. 1876. *Treasury of Botany*. 2 vols. Longmans, London.

Lovelock, Y. 1973. *The Vegetable Book: An Unnatural History*. St Martin's Press, NY.

Mansfeld, R., et al. 2001. *Mansfeld's Encyclopedia of Agricultural and Horticultural Crops (except Ornamentals)*. Springer.

Martinevski, C. S., et al. 2013. Utilização de bertalha (*Anredera cordifolia* (TEN.) Steenis) e ora-pro-nobis (*Pereskia aculeata* Mill.) na elaboração de pães. *Braz J Food Nutr* 24.3: 1-6.

Masefield, G. B., et al. 1969. *The Oxford Book of Food Plants*. OUP, London.

Maun, M. A., et al. 1990. The biological flora of coastal dunes and wetlands. 1. *Cakile edentula* (Bigel.) Hook. *J Coast Res* 6.1: 137–56.

Morton, J. F. 1962. Spanish needles (*Bidens pilosa* L.) as a wild food resource. *Econ Bot* 16.3: 173–79.

Olaeta, J. A., et al. 2007. Use of Hass avocado (*Persea americana* Mill) seed as a processed product. *Proc VI World Avocado Congress*: 1-8.

Patil, A. R., et al. 2013. *Araucaria heterophylla*: The review. *World J Pharm Pharm Sci* 3.1: 221–32.

Pliny. 1856. *The Natural History of Pliny*. (Trans. Bostock and Riley.) Bohn, London.

Rapoport, E. H., et al. 1995. Edible weeds: a scarcely used resource. *Bull Ecol Soc Am* 76.3: 163–66.

Rasool, R. and Ganai, B. A. 2013. *Prunella vulgaris* L.: A literature review on its therapeutic potentials. *Pharmacologia* 4: 441–48.

Rocha, G. F., et al. 2021. Milk-clotting and hydrolytic activities of an aspartic protease from *Salpichroa origanifolia* fruits on individual caseins. *Int J Biol Macromol* 192: 931–38.

Royal Botanic Gardens, Kew. 2020. *World Checklist of Useful Plant Species*. RBGK.

Salehi, B., et al. 2019. *Berberis* plants – drifting from farm to food applications, phytotherapy, and

phytopharmacology. *Foods* 8.522: 1-27.
Shakeri, A., et al. 2016. *Melissa officinalis L.*- A review of its traditional uses, phytochemistry and pharmacology. *J Ethnopharmacol* 188: 204-28.
Stevens, O. A. 1932. The number and weight of seeds produced by weeds. *Am J Bot* 19.9: 784-94.
Steyn, N. P., et al. 2001. A survey of wild, green, leafy vegetables and their potential in combating micronutrient deficiencies in rural populations. *S Afr J Sci* 97.7: 276-78.
Sturtevant, E. 1972. *Sturtevant's Edible Plants of the World*. Dover, NY. (First published 1919.)
Tanaka, T. 1976. *Tanaka's Cyclopedia of Edible Plants of the World*. Keigaku Pub, Tokyo.
Theophrastus. 1916. *Enquiry into Plants*. (Trans. Arthur Hort). Heinemann, London.
Tomou, E. M., et al. 2020. Genus *Stachys*: A review of traditional uses, phytochemistry and bioactivity. *Medicines* 7.63: 1-74.
Uphof, J. C. T. 1968. *Dictionary of Economic Plants*. Verlag von J. Cramer.
Usher, G. 1974. *A Dictionary of Plants Used by Man*. Constable, London.
Vaughan, J. G. and Geissler, C. A. 2009. *The New Oxford Book of Food Plants*. OUP, Oxford.
Wiersema, J. H. and Leon, B. 1999. *World Economic Plants*. CRC, FL.
Yasuda, K. and Yamaguchi, H. 2005. Genetic diversity of vegetable water pepper (*Persicaria hydropiper* (L.) Spach) as revealed by RAPD markers. *Breed Sci* 55: 7-14.
Young, R. A. 1954. Flavor qualities of some edible oriental bamboos. *Econ Bot* 8.4: 377 86.

Nutritional Assessments

References with nutritional analysis as the primary focus (including studies with a regional emphasis).

Abbasi et al. 2015 – see under **Asia**
Abdelkader, M., et al. 2015. Phytochemical study and biological activity of sage (*Salvia officinalis* L.). *Int J Bioeng Life Sci* 8.11: 1253-57.
Adiamo, O. Q., et al. 2024. Domesticated Australian wattle seeds (*Acacia* species): nutritional values, techno-functional properties and toxicological assessments after roasting. *Int J Food Sci Technol* 59.1: 573-83.
Alarcão-E-Silva, M. L., et al. 2001. The Arbutus berry: Studies on its color and chemical characteristics at two mature stages. *J Food Compos Anal* 14.1: 27-35.
Alarcón, R., et al. 2006. Nutrient and fatty acid composition of wild edible bladder campion populations [*Silene vulgaris* (Moench.) Garcke]. *Int J Food Sci Technol* 41.10: 1239-42.
Alegbejo, J. O. 2013. Nutritional value and utilization of Amaranthus (*Amaranthus* spp.) – a review. *BAJOPAS* 6.1: 136-43.
Alpinar, K., et al. 2009. Antioxidant capacities of some food plants wildly grown in Ayvalik of Turkey. *Food Sci Technol Res* 15.1: 59-64.
Arafat – see under **Global Perspective**
Araújo, S., et al. 2019. Evaluation of phytochemicals content, antioxidant activity and mineral composition of selected edible flowers. *Qual Assur Saf Crops Foods* 11.5: 471-78.
Bajracharya, D. 1980. Nutritive values of Nepalese edible wild fruits. *ZLUF* 171.5: 363-66.
Barros, L., et al. 2011. Comparing the composition and bioactivity of *Crataegus monogyna* flowers and fruits used in folk medicine. *Phytochem Anal* 22.2: 181-88.
Barros, T., et al. 2018. *Monstera deliciosa* fruit: physicochemical characterization and potential for distillate production. *J Food Meas Charact* 12.4: 2874-82.
Begum, A. and Pereira, S. M. 1977. The beta carotene content of Indian edible green leaves. *Trop Geogr Med* 29.1: 47-50.
Bianco, V. V., et al. 1996. Nutritional value and nitrate content in edible wild species used in southern Italy. *III Int Symp Diversif Veg Crops* 467: 71-90.
Bilić, V. L., et al. 2020. First extensive polyphenolic profile of *Erodium cicutarium* with novel insights to elemental composition and antioxidant activity. *Chem Biodivers* 17.9: e2000280.
Bowen-Forbes, C. S., et al. 2010. Anthocyanin content, antioxidant, anti-inflammatory and anticancer properties of blackberry and raspberry fruits. *J Food Compos Anal* 23.6: 554-60.
Brand, J. C. and Cherikoff, V. 1985. 'The nutritional composition of Australian Aboriginal food plants of the desert regions'. Ch 5 in *Plants for Arid Lands*. Springer.
Brand-Miller, J., et al. 1993. *Tables of Composition of Australian Aboriginal Foods*. Aboriginal Studies Press, Canberra.
Burrell, R. C. and Miller, H. A. 1939. The vitamin C content of spring greens. *Science* 90.2329: 164-65.
Bussmann, R. W., et al. 2020. '*Lapsana communis* L. *Lapsana grandiflora* M. Bieb. Asteraceae'. In *Ethnobotany of the Mountain Regions of Far Eastern Europe*. pp 541-46.
Butnariu, M. and Samfira, I. 2013. Vegetal metabolomics to seeds of *Galium aparine*. *J Bioequiv Availab* 5.7: e45.
Cai, Y., et al. 2004. Antioxidant activity and phenolic compounds of 112 traditional Chinese medicinal plants associated with anticancer. *Life Sci* 74.17: 2157-84.
Celik, F., et al. 2017. Determination of phenolic compounds, antioxidant capacity and organic acids contents of *Prunus domestica* L., *Prunus cerasifera* Ehrh. and *Prunus spinosa* L. fruits by HPLC. *Acta Chromatogr* 29.4: 507-10.
Cerne – see under **Europe**
Chapman – see under **Australasia**
Chib, A., et al. 2022. Effect of thermal processing on nutritional and anti-nutritional factors of amaranthus (*Amaranthus viridis Linn.*) leaves. *Pharma Innov* 11: 385-89.
Chistyakova, A. S., et al. 2022. Study of organic acids profile of genus *Persicaria* Mill species. *Pharm Pharmacol* 10.1: 44-54.

Choudhary, S. P. and Sharma, D. K. 2014. Bioactive constituents, phytochemical and pharmacological properties of *Chenopodium album*: a miracle weed. *Int. J. Pharmacogn* 1.9: 545–52.

Civelek, C. and Balkaya, A. 2013. The nutrient content of some wild plant species used as vegetables in Bafra Plain located in the Black Sea region of Turkey. *Eur J Plant Sci Biotech* 7.1: 62–65.

Clabby, G. and Osborne, B. A. 1999. *Mycelis muralis* (L.) Dumort. (*Lactuca muralis* (L.) Gaertner). *J Ecol* 87: 156–72.

Cobus, D., et al. 2023. Unconventional food plants (UFPs): an approach to the nutritional and functional properties of nasturtium (*Tropaeolum majus* L.). *Food Sci Today* 1.1: 1–6.

Couri, S., et al. 2005. Determination of inulin content of chicory roots (*Cichorium intybus* L.) cultivated organically in three regions of Rio de Janeiro state. *Embrapa Agroindustria de Alimentos*: 1–5.

Cowan, J. W., et al. 1963. Composition of edible wild plants of Lebanon. *J Sci Food Agric* 14.7: 484–88.

Damascos, M. A., et al. 2008. Fruit mineral contents of six wild species of the North Andean Patagonia, Argentina. *Biol Trace Elem Res* 125.1: 72–80.

Deng, P., et al. 2023. Optimisation of the controlled atmosphere storage and shelf life of *Lilium longiflorum*. *Qual Assur Saf Crops Foods* 15.SP1: 1–15.

Dragomir, N, et al. 2011. Forage quality determined by botanic species' contribution on permanent pastures. *Anim Sci Biotechnol* 44.2: 205–07.

Edmonds, J. M. and Chweya, J. A. 1997. *Black Nightshades,* Solanum nigrum *L. and Related Species*. IPGRI, Rome.

Ekeanyanwu, R. C. and Ononogbu, C. I. 2010. Nutritive value of Nigerian tigernut (*Cyperus esculentus* L.). *Agric Res J* 5.5: 297–302.

Ershow, A. G. and Wong-Chen, K. 1990. Chinese food composition tables – An annotated translation of the 1981 edition published by the INFH, CAPM, Beijing. *J Food Compos Anal* 3.3–4: 191–434.

Fernandes, L., et al. 2019. Phytochemical characterization of *Borago officinalis* L. and *Centaurea cyanus* L. during flower development. *Food Res Int* 123: 771–78.

Francis – see under **Americas**

Franke, W. 1978. On the contents of vitamin C and thiamin during the vegetation period in leaves of three spice plants (*Allium schoenoprasum* L., *Melissa officinalis* L. and *Petroselinum crispum* (mill.) nym. ssp. *crispum*). *Acta Hortic* (ISHS) 73: 205–12.

Gauchan, D. P., et al. 2008. Nutrient analysis of *Nephrolepis cordifolia* (L.) C. Presl. *KUSET* 4.1: 68–72.

Ginocchio, R., et al. 2021. Mayten tree seed oil: Nutritional value evaluation according to antioxidant capacity and bioactive properties. *Foods* 10.729: 1–13.

Grlić – see **Europe**

Guil, J. L., et al. 1997. Nutritional and toxic factors in selected wild edible plants. *Plant Foods Hum Nutr* 51.2: 99–107.

Guil-Guerrero, J. L., et al. 1999. Mineral elements determination in wild edible plants. *Ecol Food Nutr* 38.3: 209–22.

Hadi, S., et al. 2023. Uji antioksidan dan penetapan flavonoid tuber pakis kinca (*Nephrolepis cordifolia* (L) C. Presl). *IJCA* 6.1: 1–9.

Harrold, R. L. and Nalejawa, J. D. 1977. Proximate, mineral and amino acid composition of 15 weed seeds. *J Anim Sci* 44.3: 389–94.

Heinrich – see under **Europe**

Herzog, F., et al. 1994. Composition and consumption of gathered wild fruits in the V-Baoulé, Côte d'Ivoire. *Ecol Food Nutr* 32: 181–96.

Howard, J. L. 1992. *Erodium cicutarium*. In Fire Effects Information System [Online]. USFS, RMRS, Fire Sci Lab: https://www.fs.usda.gov/database/feis/plants/forb/erocic/all.html [2023, April 24].

Imanishi, H. 2011. Characteristics and breeding of underutilized Japanese *Rubus* genetic resources. *Acta Hort* 918: 625–630.

Islam, M. N., et al. 1987. Nutritional and sensory evaluation of *Atriplex triangularis* leaves. *Food Chem* 25.4: 279–84.

Iyda, J. H., et al. 2019. Nutritional composition and bioactivity of Umbilicus rupestris (Salisb.) Dandy. *Food Chem* 295: 341–49.

Jabłońska-Ryś, E., et al. 2009. Antioxidant capacity, ascorbic acid and phenolics content in wild edible fruits. *J Fruit Ornam Plant Res* 17.2: 115–20.

Jain – see under **Asia**

Jansson, O. 1974. Phylloquinone (Vitamin K1) levels in leaves of plant species differing in susceptibility to 2, 4-dichlorophenoxyacetic acid. *Physiol Plant* 31.4: 323–25.

Jimoh, F. O., et al. 2010. Assessing the polyphenolic, nutritive and biological activities of acetone, methanol and aqueous extracts of *Rumex sagittatus* Thunb. *Afr J Pharm Pharmacol* 4.9: 630–35.

Jimoh, F. O., et al. 2011. Comparison of the nutritive value, antioxidant and antibacterial activities of *Sonchus asper* and *Sonchus oleraceus*. *Rec Nat Prod* 5.1: 29–42.

Jobson, H. T. and Thomas, B. 1964. The composition of gorse (*Ulex europaeus*). *J Sci Food Agric* 15.9: 652–56.

Jones, E. and Hughes, R. E. 1983. Foliar ascorbic acid in some angiosperms. *Phytochem* 22.11: 2493–99.

Karpiuk, V. and Konechna, R. 2021. Total phenolic and flavonoid content, antioxidant activity of *Ficaria verna*. *PNAP* 46.3: 229–34.

Katanić Stanković, J. S., et al. 2022. The qualitative composition and comparative biological potential of *Lunaria annua* L. (Brassicaceae) extracts. *Kragujevac J Sci* 44: 75–89.

Keser, S., et al. 2015. Vitamin, sterol and fatty acid contents of some edible and medicinal plants from East and Southeast Anatolia (Turkey). *Turk J Pharm Sci* 12.2: 133–46.

Keskin, S., et al. 2019. Phenolic composition and antioxidant properties of *Wisteria sinensis*. *Int J Sci Tech Res* 5.2: 98–103.

Khare – see under **Asia**

Khatun, S. 2020. Analysis of nutritional composition,

in vitro antioxidant and antidiabetic effect of three *Chenopodium* species. Master's thesis, CVASU, Bangladesh.

Khlifi, S., et al. 2006. In vitro antioxidant properties of *Salvia verbenaca* L. hydromethanolic extract. *Indian J Pharmacol* 38.4: 276.

Kinupp, V. F. 2007. Plantas alimentícias não-convencionais da região metropolitana de Porto Alegre, RS. Thesis, UFRGS, Brazil.

Kinupp, V. F. and Barros, I. B. I. D. 2008. Teores de proteína e minerais de espécies nativas, potenciais hortaliças e frutas. *Food Sci Technol* 28: 846–57.

Knudsen, B. F. and Kaack, K. V. 2015. A review of human health and disease claims for elderberry (*Sambucus nigra*) fruit. *Acta Hort* 1061: 121–31.

Konsam, S. C., et al. 2016. Biochemical constituents and nutritive evaluation of some less known wild edible plants from Senapati District, Manipur, India. *Not Sci Biol* 8.3: 370–72.

Kossah, R., et al. 2009. Comparative study on the chemical composition of Syrian sumac (*Rhus coriaria* L.) and Chinese sumac (*Rhus typhina* L.) fruits. *Pak J Nutr* 8.10: 1570–74.

Krishnan, G., et al. 2019. Phytochemical analysis, anti-microbial and anti-oxidant potential of *Oxalis latifolia* Kunth. *Eur J Biotech Biosci* 7.3: 88–93.

Kuhnlein, H. V., et al. 2009. *Indigenous Peoples' Food Systems*. FAO, Roma.

Kūka, M., et al. 2013. Determination of bioactive compounds and mineral substances in Latvian birch and maple saps. *Proc Latv Acad Sci B: Nat Exact Appl Sci* 67.4/5: 437–41.

Kumar, V., et al. 2011. Therapeutic potentials of *Brassica juncea*: an overview. *TANG* 1.1: 8–23.

Laferriere, J. E., et al. 1991. Use and nutritional composition of some traditional Mountain Pima plant foods. *J Ethnobiol* 11.1: 93–114.

Lara-Cortés, E., et al. 2014. Antioxidant capacity, nutritional and functional composition of edible *Dahlia* flowers. *RCSH* 20.1: 101–16.

Leterme, P., et al. 2006. Mineral content of tropical fruits and unconventional foods of the Andes and the rain forest of Colombia. *Food Chem* 95.4: 644–52.

Lewis, H. B., et al. 1948. The nutritive value of some legumes. Lathyrism in the rat. The sweet pea (*Lathyrus odoratus*), *Lathyrus sativus*, *Lathyrus cicera* and some other species of *Lathyrus*. *J Nutr* 36.5: 537–59.

Li, S., et al. 2013. Antioxidant capacities and total phenolic contents of infusions from 223 medicinal plants. *Ind Crops Prod* 51: 289–98.

Lim – see under **Global Perspective**

Łuczaj, Ł., et al. 2014. Sugar content in the sap of birches, hornbeams and maples in southeastern Poland. *Open Life Sci* 9.4: 410–16.

Luis, G., et al. 2012. Palm tree syrup; nutritional composition of a natural edulcorant. *Nutr Hosp* 27.2: 548–52.

Luta, G., et al. 2020. Bioactive compounds and antioxidant properties of some wild plants with potential culinary uses. *Rev Chim* 71.2: 179–84.

Mahbub, A., et al. 2010. Investigation of some constituents of two plants (*Alternanthera philoxeroides* and *Alternanthera sessilis*) of Amaranthaceae family. *Dhaka Univ J Sci* 58.2: 327–28.

Makobo, N. D., et al. 2010. Nutrient content of vegetable amaranth (*Amaranthus cruentus* L.) at different harvesting stages. *World J Agric Sci* 6.3: 285–89.

Mariod, A. A. (ed). 2019. *Wild Fruits: Composition, Nutritional Value and Products*. Springer.

Menacer, A., et al. 2017. In vitro antioxidant activity of different extracts of Algerian *Allium* plant (*Allium triquetrum* L.). *Revue des Bio Res* 7.1: 80–91.

Mendes, M. D., et al. 2009. Volatile and molecular characterization of two Portuguese endemic species: *Angelica lignescens* and *Melanoselinum decipiens*. *Biochem Syst Ecol* 37.2: 98–105.

Mikulic-Petkovsek, M., et al. 2012. Composition of sugars, organic acids, and total phenolics in 25 wild or cultivated berry species. *J Food Sci* 77.10: C1064–70.

Mishra, A. P., et al. 2017. Himalayan dogwood (*Cornus capitata* Wall ex. Roxb., Cornaceae): Nutritional and bioactive properties. *Oxid Commun* 40.1: 168–77.

Morales, P., et al. 2012. Tocopherol composition and antioxidant activity of Spanish wild vegetables. *Genet Resour Crop Evol* 59.5: 851–63.

Moteetee et al. 2019 – see under **Africa**

Mou, B. 2005. Genetic variation of beta-carotene and lutein contents in lettuce. *J Am Soc Hortic Sci* 130.6: 870–76.

Mutwa, N. K., et al. 2015. Identification and nutritional characterization of edible wild cactus varieties from Kenya. Annals. *Food Sci Technol* 16.2: 379–87.

Nagai, T., et al. 2005. Antioxidative activities of water extract and ethanol extract from field horsetail (tsukushi) *Equisetum arvense* L. *Food Chem* 91.3: 389–94.

Nergiz, C. and Dönmez, I. 2004. Chemical composition and nutritive value of *Pinus pinea* L. seeds. *Food Chem* 86.3: 365–68.

Netzel, M., et al. 2007. Native Australian fruits – a novel source of antioxidants for food. Innovative *Food Sci Emerg Technol* 8.3: 339–46.

Nguyen, V. T., et al. 2020. Phytochemical screening, antioxidant activities, total phenolics and flavonoids content of leaves from *Persicaria odorata* Polygonaceae. *IOP Conf Ser: Mater Sci Eng* 991.012029: 1–6.

Niizu, P. Y. and Rodriguez-Amaya, D. B. 2005. Flowers and leaves of *Tropaeolum majus* L. as rich sources of lutein. *J Food Sci* 70.9: S605–S609.

Nwaogu, L. A., et al. 2017. Chemical composition of *Siegesbeckia orientalis*: A valuable, but less known ethnomedicinal plant. *Biokemistri* 29.2: 54–60.

Odhav, B., et al. 2007. Preliminary assessment of nutritional value of traditional leafy vegetables in KwaZulu-Natal, South Africa. *J Food Compos Anal* 20.5: 430–35.

Ogundare, D. O. and Tanimola, A. R. 2022. Nutritional composition of some selected, unprocessed amaranth grain (Amaranthus spp) varieties in Nigeria. *Afr J Food Agric Nutr Dev* 22.8: 21383–96.

Orech, F. O., et al. 2007. Mineral content of traditional leafy vegetables from western Kenya. *Int J Food Sci Nutr* 58.8: 595–602.

Osei-Owusu, J., et al. 2023. Evaluation of phytochemical, proximate, antioxidant, and anti-nutrient properties of *Corchorus olitorius*, *Solanum macrocarpon* and *Amaranthus cruentus* in Ghana. *Int J Biochem Mol Biol* 14.2: 17–24.

Özcan, T. 2006. Total protein and amino acid compositions in the acorns of Turkish Quercus L. taxa. *Genet Resour Crop Evol* 53.2: 419–29.

Panfili, G., et al. 2020. Bioactive compounds in wild Asteraceae edible plants consumed in the Mediterranean diet. *Plant Foods Hum Nutr* 75: 540–46.

Pereira, C., et al. 2013. Use of UFLC-PDA for the analysis of organic acids in thirty-five species of food and medicinal plants. *Food Anal Methods* 6.5: 1337–44.

Pereira, O. R., et al. 2018. *Salvia elegans*, *Salvia greggii* and *Salvia officinalis* decoctions: Antioxidant activities and inhibition of carbohydrate and lipid metabolic enzymes. *Molecules* 23: 3169.

Peters, R. E. and Lee, T. H. 1977. Composition and physiology of *Monstera deliciosa* fruit and juice. *J Food Sci* 42.4: 1132–33.

Petrova, I., et al. 2016. Five edible flowers - Valuable source of antioxidants in human nutrition. *Int J Pharmacogn Phytochem* 8.4: 604–10.

Petzold, G., et al. 2006. Caracterización fisicoquímica de pecíolos del pangue (*Gunnera tinctoria*). *Rev Chil Nutr* 33.3: 539–43.

Pieterse, E., et al. 2023. Consumption of edible flowers in South Africa. *Br Food J* 125.6: 2099–2122.

Prohens, J. and Nuez, F. 2001. The tamarillo (*Cyphomandra betacea*): A review of a promising small fruit crop. *Small Fruits Rev* 1.2: 43–68.

Rahayu, E. S. and Pribadi, P. 2012. Kadar vitamin dan mineral dalam buah segar dan manisan basah karika dieng (*Carica pubescens* Lenne & K. Koch). *Biosantifika* 4.2: 89–91.

Ramadan, M. F. and El-Shamy, H. 2013. Snapdragon (*Antirrhinum majus*) seed oil: Characterization of fatty acids, bioactive lipids and radical scavenging potential. *Ind Crops Prod* 42: 373–79.

Rana, M. K. (ed). 2017. *Vegetable Crop Science*. CRC, FL.

Ranfa et al. – see under **Europe**

Rashed, A. N., et al. 2004. Investigation of the active constituents of *Portulaca oleracea* L. (Portulacaceae) growing in Jordan. *Pak J Pharm Sci* 17.1: 37–45.

Redžić – see under **Europe**

Renna, M. 2017. Wild edible plants as a source of mineral elements in the daily diet. *Prog Nutr* 19.2: 219–22.

Rezgui, M., et al. 2021. Evaluation of *Marrubium vulgare* growing wild in Tunisia for its potential as a dietary supplement. *Foods* 10.11: 2864.

Ribeiro, A. B., et al. 2014. *Psidium cattleianum* fruit extracts are efficient in vitro scavengers of physiologically relevant reactive oxygen and nitrogen species. *Food Chem* 165: 140–48.

RIRDC. 2014. *Focus on Wattle Seed*. RIRDC Report, Canberra.

Romojaro, A., et al. 2013. Nutritional and antioxidant properties of wild edible plants and their use as potential ingredients in the modern diet. *Int J Food Sci Nutr* 64.8: 944–52.

Ruskin 1989 – see under **Americas**

Sabir, S., et al. 2015. Pharmacognostic and clinical aspects of *Cydonia oblonga*: A review. *Asian Pac J Trop Dis* 5.11: 850–55.

Saha, D., et al. 2014. Diversity of food composition and nutritive analysis of edible wild plants in a multi-ethnic tribal land, Northeast India: an important facet for food supply. *Indian J Tradit Knowl* 13.4: 698–705.

Salvatore, S., et al. 2005. Antioxidant characterization of some Sicilian edible wild greens. *J Agric Food Chem* 53.24: 9465–71.

Sánchez-Mata & Tardio 2016 – see under **Europe**

Santos, J., et al. 2014. Multi-elemental analysis of ready-to-eat 'baby leaf' vegetables using microwave digestion and high-resolution continuum source atomic absorption spectrometry. *Food Chem* 151: 311–16.

Sartori et al. – see under **Americas**

Schelstraete, M. and Kennedy, B. M. 1980. Composition of miner's lettuce (*Montia perfoliata*). *J Am Diet Assoc* 77.1: 21–25.

Sengupta, S. R. and Pal, B. 1970. Composition of edible wild greens. *J Sci Food Agric* 21: 215.

Shad, A. A., et al. 2013. Ethnobotanical assessment and nutritive potential of wild food plants. *J Anim Plant Sci* 23.1: 92–97.

Shan, Y., et al. 2010. Amino-acid and mineral composition of *Stellaria media*. *Chem Nat Compd* 46.4: 667–68.

Sharifi-Rad, J., et al. 2018. In vitro and in vivo assessment of free radical scavenging and antioxidant activities of *Veronica persica* Poir. *Cell Mol Biol* 64.8: 57–64.

Shitasue, S., et al. 2016. Nutrient content of wild edible plants growing in the natural environment. *J Sugiyama Jyogakuen* 47: 53–58.

Sim, W-S., et al. 2020. Antioxidant and anti-inflammatory effects of *Lilium lancifolium* bulbs extract. *J Food Biochem* 44.5: e13176.

Singh et al. 2019 – see under **Asia**

Siol, M. and Sadowska, A. 2023. Chemical composition, physicochemical and bioactive properties of avocado (*Persea americana*) seed and its potential use in functional food design. *Agriculture* 13.316: 1–13.

Sundarapandian, M., et al. 2016. Nutritional assessment of the plant, *Spergula arvensis* L. *Indian J Nat Prod Resour* 7.2: 150–54.

Suzuki, H., et al. 1978. Polyphenol components in cultured cells of amacha (*Hydrangea macrophylla* Seringe var. *thunbergii* Makino). *Agric Biol Chem* 42.6: 1133–37.

Tegin, I., et al. 2019. Evaluation of chemical content and radical scavenging activity of *Allium vineale* L. extract and its elemental analysis. *Rev Roum Chim* 64.8: 673–79.

Terninko, I. I., et al. 2018. Comparative study of mineral

composition of catnip herb (*Nepeta cataria* L.) from different regions. *Drug Dev* 3.24: 152–56. (In Russian.)
Uddin, M. K., et al. 2014. Purslane weed (*Portulaca oleracea*): a prospective plant source of nutrition, omega-3 fatty acid, and antioxidant attributes. *Sci World J* 2014: 1–6.
Uggla, M., et al. 2003. Variation among and within dogrose taxa (*Rosa* sect. *caninae*) in fruit weight, percentages of fruit flesh and dry matter, and vitamin C content. *Acta Agric Scand – B Soil Plant Sci* 53.3: 147–55.
USDA Food Composition Database (accessed 2017–24): https://ndb.nal.usda.gov/
Vanzani, P., et al. 2011. Wild Mediterranean plants as traditional food: a valuable source of antioxidants. *J Food Sci* 76.1: C46–C51.
Vardavas, C. I., et al. 2006. The antioxidant and phylloquinone content of wildly grown greens in Crete. *Food Chem* 99.4: 813–21.
Vasco, C., et al. 2008. Total phenolic compounds and antioxidant capacities of major fruits from Ecuador. *Food Chem* 111.4: 816–23.
Vasilisin, L., et al. 2018. Comparison of chemical composition and antioxidant activity between Indian strawberry (*Duchesnea indica* (Jacks.) Focke) and other species of strawberries. *Agrosym* 2018: 2114–20.
Vaughan & Geissler 2009 – see under **Global Perspective**
Veberic, R., et al. 2015. Anthocyanin composition of different wild and cultivated berry species. *LWT* 60.1: 509–17.
Wang, Y., et al. 2018. Analysis of nutritional components of the fruits of *Pyracantha angustifolia* and *Pyracantha fortunaeana*. *IOP Conf Ser: Earth Environ Sci* 199: 1–5.
Wehmeyer, A. S. 1986. *Edible Wild Plants of Southern Africa: Data on the nutrient contents of over 300 species*. CSIR: NFRI, Pretoria.
Whitley, G. R. 1985. The medicinal and nutritional properties of *Dahlia* spp. *J Ethnopharmacol* 14: 75–82.
Yamada, H., et al. 1992. Osladin, a sweet principle of *Polypodium vulgare*. Structure revision. *Tetrahedron Lett* 33.28: 4009–10.
Yánez, E., et al. 1994. Chemical and nutritional characterization of amaranthus (*Amaranthus cruentus*). *Arch Latinoam Nutr* 44.1: 57–62.
Yanovsky – see under **Americas**
Yemata – see under **Africa**
Zamorano, P., et al. 2018. Composición química proximal, capacidad antioxidante y actividad antifúngica de peciolo de nalca (*Gunnera tinctoria*). *Inf Tecnol* 29.2: 185–94.
Zeghichi, S., et al. 2003. 'Nutritional composition of selected wild plants in the diet of Crete'. In *Plants in Human Health and Nutrition Policy*. pp 22–40. Karger, Basel.
Zennie, T. M. and Ogzewalla, C. D. 1977. Ascorbic acid and vitamin A content of edible wild plants of Ohio and Kentucky. *Econ Bot* 31: 76–79.

Toxicity Studies

References with a focus on safety assessments, including absorption of potential pollutants and the prevalence and treatment of antinutrients (including studies with a regional emphasis).

Abbasi 2015 – see under **Asia**
Abdel-Aal, E. M., et al. 1997. Structural and compositional characteristics of canaryseed (*Phalaris canariensis* L.). *J Agric Food Chem* 45: 3049–55.
Abe, T., et al. 2008. Cadmium accumulation in the shoots and roots of 93 weed species. *J Soil Sci Plant Nutr* 54: 566–73.
Adler, L. S., and Kittelson, P. M. 2004. Variation in *Lupinus arboreus* alkaloid profiles and relationships with multiple herbivores. *Biochem Syst Ecol* 32: 371–90.
Adiamo 2024 – see under **Nutritional Assessments**
Ahmad, K., et al. 2018. Metal accumulation in *Raphanus sativus* and *Brassica rapa*: an assessment of potential health risk for inhabitants in Punjab, Pakistan. *Environ Sci Pollut Res* 25: 16676–85.
Aksoy, A., et al. 2012. Spreading pellitory (*Parietaria judaica L.*): A possible biomonitor of heavy metal pollution. *Pak J Bot* 44: 123–27.
Anywar, G. 2023. '*Agapanthus orientalis* (Lily of the Nile)'. Ch 8 in *Exploring Poisonous Plants*. CRC, FL.
Ashrafi, K., et al. 2006. Plant-borne human contamination by fascioliasis. *Am J Trop Med Hyg* 75.2: 295–302.
Auguy, F., et al. 2013. Lead tolerance and accumulation in *Hirschfeldia incana*, a Mediterranean Brassicaceae from metalliferous mine spoils. *PLoS ONE* 8.5: e61932.
Bakerink, J. A., et al. 1996. Multiple organ failure after ingestion of pennyroyal oil from herbal tea in two infants. *Pediatrics* 98.5: 944–47.
Baroni, F., et al. 2004. Arsenic in soil and vegetation of contaminated areas in southern Tuscany (Italy). *J Geochem Explor* 81.1: 1–14.
Bell, E. A. 1958. Canavanine and related compounds in Leguminosae. *Biochem J* 70.4: 617–19.
Besharat, S., et al. 2009. Wild lettuce (*Lactuca virosa*) toxicity. *BMJ Case Reports*, bcr0620080134.
Bizimana, N. 1994. Traditional Veterinary Practice in Africa. *DGTZ*, Eschborn.
Bonamonte, D., et al. 2021. 'Plant Contact Dermatitis'. Ch 16 in *Clinical Contact Dermatitis: A Practical Approach*. Springer.
Bonora, A., et al. 1988. Organ-specific distribution and accumulation of protoanemonin in *Ranunculus ficaria* L. *Biochem Physiol Pflanzen* 183.5: 443–47.
Boughton, B. A., et al. 2015. Non-protein amino acids in Australian acacia seed: Implications for food security and recommended processing methods to reduce djenkolic acid. *Food Chem* 179: 109–15.
Brown, A. C. 2002. Potentially life-threatening herbs: Reported cases in MEDLINE of liver toxicity, renal toxicity, cardiotoxicity, cancer, and death. Poster Presentation #489.29. *Experimental Biology*, New Orleans, Apr 20–24.
Burrows, G. E. and Tyrl, R. J. 2013. *Toxic Plants of North*

America. John Wiley, Iowa.
Chai, W. and Liebman, M. 2005. Effect of different cooking methods on vegetable oxalate content. *J Agric Food Chem* 53: 3027-30.
Chan, T. Y. K. 2011. Vegetable-borne nitrate and nitrite and the risk of methaemoglobinaemia. *Toxicol Lett* 200: 107-8.
Chari, L. D., et al. 2020. Biology of invasive plants 1. *Pyracantha angustifolia* (Franch.) CK Schneid. *Invasive Plant Sci Manag* 13: 120-42.
Chongtham, N., et al. 2021. Quality improvement of bamboo shoots by removal of antinutrients using different processing techniques: A review. *J Food Sci Technol* 59.1: 1-11.
Ciprandi, G., et al. 2018. *Parietaria* allergy: An intriguing challenge for the allergist. *Medicina* 54.6: 106.
Coakley, S., et al. 2019. Cadmium hyperaccumulation and translocation in *Impatiens glandulifera*: From foe to friend? *Sustainability* 11: 5018.
Collett, M. G. 2019. Photosensitisation diseases of animals: Classification and a weight of evidence approach to primary causes. *Toxicon: X* 3: 100012.
Colombo, M. L., et al. 2010. Most commonly plant exposures and intoxications from outdoor toxic plants. *J Pharm Sci Res* 2: 417-25.
Connor, H. E. 1977. *The Poisonous Plants in New Zealand*. GP, Wellington.
De Smet, P. A. G. M., et al. (eds). 2012. *Adverse Effects of Herbal Drugs*. 3 vols. Springer.
Dreyfuss, G. 2011. *Fasciola hepatica*. Data sheet on foodborne biological hazards, Anses, France.
Dugdale, T. M., et al. 2015. The biology of Australian weeds 65. '*Tradescantia fluminensis*' Vell. *Plant Prot Q* 30.4: 116-25.
Dymond, J. R., et al. 2013. Nitrate and phosphorus leaching in New Zealand: a national perspective. *N Z J Agric Res* 56.1: 49-59.
Egebjerg, M. M., et al. 2018. Are wild and cultivated flowers served in restaurants or sold by local producers in Denmark safe for the consumer? *Food Chem Toxicol* 120: 129-42.
Essack, H., et al. 2017. Screening of traditional South African leafy vegetables for specific anti-nutritional factors before and after processing. *Food Sci Technol* 37: 462-71.
Fateh, A. H., et al. 2019. Prenatal developmental toxicity evaluation of *Verbena officinalis* during gestation period in female Sprague-Dawley rats. *Chem Biol Interact* 304: 28-42.
Foca, G., et al. 2011. 'Seeds of horse chestnut (*Aesculus hippocastanum* L.) and their possible utilization for human consumption'. Ch 76 in *Nuts and Seeds in Health and Disease Prevention*. Acad Press.
Freitas, H. and Breckle, S. W. 1992. Importance of bladder hairs for salt tolerance of field-grown *Atriplex* species from a Portuguese salt marsh. *Flora* 187: 283-97.
FSANZ (Food Standards Australia New Zealand). 2005. Cyanogenic Glycosides in Cassava and Bamboo Shoots: A Human Health Risk Assessment. *Tech Rep Ser* 28.
Górski, P. M., et al. 1984. Studies on *Medicago lupulina* saponins. 3. Effect of *M. lupulina* saponins on the growth and feed utilization by mice. *Acta Soc Bot Pol* 53.4: 535-41.
Grayson, D. H. 2000. Monoterpenoids. *Nat Prod Rep* 17.4: 385-419.
Greer, F. R., 2005. Infant methemoglobinemia: the role of dietary nitrate in food and water. *Pediatrics* 116.3: 784-86.
Guil-Guerrero, J. L., et al. 1996. Oxalic acid and calcium determination in wild edible plants. *J Agric Food Chem* 44.7: 1821-23.
Günaydın, Y. K., et al. 2015. Intoxication due to *Papaver rhoeas* (Corn Poppy): Five case reports. *Case Rep Med* 321360: 1-3.
Hall, J. O. 2018. 'Nitrate-and nitrite-accumulating plants'. Ch 65 in *Veterinary Toxicology*. Acad Press.
Hane, J. K., et al. 2017. A comprehensive draft genome sequence for lupin (*Lupinus angustifolius*), an emerging health food: insights into plant-microbe interactions and legume evolution. *Plant Biotechnol J* 15.3: 318-30.
Hardin, J. W. and Arena, J. M. 1969. *Human Poisoning from Native and Cultivated Plants*. DUP, Durham, NC.
Hegarty M. P., et al. 2001. *Food Safety of Australian Plant Bushfoods*. RIRDC publication 01/28, Canberra.
Highfield, E. S. and Kemper, K. J. 1999. White willow bark (*Salix alba*). *Longwood Herbal Task Force*. Rev July 13. pp 1-12.
Irvine, F. R. 1953. Waterlilies as food. *Kew Bull* 8.3: 363-70.
Khandker, S. S., et al. 2022. Subchronic toxicity study of *Alternanthera philoxeroides* in Swiss albino mice having antioxidant and anticoagulant activities. *J Toxicol* 2022: 8152820
Kicel, A., 2020. An overview of the genus *Cotoneaster* (Rosaceae): Phytochemistry, biological activity, and toxicology. *Antioxidants* 9.1002: 1-26.
Koçak, S., et al. 2016. Red poppy (*Papaver Rhoeas*) poisoning: A report of three cases. *Cyprus J Med Sci* 1: 11-13.
Kristanc, L. and Kreft, S. 2016. European medicinal and edible plants associated with subacute and chronic toxicity. Parts I & II. *Food Chem Toxicol* 92: 38-49; 150-64.
Kumar, A., et al. (eds). 2010. *Working with Ferns*. Springer.
Lancaster, M. J., et al. 2009. *Lythrum hyssopifolia* (lesser loosestrife) poisoning of sheep in Victoria. *Aust Vet J* 87.12: 476-79.
Lechkova, B., et al. 2023. A study of the chemical composition, acute and subacute toxicity of Bulgarian *Tanacetum parthenium* essential oil. *Molecules* 28: 4906.
Lewis, W. H. and Smith, P. R. 1979. Poke root herbal tea poisoning. *JAMA* 242.25: 2759-60.
Magnuson, B. A., et al. 2014. Safety assessment of consumption of glabrous canary seed (*Phalaris canariensis* L.) in rats. *Food Chem Toxicol* 63: 91-103.
Mukherjee, S. 2001. Cypselar features in nineteen taxa of the tribe Senecioneae (Asteraceae) and their taxonomic

significance. *J Econ Taxon Bot Addit Ser* 19: 253–74.
Murray, V. 1994. Hazard Assessment of Poisonous Plants in the Horticultural Trade. *HNS* 48. Nat Poisons Unit, London.
Muthee, J. K., et al. 2011. Clinical, haematological, biochemical and pathological manifestations of sub-acute toxicity of *Nicandra physaloides* (L) Gaertn in calves. *Bull Anim Health Prod Afr* 59.1: 17–24.
Nelson, L. S., et al. 2007. *Handbook of Poisonous and Injurious Plants*. NY Bot Gdn.
Njoki, J. W, et al. 2014. Impact of processing techniques on nutrient and anti-nutrient content of grain amaranth (*A. albus*). *FSQM* 25: 10–17.
Noonan, S. C. and Savage, G. P. 1999. Oxalate content of foods and its effect on humans. *Asia Pac J Clin Nutr* 8: 64–74.
Oladeji, O. S. and Oyebamiji, A. K. 2020. *Stellaria media* (L.) Vill. – A plant with immense therapeutic potentials: phytochemistry and pharmacology. *Heliyon* 6. e04150.
Orabueze, I. C., et al. 2021. Evaluation of possible effects of *Persea americana* seeds on female reproductive hormonal and toxicity profile. *J Ethnopharmacol* 273: 113870.
Paura 2021 – see under **Europe**
Petrevska, C., et al. 2016. HPLC determination of amygdalin in different plant material. *Maced Pharm Bull* 62 (suppl) 673–74.
Pilegaard, K. and Gry, J. 2008. *Alkaloids in Edible Lupin Seeds*. TemaNord, Copenhagen.
Prasad, M. N. V. 2007. Emerging phytotechnologies for remediation of heavy metal contaminated/ polluted soil and water. *Environ Bioremediat Tech* 54.1: 39–43.
Rawat, K., et al. 2015. Processing techniques for reduction of cyanogenic glycosides from bamboo shoots. 10th World Bamboo Congress paper, Korea.
Riccardi, A., et al. 2006. Spanish broom flower ingestion: A very unusual poisoning. *Eur J Emerg Med* 13.5: 317–18.
Ridker, P. M. 1987. Toxic effects of herbal teas. *Arch Environ Health* 42.3: 133–36.
Rumyantseva, A., et al. 2021. Estimation of the phytoremediation potential of *Alisma plantago-aquatica* L. taken from different stations during water contamination by Cu and Pb (Russia, Vologda region). *E3S Web of Conferences* 265.04004.
Schultheiss, P. C., et al. 1995. Toxicity of field bindweed (*Convolvulus arvensis*) to mice. *Vet Hum Toxicol* 37.5: 452–54.
Senica, M., et al. 2017. Fruit seeds of the Rosaceae family: A waste, new life, or a danger to human health? *J Agric Food Chem* 65.48: 10621–29.
Sharma, R. K., et al. 2008. Heavy metal (Cu, Zn, Cd and Pb) contamination of vegetables in urban India: A case study in Varanasi. *Environ Pollut* 154.2: 254–63.
Simkova & Polesny 2015 – see under **Europe**
Slaughter, R. J., et al. 2012. Poisonous plants in New Zealand: a review of those that are most commonly enquired about to the National Poisons Centre. *NZ Med J* 125.1367: 87–118.
Sultana, N., et al. 2020. *Prunus domestica*: a review. *Asian J Pharmacogn* 4.3: 21–9.
Tanaka, T., et al. 2020. Quantification of amygdalin, prunasin, total cyanide and free cyanide in powdered loquat seeds. *Food Addit Contam*: Part A 37.9: 1503–09.
Tate, M. E. and Enneking, D. 1992. A mess of red pottage. *Nature* 359.6394: 357–58.
Turker, A. U. and Gurel, E. 2005. Common mullein (*Verbascum thapsus* L.): Recent advances in research. *Phytother Res* 19: 733–39.
Ward, M. H., et al. 2018. Drinking water nitrate and human health: An updated review. *Int J Environ Res Public Health* 15.7: 1557.
WHO (World Health Organization). 1989. *Pyrrolizidine Alkaloids*. Health and Safety Guide 26, WHO, Geneva.
Wu, I-L, et al. 2017. Fatal cardiac glycoside poisoning due to mistaking foxglove for comfrey. *Clin Toxicol* 55.7: 670–73.
Zeng, Z., et al. 2024. Subchronic toxicity evaluation of *Idesia polycarpa* fruit oil by 90-day oral exposure in Wistar rats. *J Med Food* 27.6: 510–20.
Zhakypbek, Y., et al. 2024. Reducing heavy metal contamination in soil and water using phytoremediation. *Plants* 13.1534: 1–26.

Index

(Where several page numbers are given, **bold** refers to the main entry.)

PENGUIN

UK | USA | Canada | Ireland | Australia
India | New Zealand | South Africa | China

Penguin is an imprint of the Penguin Random House group of companies,
whose addresses can be found at global.penguinrandomhouse.com

First published by Penguin Random House New Zealand, 2025

Design by Cat Taylor © Penguin Random House New Zealand
Design concept and plant distribution maps by Andrew Crowe
Front cover photograph: Ines Porada/stock.adobe.com
Back cover photograph: Andrew Crowe
Printed and bound in China by 1010 Printing International

A catalogue record for this book is available from the National Library of New Zealand.

ISBN 978-1-77695-085-0